FREE DERRY
Protest and Resistance

Adrian Kerr

GUILDHALL PRESS

ISBN: 978 1 906271 56 5

Copyright © Adrian Kerr/Guildhall Press 2013

The author asserts his moral rights in this work in accordance with the Copyright, Designs and Patents Act 1998.

Published in January 2013 by
GUILDHALL PRESS
Ráth Mór Business Park
Bligh's Lane, Derry
BT48 0LZ
00 44 28 7136 4413
info@ghpress.com
www.ghpress.com

Designed by Guildhall Press.

A catalogue record for this title is available from the British Library.

For Eileen and Mickey

About the Author

Adrian Kerr is the manager of the Museum of Free Derry, the Bogside museum set up by the Bloody Sunday Trust to tell the story of the civil rights and Free Derry eras in the late 1960s and early 1970s from the point of view of those who were most involved in and affected by events of that time. A native of Lurgan, Co Armagh, who has lived and worked in Derry since 1991, he has compiled, contributed to and/or edited a number of books on the conflict in the North of Ireland, including *Perceptions: Cultures in Conflict* (Guildhall Press, 1996), *No Go: A Photographic Record of Free Derry* (Guildhall Press, 1997), *Free Derry Wall* (Guildhall Press, 2009, with Jim Collins) and *Museums of Ideas: Commitment and Conflict* (MuseumsEtc, 2010).

Acknowledgements

Special thanks are due to Irene for constructive criticism, words of encouragement, and the occasional well-placed threat to make me keep writing; Anne for essential tea breaks; and Sarah and Tracey for support through the long summer nights when I was writing what I had planned to write to fill the cold nights of the previous winter. They, along with plenty of good soul music, helped me to Keep The Faith.

Thanks also to Colm Barton and Eamonn McCann, co-authors of the narrative in the Museum of Free Derry which inspired this work, and whose other work for or on behalf of the Bloody Sunday Trust/Museum of Free Derry was also a great help (and occasionally 'borrowed'), and to John Kelly, Jean Hegarty and all at the Bloody Sunday Trust, where I get to do a job that is consistently interesting and fulfilling.

And thanks to all at Guildhall Press – Joe McAllister, Declan Carlin, Peter Mc-Cartney, Kevin Hippsley and Paul Hippsley – for their professional input and usual top-quality job. I've worked with them on and off for the past eighteen years and again it's been a great experience, though this time there wasn't a flip chart in sight.

I am also indebted to the many people who kindly gave permission for the use of their photographs, posters, leaflets etc, namely Robert White, Eamon Melaugh (www.cain.ulst.ac.uk/melaugh), Barney McMonagle, George Sweeney, Jim Davies, James McCloskey, Peter Moloney, Fulvio Grimaldi, Hugh Gallagher, Lorcan Doherty, Charlie McMenamin and Frankie McMenamin. Also to the *Derry Journal*, MoFD collection and Willie Carson collection for a range of source material and images.

Foreword

A few days before he died a couple of years back, dozy from drugs that didn't ease the pain, Johnnie White managed a smile: 'Nineteen sixty-nine, McCann, that was the best.'

Johnnie had been Officer Commanding the IRA in Derry back then. Not that there had been much to command, maybe a dozen volunteers with little in the way of hardware. But rage was rising and reaching for guns beginning gradually to become less fanciful. Republicans were soon to split into the Officials and Provisionals. Johnnie went with the Officials who, for all their ideological eccentricities, were widely seen as more left-wing than the Provos.

Johnnie didn't care much for nationalism, and didn't believe the British were much concerned, either. 'The British ruling class doesn't give a fuck whether there's a united Ireland. But Free Derry frightens them to death.'

Looked at solely and starkly in Orange-Green perspective, the emergence of Free Derry appears as an elemental upsurge of Catholic-nationalism against Protestant-unionism with the British Army operating as the front-line attack force for entrenched Orange power. There is truth in this, but it isn't the whole of the truth.

Free Derry was shapeless, spontaneous, fractious, contradictory, creative, courageous, unpredictable, episodic, heroic and fun. That is, it was an authentic uprising by the ground-down and marginalised against injustice, in the early stages at least unconstrained by ideological dogma or obedience to leaders. It was a heady celebration of the freedom it foreshadowed.

Documents unearthed by the Bloody Sunday Inquiry leave no room for doubt that the most senior British officers in the North seethed with anger at Free Derry. This had less to do with the politics of the people behind the barricades than with the fact that they had enclosed themselves within barricades in the first place. They hadn't just rejected but had removed themselves from the rule of law which the armed forces existed to uphold, had declared their own independence of the State – an intolerable insult to all established notions of good order.

Thus the disdain of Major General Robert Ford, Commander of Land Forces NI, in 1971–72 for regiments stationed in Derry which had stood back from the barricades and not tried to smash through. The reasoning of local commanders – that it was preferable to play the long game rather than precipitate a confrontation with dangerously unpredictable consequences – was seen by Ford and other top brass as shameful weakness. As evidence to Saville was to confirm, it was for this reason that at the beginning of January 1972 Ford asked Brigadier Frank Kitson in Belfast to 'loan' him a battalion of Paras to go to Derry and show how it's done.

Herein lies the direct connection between Free Derry and Bloody Sunday, and so between Free Derry and all that was to follow.

While it lasted, though, particularly in its early phases, Free Derry was a remarkably relaxed and fulfilling place to be. We marvelled at our own daring, swaggered as we showed ourselves off to the world.

But Free Derry was to shape the future in ways no-one predicted – albeit there is now no shortage of people to explain that they saw it all coming. The fact that after the RUC had been repulsed in August 1969 it was the British Army which surrounded the area, threatened invasion and opened or returned fire against increasingly better-armed republican groups established a pattern of play which conformed to traditional republican thinking: the Catholic community pitched against British oppression. Implicitly, the solution now was to get the Brits Out and establish a united Ireland. The revolutionary flourishes which had found some resonance in the first flush of Free Derry gave way to a grimmer reality.

Free Derry had excited people far beyond Ireland. This was the era of the American civil rights movement, mass resistance to the war on Vietnam, student uprisings from Australia to Czechoslovakia, the defence of democracy by students and workers in face of state massacre in Mexico, etc. Free Derry seemed to many including, at least for a time, many behind the barricades, to be an Irish component of and contribution to the same global phenomenon – that what we were about was playing our part in turning the world upside down.

There was a ferment of ideas, heated exchanges in the Bogside Inn between adherents of Marxism, anarchism, nationalism/republicanism and belief systems of more exotic varieties. But as time went on through the phases of Free Derry, under pressure of British military belligerence and political obduracy in Belfast and London, attitudes hardened towards a conviction that accounts would first have to be settled with the besieging force. More and more, proponents of armed struggle matched the mood of the area – particularly of a younger generation no longer daunted by armoured cars and tanks and guns.

The introduction of internment in August 1971 stiffened communal resolve. Bloody Sunday six months later, as far as Free Derry was concerned, dispelled the cloudy thinking of the world revolutionists, leaving the harbingers of a renewed and sharper-edged variant of nationalism as the most dynamic presence within the area.

The fact that Free Derry proved the incubator of militant republicanism has encouraged an assumption that this was the shape and direction that events were bound to take, as if all that followed has been inevitable, natural, unavoidable. Certainly, the seeds of the armed campaign which was to dictate the political trajectory of the next twenty years had been just under the surface of the area, needing only appropriate conditions to germinate, scatter and bloom. These were not the only seeds, but they were to prove the most suitable and sturdy in the patch of earth that constituted Free Derry.

For all that, the role of Free Derry in facilitating armed struggle was not the most significant aspect of the experience. The creation of Free Derry, the seizure of control by a downtrodden community, the breaking of chains by those who had borne them, was a dizzying achievement which has left an indelible trace on the area and beyond.

Johnnie White was right: it was the best of times, the time when we were at our best, the closest we came in the decades of smoke and sulphur to the clear high ground of a shared freedom, giving us a glimpse of a future we still hurtle towards.

It is startling that Adrian's book is the first to focus on Free Derry in a way that lends it the centrality and significance which history demands it be accorded. Free Derry endures, and will for as long as freedom is fought for.

Eamonn McCann

Contents

Glossary   10

Introduction: A Community Without   15

Settlement to Stormont   18

Partition to Protest   26

Early Rising   39

Fifty Days of Revolution   47

You Are Now Entering Free Derry   56

Public Disorder and Division   63

The Battle of the Bogside   84

Free Derry and Brits In   91

Petrol Bombs and CS Storms   100

Towards War   116

Internment and Free Derry   120

The Darkest Year Dawns   136

Bloody Sunday   141

Motorman and the End of Free Derry   165

Epilogue   191

Civil Rights and Bloody Sunday Posters   193

Glossary

Apprentice Boys of Derry: One of the Protestant loyal orders set up to commemorate the Siege of Derry and named after the apprentices who closed the city gates against the besieging forces. The Apprentice Boys hold two main marches in Derry every year, in August and December.

B Specials/Ulster Special Constabulary (USC): The USC were a 100 per cent unionist police reserve force set up after partition. The A and C Specials were soon disbanded, but the part-time B Specials, a notoriously sectarian force, was not disbanded until 1970, when it was replaced by the equally sectarian Ulster Defence Regiment under the command of the British Army.

Bloody Sunday Initiative: A group of Bloody Sunday relatives and campaigners set up in 1987 to reawaken Bloody Sunday as an issue in the wider public consciousness.

Bloody Sunday Inquiry (BSI): The second inquiry into Bloody Sunday, set up in 1998 under the chairmanship of Law Lord Mark Saville. The inquiry reported in 2010.

Bloody Sunday Justice Campaign (BSJC): Campaign group, led by the Bloody Sunday families, set up to force the British Government to admit the truth about Bloody Sunday. Formed in 1992, it was effectively disbanded after the setting up of the BSI in 1998.

Bloody Sunday Trust: Voluntary organisation made up of family members and campaigners, set up in 1997 to help the Bloody Sunday families through the course of the BSI, and to preserve the history of the era that led to Bloody Sunday. BST founded and runs the Museum of Free Derry.

Cameron Commission: Commission of Inquiry set up in January 1969 to look at the causes of violence in the North since October 1968. Report published in September 1969.

Campaign for Social Justice (CSJ): The first formal civil rights organisation in the North. Formed in Dungannon in 1964 by Conn and Patricia McCluskey, it was effectively the birth of the civil rights campaign in the North.

Cityside: West bank of the River Foyle.

CS Gas: Form of tear gas used by the RUC and British Army in the North during riots in the late 1960s and early 1970s.

Dáil/Dáil Éireann: Parliament of the Republic of Ireland.

Democratic Unionist Party (DUP): Hardline unionist political party formed by Ian Paisley in 1971. Currently the largest unionist party in the North.

Derry Citizens' Action Committee (DCAC): Co-ordinating committee for civil rights agitation formed in Derry in October 1968. A moderate organisation, it faded out of existence in the latter part of 1969.

Derry Citizens' Central Council (DCCC): A successor to the DCAC, formed in the summer of 1970.

Derry Citizens' Defence Association (DCDA): Organisation set up to co-ordinate the defence of Free Derry in August 1969. Disbanded in October 1969.

Derry City Council: More democratic successor to the Londonderry Corporation. Set up as Londonderry City Council in 1973, it changed its name in 1984.

Derry Civil Rights Association (DCRA): Derry branch of the Northern Ireland Civil Rights Association.

Derry Civil Rights Committee (DCRC): Civil rights organisation that appeared briefly in 1969 in opposition to the DCAC.

Derry Development Commission: Temporary, unelected 'council' for Derry that operated between the end of the Londonderry Corporation in 1969 and the setting up of Londonderry City Council in 1973.

Derry Housing Action Committee (DHAC): Ad hoc group of republicans and socialists formed in March 1968 to agitate on housing issues.

Derry Labour Party: Derry branch of the Northern Ireland Labour Party, close to but not a part of the British Labour Party.

Derry Unemployed Action Committee (DUAC): Similar to the DHAC, with a lot of dual membership, set up in 1965 to protest about the high levels of unemployment in the city.

Derry Young Hooligans (DYH): British Army term for the rioters in Free Derry.

Gerrymander: Deliberate manipulation of electoral boundaries to give a minority an advantage over the majority.

Historical Enquiries Team (HET): A police investigation unit, answerable to the Chief Constable of the Police Service of Northern Ireland, set up in 2005 to re-examine killings from the conflict in the North.

Hunt Report: Inquiry into reforms of the police in the North of Ireland in 1969. It recommended that the USC be disbanded and the RUC disarmed.

Independent Organisation: Set up to support the work of then Independent MP John Hume in May 1969, it formed the basis of the SDLP in the city when it was formed.

Internment: Imprisonment without charge or trial, used against nationalists and republicans by the Stormont Government in every decade of its existence from the 1920s to the 1970s.

Irish Republican Army (IRA): Irish republican military organisation set up to fight against British rule in Ireland. The name was first used in Ireland during the 1916 rising (although it had previously been used during a brief skirmish on the American-Canadian border in 1866). The IRA split in 1969 (see below).

Londonderry Corporation: Partisan Unionist-controlled council for Derry that was abolished by the reforms announced at the end of 1968.

Loyalists: General term used for those who wish to retain the constitutional link with Britain and are prepared to resort to violent means to do so. Mainly Protestant.

Nationalist Party: The main anti-partition party operating in the North under the Stormont regime. Faded into irrelevance as the political situation in the North changed dramatically in the late 1960s and the SDLP emerged.

Nationalists: General term used for those who wish to re-unite Ireland using constitutional (non-violent) methods. Mainly Catholic.

Northern Ireland Civil Rights Association (NICRA): Formed in January 1967, the Northern Ireland Civil Rights Association (NICRA) 'evolved from a diverse set of political aims and ideals which slowly came together to forge a unity based on a common frustration with unionism, a broad rejection of crude nationalism and a growing awareness of the need for an effective vehicle for political and legislative reform'.

Despite the organisation's origins, in a proposal forwarded by the Wolfe Tone Society, and later unionist accusations that NICRA was merely a front for active republicanism, the organisation was never republican, and of the fourteen original NICRA committee members, only four were members of republican organisations.

From 1967 to 1972, NICRA engaged in a programme of street demonstrations and civil disobedience demanding universal adult suffrage in all elections, an end to gerrymandering, allocation of housing on the basis of need, repeal of the Special Powers Act and the disbandment of the B Specials, the ending of discrimination in employment and, later, the ending of internment. NICRA's use of street protests as a tactic virtually ended after thirteen people were shot dead and a further eighteen injured on a NICRA-organised anti-internment march in Derry on 30 January 1972, Bloody Sunday.

Official Irish Republican Army (OIRA): Formed after the IRA split in 1969, the OIRA was comprised of those who supported former IRA leader Cathal Goulding's attempts to steer the IRA towards a more left-wing political path and end abstentionism (refusal to take seats in London, Dublin or Belfast parliaments, or local councils, if elected). The OIRA declared a ceasefire in 1972.

Paras (Parachute Regiment): Elite parachute regiment of the British Army responsible for many deaths during the conflict in the North, including the Ballymurphy Massacre in Belfast and Bloody Sunday in Derry.

People's Democracy (PD): Left-wing student organisation formed at Queen's University in Belfast in 1968 to campaign for civil rights.

Provisional Irish Republican Army (PIRA): Formed after the IRA split in 1969, the PIRA was comprised of those who opposed the attempts to steer the IRA towards a more political path, believing that military tactics were still necessary. The PIRA was the largest republican paramilitary organisation in the North throughout the conflict.

Republicans: General term used for those who wish to re-unite Ireland and are prepared to use military methods. Mainly Catholic.

Royal Ulster Constabulary (RUC): Police force in the North of Ireland, set up after partition and regarded by most nationalists and republicans as being a partisan unionist force. Renamed as the Police Service of Northern Ireland in 2001.

Scarman Tribunal: Inquiry set up to examine the causes of the conflict in the North in 1969. It published its report in April 1972.

Sinn Féin: Political wing of the IRA; its split in 1970 mirrored that of the IRA in 1969. The wing linked to the PIRA launched its political strategy in the aftermath of the hunger strikes in 1981 and is now the largest nationalist/republican party in the North. The wing attached to the OIRA eventually became The Workers' Party.

Social Democratic and Labour Party (SDLP): Constitutional nationalist party set up in August 1970. The SDLP remained the largest nationalist party in the North until it was overtaken by Sinn Féin in the early years of the twenty-first century.

Special Powers Act: Draconian legislation enacted by the Stormont Government in 1922 giving it extensive powers of repression.

Stormont Government: Term used to describe the one-party Unionist government parliament at Stormont in Belfast.

Ulster Volunteer Force (UVF): Unionist/loyalist paramilitary organisation. Named after the organisation formed to fight Home Rule in 1912, it re-emerged in 1966 around the period of the fiftieth anniversary of the 1916 rising and remained active throughout the conflict.

Ulster Unionist Party: Unionist political party that formed the government in the North from partition until 1972. Remained the largest unionist party in the North until it was overtaken by the DUP in the early part of the twenty-first century.

Unionists: General term used for those who wish to retain the constitutional link with Britain using non-violent methods. Mainly Protestant.

Waterside: East bank of the River Foyle.

Westminster: Seat of the British Parliament.

Widgery Inquiry/Tribunal/Report: First British Government inquiry into the events of Bloody Sunday, which reported in April 1972. The report is widely recognised as an integral part of the organised cover-up of the events of the day.

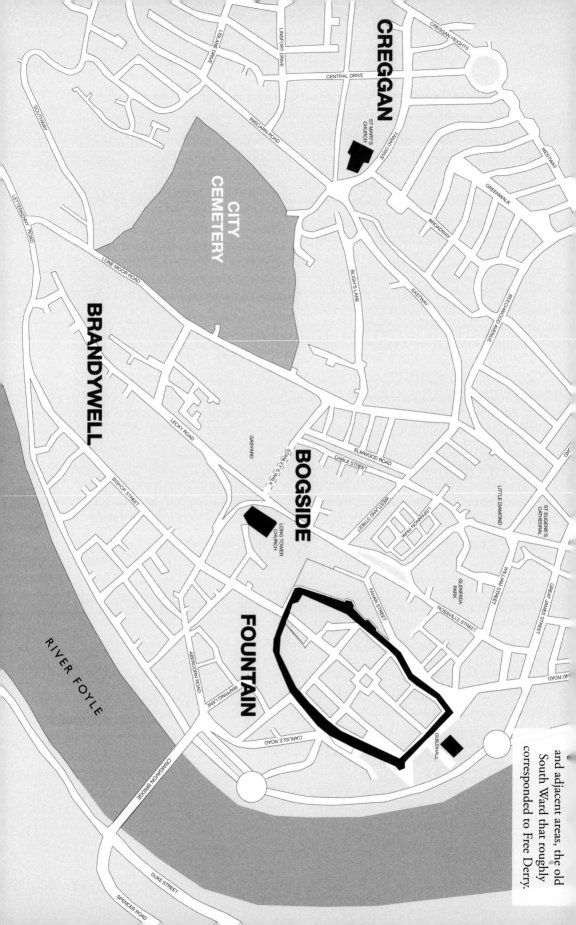

CREGGAN

CREGGAN HEIGHTS

CENTRAL DRIVE

LISLANE DRIVE

LINSFORT DRIVE

INISCARN ROAD

ST MARY'S CHURCH

FANAD DRIVE

WESTWAY

SOUTHWAY

GREENWALK

BROADWAY

BEECHWOOD AVENUE

LETTERKENNY ROAD

LONE MOOR ROAD

CITY CEMETERY

BLIGH'S LANE

EASTWAY

BRANDYWELL

LECKY ROAD

GASYARD

STANLEY'S WALK

ELMWOOD ROAD

CABLE STREET

LITTLE DIAMOND

ST EUGENE'S CATHEDRAL

BOGSIDE

LONG TOWER CHURCH

WESTLAND STREET

LISFANNON PARK

WILLIAM STREET

GREAT JAMES STREET

BISHOP STREET

FAHAN STREET

GLENFADA PARK

ROSSVILLE STREET

RIVER FOYLE

FOUNTAIN

ABERCORN ROAD

WAPPING LANE

CARLISLE ROAD

GUILDHALL

CRAIGAVON BRIDGE

DUKE STREET

SPENCER ROAD

and adjacent areas, the old
South Ward that roughly
corresponded to Free Derry.

Introduction: A Community Without

'. . . the barricades mark our frontiers. We hold 888 acres and two roods. Within this area we have 25,000 people. This indicates the extent of our strength and the massive nature of our protest . . .'[1]

Free Derry may have been only 888 acres in size, with a population of 25,000 people, but its impact, and the impact of its populace, before, during and after its short existence, was to have a massive effect on the city of Derry and beyond. Derry today is a product of the events that created Free Derry and the events that occurred in and emanated from it, more so than any other period in its history.

The history of Free Derry is one characterised by the relationship between two communities – one within the Walls, safe, secure and powerful, the other without, powerless, dispossessed and oppressed. From the 1600s to the 1900s it was a place apart, looked down on from a height by those with power and privilege. It is the story of the people of the working-class community without, who endured oppression from those within, rose up against it and brought down those who imposed it.

It is a violent and heart-rending story, as a peaceful campaign for civil rights was met with violence, beginning a spiral into conflict that was to lead to massacre on the streets and the deaths of hundreds locally and thousands across the North as the longest single period of violent opposition to British rule in Ireland erupted in the late 1960s. It was also a period that split the city, with thousands of Protestants leaving the west bank forever and irrevocably changing the demography of the city.

But it is also a positive story, one of a community uniting to tackle the major oppression that they faced and eventually defeating it. One that shows the indomitable nature of the human spirit in how ordinary people faced extraordinary odds and overcame them, nowhere more so than in the case of the Bloody Sunday families, who suffered personal tragedy and responded by creating history in forcing a sovereign government to face up to its own violent actions.

By the 1960s, nationalist Derry had suffered four decades of oppression and sectarian discrimination, and was the starkest example of what nationalists across the North were being forced to endure under the one-party Unionist Government. It was in Derry that the inequalities in jobs, voting and housing – the issues that would make up the core of the later civil rights demands – were most stark, where the majority were treated like a very much-unwanted minority.

And it was in Derry, from the people of the overcrowded and underestimated South Ward – covering the Bogside, Brandywell and Creggan – that the impetus for the reaction against such treatment would come. With centuries of experience of being on the outside, the people of the Bogside were well used to defying authority and in the 1960s and early 1970s they did it again, and they succeeded.

The civil rights movement in Ireland had its deepest roots in Derry. It was in Derry on 5 October 1968 that the issue of civil rights in the North first came to the attention

---

1 *DCDA Newsletter*, 27 August 1969. (MoFD collection)

of the world, when the RUC attacked a peaceful demonstration in Duke Street. It was in Derry that a short, concentrated period of protests and marches forced the first and only real positive change out of the Unionist government in its entire existence when they announced reforms in November 1968.

It was in Derry that the first 'No Go' area was declared in January 1969, when the defiant slogan 'You Are Now Entering Free Derry' appeared on a gable wall in the Bogside. It was in Derry that the community took on the force of the RUC and fought them to exhaustion during the Battle of the Bogside, forcing them to call in the British Army for support.

Free Derry, which existed for three separate periods during these years – in January 1969, August to October 1969 and August 1971 to July 1972 – was the ultimate expression of the people taking charge of their own destiny, when they put up the barricades and shut out the State and all it stood for, when they claimed their own freedom. It became a place 'not easily passable . . .'

But a price was paid for Free Derry. It was in Free Derry on 30 January 1972, Bloody Sunday, that the British Army shot dead thirteen unarmed demonstrators and injured eighteen others, and in doing so also succeeded in killing the peaceful civil rights movement. Many others lost their lives in and around Free Derry – unarmed civilians, British soldiers, republican volunteers and RUC officers. It was a high price.

And it ended with invasion and occupation when the British Army, using a level of force not seen since the Suez Crisis, poured into Free Derry and the other republican No Go areas in the North and swamped them with military might in July 1972.

This is the story of that era and that area, the story of the community below the Walls, the community without, from the 1600s when the area literally emerged from a bog to become a community, through the centuries of neglect and oppression to those tumultuous few years in the latter part of the twentieth century when it became the centre of world attention.

It is the history of a community through good and bad.

The story told here is based on the narrative used in the Museum of Free Derry, and as such it shares the same subjectivity and uses many of the same definitions as the museum. It is not the official story that has appeared in the wider media and other histories over the years but an attempt to give it from a local perspective. Subjectivity in the telling of history is not wrong as long as it is made clear from the outset. It is those who claim to be giving an objective view, especially of recent and contested history, who are in denial. It is impossible to write an objective history of events that have in any way impacted on your own life.

This also determined the sources used for the book. As the main local newspaper during this period, the *Derry Journal* was reporting the immediate reaction to events as they happened, and therefore also giving the immediate perception of those events. It was the perception of events as they happened that shaped what happened next and is therefore the most important. For example, a historian's view of the events of 5 October 1968, written years later, may be more factually accurate, but it was how the people of Derry felt in the immediate aftermath that caused it to become such a pivotal event, and this is best found in the local press from the time where hindsight and revisionism, for whatever motive, have not yet had a chance to affect the story. Therefore the *Derry Journal* became the main source of information for this book and was used extensively throughout.

There is no exact geographical definition of Free Derry that can cover its entire existence, and, of course, many of the integral parts of the story happened when Free Derry didn't technically exist. For the purposes of some sort of geographical definition, this book uses an area roughly akin to the old South electoral ward, where Derry's nationalists were forced to live in order to nullify their voting power in local-government elections. This area includes neighbourhoods that were never actually 'inside the barricades', such as parts of Bishop Street and Foyle Road, but that played a major part in the Free Derry story.

Within the book, certain deaths – those that occurred within the area defined as Free Derry for the purposes of the narrative – have been highlighted. This is not to minimise the impact of deaths that occurred just outside Free Derry, or in other parts of the city, but to show the scale and regularity with which people were dying inside such a small area as Free Derry. It was an area that suffered inordinately, not just in the early years but throughout the conflict, and it is important that the scale of this is made very clear. The Free Derry area, especially the Bogside, had an international reputation as a very violent area, and is best known for the violent events that occurred there, but the fact that all sides both perpetrated and suffered from the violence needs to be made clear to enable people to reach a proper understanding of it.

And that is why our recent history needs to be told: to reach an understanding of it. There are some who would prefer to draw a line under it, pretend it is over and done with, and try to move on. But until we reach a proper understanding of our recent history and the diverse perceptions of it, and agree to disagree on this diversity, we can never properly move on from it and therefore run the danger of having to live it again. The intention of this book, and the Museum of Free Derry that inspired it, is to try to promote a better understanding of this area and this era.

Adrian Kerr

Settlement to Stormont

The area that is now known as the Bogside was originally mainly underwater, as a branch of the River Foyle flowed between two hills before re-entering the main stream of the river. One hill, made an island by the split in the river, was known as *Doire Calgach* (the Oak Grove, hence the oak leaf commonly used as a symbol for the city, including the logo of the Derry Civil Rights Association designed by Sheila McClean in the 1960s) and eventually became the walled city of Derry. The other, looking down on the island from an even greater height to the west, was centuries later to become Creggan, an integral part of the Free Derry story.

Derry had been an occupied settlement in one form or another since the sixth century, but it was during the sixteenth century, as the English crown tried to crush the last remaining power of the old Ulster lords, that it came to be seen as a site of strategic importance for the English.

The first English soldiers arrived in Derry in 1566 and expelled the inhabitants of the monastic settlement that occupied the island site, but they withdrew again in 1567 after the majority of the soldiers succumbed to illness and an explosion in an ammunition store destroyed most of their camp.

Around this time (fifteenth/sixteenth century), the section of the river that flowed to the west of the island was slowly diverting back onto its main course and the land drying out into marshland, hence the literal name 'Bogside' for what was once the marshy area below the original settlement.

The first known reference to 'the bog' came in a report from Sir Henry Docwra, who arrived in Derry with a second English force in 1600. He described what is now the Bogside as:

> . . . a bog most commonlie wett, and not easily passable except in two or three places dividing it from the maine land.

As Brian Lacey noted in *Discover Derry*, he was not the last British Army officer to find the Bogside 'not easily passable . . .'[2]

Docwra reinstated the British settlement at Doire, which was renamed 'Derrie' by a charter of James I in 1604. It was renamed 'Londonderry' by a second charter in 1613 after the London Guilds were persuaded to take financial responsibility for development of the city, including the building of its fortification Walls.

The first known inhabitants of the 'Bogg Side' were sixty-one 'British families' listed as living there in a 1622 survey. This survey would have ignored any native Irish inhabitants.

From the beginning, the relationship between the Bogside and the walled city was antagonistic. When the English settlement was attacked in 1600, and then attacked again and destroyed by Donegal chieftain Cahir O'Doherty in 1608, the attackers came through the bog. The 1608 attack was the one and only time that a British

---

2   Brian Lacey, *Discover Derry* (Guildhall Press, 2011) p22.

settlement in Derry was successfully stormed and destroyed by the native Irish, and obviously contributed to the decision to build the city's Walls, which were constructed between 1613 and 1618. During the 'Great Siege' of 1688–89, when one group of royalists inside the city held off an opposing group of royalists outside the city, many of the attacking forces were based in what is now the Bogside, Brandywell and Creggan – the area that was to become Free Derry.

In October 1798, Theobald Wolfe Tone, regarded by many as one of the leading figures of Irish republicanism, was captured on a French ship on Lough Swilly near Buncrana and held for one night in Derry Jail before being taken on to Dublin for his trial.

The influx of migrants from Donegal throughout the eighteenth century began to create a sizeable Catholic population in Derry. Since Catholics were forbidden from living inside the city, most of the migrants settled in the area below the Walls, in the Bogside. The building of Long Tower Church in 1784 (on a site where Catholics used to gather to hear Mass in secret during the worst days of the penal laws) and St Eugene's Cathedral between 1851 and 1873 reflected the growth in the Catholic population in the area. The local press caught the change in mood early and in 1829 the *Londonderry Journal* changed its stance to a pro-Catholic one and the editor, who resigned in disgust at the move, founded the *Londonderry Sentinel*, which became, and remains, the 'Protestant' newspaper in the city. The *Derry Journal* dropped the 'London' prefix in 1880.

By the early nineteenth century, the Bogside was predominantly Catholic but still had a substantial Protestant minority. The Ordnance Survey Memoir of the 1830s recorded that most of the poorest inhabitants of Derry lived in the Bogside.

By 1834, Catholics accounted for just over fifty per cent of the population of Derry as a whole, and the further influx of migrants during the potato famine of the 1840s meant that by the 1851 census, Catholics were a clear majority in the city. The port of Derry serviced a very large hinterland, including a lot of the rural counties of the northwest of Ireland, which had suffered greatly during the famine. Many thousands of those who arrived in the city from rural counties – Derry, Donegal, Tyrone, Fermanagh and elsewhere – planning on onward passage to America or Britain, got no further than the shadow of the city's Walls, where they settled into an urban poverty that was little better than the rural one they had fled. But it would be over 120 years before this majority would translate into political power in the city.

The Bogside was hugely overcrowded. Small houses and large families were the order of the day. By 1832, Abbey Street, which held forty-two houses, was home to sixty-three families. Fahan Street, with 164 houses, was home to 244 families. The Bogside had not been included in a piped-water scheme for the city in 1809, which did include the walled city and Protestant Fountain area, so sanitary conditions in the Bogside, where the residents had to rely on wells, were extremely poor and the associated diseases rife. A cholera epidemic in the city in 1832 killed 188 people, mostly Bogsiders, but none in the less crowded Waterside.

Poverty and unemployment was the norm, with little work available for men and, in a tradition that was to last in the city until well into the twentieth century, the women went to work in the sweatshop shirt factories that encircled the area. One of the few forms of livelihood available for men in the area was 'poteen' (illegal alcohol) making, and the presence of organised and armed poteen gangs meant that the authorities could sometimes only come into the area with military force behind them – an early, non-political manifestation of Free Derry.

Sectarian tensions were a feature in Derry throughout the nineteenth century, with serious rioting on many occasions. In 1841, Catholics from the Bogside tried to march into the city centre but were beaten back by Protestants and the military. (It would not be until the end of 1968 that nationalists could easily march inside the Walls.) In 1849, rioting broke out when Protestants attempted to stop a St Patrick's Day parade in the city. In April 1869, three people were shot dead during trouble between Apprentice Boys, the Royal Irish Constabulary (RIC) and Bogsiders after Prince Arthur, son of the English Queen Victoria, visited the city. The Catholic Working Men's Defence Association was set up in the Bogside in August 1869, a precursor to the Derry Citizens' Defence Association of exactly a century later. In August 1870, serious rioting erupted when a Catholic counter-demonstration against an Apprentice Boys' parade was banned. The 'ribbon-men', a term applied to members of Catholic and anti-Orange secret societies, who wore small red or green ribbons for identification, were particularly active in Derry around this time, providing protection and support for working-class Catholics and actively opposing and attacking loyal-order parades.

By the end of the nineteenth century, Catholics had a clear voting majority in Derry and took the City of Derry seat in the parliamentary election in 1884. In response to this, the 1895 Londonderry Improvement Bill was passed, the first recognised gerrymander[3] in Derry. As a result of the bill, and despite a 4,500 Catholic voting majority, Protestants were able to take twenty-four out of the forty seats on the Londonderry Corporation. As the demography of the city changed and the Catholic voting population continued to increase, the gerrymander was repeated in 1919, 1922 and 1936.

At the beginning of the twentieth century, there was no strong republican tradition in Derry, with Catholic Derry dominated by parliamentary Irish nationalism.[4] Nationalist leaders and the local Catholic clergy resisted any moves towards the development of any republican organisation, even opposing the Gaelic Athletic Association as a 'republican influence' (hence the domination of soccer in the city that continues to this day).

---

3   The redrawing of electoral boundaries in such a way that it gives one party an unfair advantage over its rivals. The term is derived from the name of Governor Elbridge Gerry of Massachusetts, whose administration enacted a law in 1812 defining new state senatorial districts to benefit his own party. The outline of one of these new districts resembled a salamander, a description that was combined with the governor's name to give the term gerrymander.

4   By the end of the nineteenth century, with Home Rule, and opposition to Home Rule, becoming major political issues in Ireland, political rather than religious terms become more accurate forms of description for the opposing sides, with nationalist or republican referring to the majority of Catholics and unionist or loyalist to the majority of Protestants. By this stage theological differences had long since ceased to be relevant, with political differences over the future of Ireland becoming the real divisive issue.

After the 1916 rising, which the *Derry Journal* reported under the quirkily Derry headline of 'Wild Doings in Dublin', martial law was declared in the city, and raids led to the arrest of nine men 'associated with the Sinn Féin movement in the city' and the recovery of a small quantity of arms, including a 'rusty sword'. While crowds gathered as the men were arrested and taken to Derry Jail, there were no real protests either against or in support of those arrested. All those arrested were from in and around the Bogside area, and were named as:

> Eamonn MacDermott, Westland Avenue, book keeper; Patrick Hegarty, West-land Avenue, traveller for a local tobacconist firm; Charles O'Breslin, William Street, National Teacher and newsagent; Edward J O'Duffy, Foyle Street, book keeper and one of the founders of the Derry Town Tenants Association; Joseph O'Doherty, Creggan Street; Vincent O'Doherty, Creggan Street, butcher; James Kavanagh, Alexandra Place, foundry worker; Patrick Shiels, Bogside and John Fox, St Columb's Wells, labourer.[5]

It was not until 1917 that the first formal Sinn Féin 'club', named after Pádraig Pearse, was formed in the city. It was described as 'probably the first [Catholic] move-ment in Derry . . . where the clergy were not the directing influence'. Sinn Féin won the City of Derry Westminster seat in 1918 after an electoral deal with nationalists and by 1919, poor housing and social conditions in the city were generating even more support for the party.

In 1920, this alliance secured a majority in the Corporation election, and nation-alist Hugh C O'Doherty became the first Catholic mayor of the city since 1688. A further gerrymander in 1922 restored Unionist minority rule; in response, nationalist councillors boycotted the Corporation for the next ten years.

As tensions grew across Ireland during the War of Independence, and with ru-mours that Derry was to remain in the North under a partitionist settlement, sectar-ian tensions again erupted in Derry.

In August 1919, there were major riots when nationalists demanded the right to march along the city's Walls. Throughout 1920, there were numerous clashes between armed groups on both sides, with the Irish Republican Amy (IRA) and loyalist Ulster Volunteer Force (UVF) both active in the city. But when the British Army intervened in June and imposed a curfew, they surrounded nationalist areas whereas members of the UVF were not disarmed and were allowed to patrol openly in the city. During this period in the summer of 1920, forty people were killed in the city in clashes between republicans and an alliance of loyalists and British forces.

Bogside man Michael Doherty was active in the IRA in Derry and Donegal during the War of Independence, and was awarded a medal in 1971 to mark the fiftieth an-niversary of the end of the war. With the medal was a list of actions he was credited with being involved in, which stated:

> This was the most active Company in all Inishowen [County Donegal] . . .

5 *Derry Journal*, 5 May 1916.

The Company engaged in cutting off communications between Derry and Lower Inishowen by continually raiding post offices, holding up trains, tumbling bridges and tearing up roads . . .

Engaged with the Flying Column (ASU) in raiding Military Stores in Buncrana . . .

Raided the residential area between Moville and Greencastle and securing supply of arms and ammunition, meeting with armed resistance in one instance and being beaten off . . .

Hold up of train on Swilly line between Derry and Buncrana, when fire was opened by British Officers in mufti (whom our scout did not recognise). All volunteers escaped after replying to attack . . .

Burning of Quigley's Point Police Barracks . . .

Burning of Quigley's Point Military Occupation Hall . . .

Holding up of mail car at Quigley's Point when the Military were only up the road raiding for volunteers . . .

Assisting in Derry riots, 1920 . . .

Continually sought after during 1920 and 1921 by military and police . . .[6]

When the Government of Ireland Act was passed in 1920, and partition formally accepted by the Dáil (Irish Parliament) in 1921, nationalist Derry remained a very reluctant part of the North.

As former *Derry Journal* editor Frank Curran wrote, nationalists were:

. . . denied inclusion in the part of Ireland to which they gave allegiance, isolated by the nearby border from their natural and historic Donegal hinterland where so many of them had their roots, refused the municipal power to which their numbers democratically entitled them. Derry's Catholics seethed with a sense of community deprivation that set the tone for the future political warfare.[7]

It is quite possible that if Derry hadn't contained so much of value to unionist heritage in the shape of the city's Walls, the siege connections etc, that all, or at least part, of the city would have been quietly left to the South, avoiding the problem of having a city with such a troublesome nationalist majority under the guaranteed

---

6   Museum of Free Derry (MoFD) collection.
7   Frank Curran, *Derry: Countdown to Disaster* (Gill & MacMillan, 1986) p9.

Unionist Government at Stormont. But unionist tradition prevailed and, with Stormont sowing the eventual seeds of its own destruction, nationalist Derry remained in the North, becoming a target for decades of oppression and neglect.

Mural on the wall of Watt's Distillery in the Bogside, 1920, satirising one of the British Army regiments stationed in the city.

'No King Here', republican graffiti in Bishop Street in the 1940s. (George Sweeney)

Irish Taoiseach Éamon de Valera visits nationalist areas of Derry in 1951. (George Sweeney)

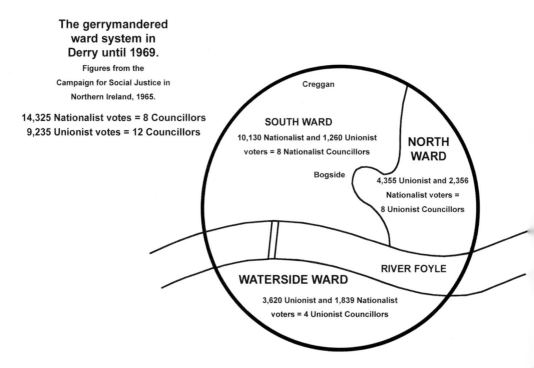

The gerrymandered ward system in Derry until 1969.

Figures from the Campaign for Social Justice in Northern Ireland, 1965.

14,325 Nationalist votes = 8 Councillors
9,235 Unionist votes = 12 Councillors

Creggan

SOUTH WARD
10,130 Nationalist and 1,260 Unionist voters = 8 Nationalist Councillors

NORTH WARD

Bogside

4,355 Unionist and 2,356 Nationalist voters = 8 Unionist Councillors

RIVER FOYLE

WATERSIDE WARD
3,620 Unionist and 1,839 Nationalist voters = 4 Unionist Councillors

The gerrymandered ward system in Derry in the 1960s, showing how a unionist minority were guaranteed elect a majority of members to the Londonderry Corporation.

The old Bogside, neglected, overcrowded and dilapidated. (Eamon Melaugh)

Partition to Protest

After partition, the Unionist Party set about creating a one-party 'Protestant state for a Protestant people' – built on a 'foundation of sectarian discrimination, biased administration and a barrage of totalitarian legislation, which both protected unionism and instilled a deep sense of social injustice in the non-unionist population'.[8]

Partition was followed by a period of sustained sectarian violence, mainly in Belfast, where between July 1920 and July 1922, 303 nationalists, 172 unionists and eighty-two members of the security forces were killed. Stormont did little or nothing to prevent this, and this was recognised even in England, where the *Manchester Guardian* claimed that '[Stormont] are voting themselves power to use torture and capital punishment against citizens whom they forbid to defend themselves while they scarcely attempt to protect them from massacre'.

The Unionist Party allowed no opposition to their rule, and under the Stormont regime their nationalist opponents were ignored and their republican antagonists interned. When internment was introduced in May 1922, 200 alleged republicans, but no loyalists, were interned. They passed the Special Powers Act, which was used almost exclusively to repress any nationalist or republican opposition to the government. All of the groups originally banned under the act were nationalist or republican – the UVF were not banned until 1966. The Special Powers Act was so wide ranging and draconian that the South African apartheid government expressed their envy at it. It gave Stormont's security forces the power to:

- Arrest without warrant;
- Imprison without charge or trial and deny recourse to *habeas corpus* or court of law;
- Enter and search homes without warrant, and with force, at any hour of the day or night;
- Declare a curfew and prohibit meetings, assemblies (including fairs and markets) and processions;
- Permit punishment by flogging;
- Deny claim to a trial by jury;
- Arrest persons it desired to examine as witnesses, forcibly detain them and compel them to answer questions, under penalties, even if answers may incriminate them. Such a person is guilty of an offence if he refuses to be sworn or answer a question;
- Do any act involving interference with the rights of private property;
- Prevent access of relatives or legal advisers to a person imprisoned without trial;
- Prohibit the holding of an inquest after a prisoner's death;

---

8 *We Shall Overcome* (Northern Ireland Civil Rights Association, 1978).

- Arrest a person who 'by word of mouth' spreads false reports or makes false statements;
- Prohibit the circulation of any newspaper;
- Prohibit the possession of any film or gramophone record;
- Arrest a person who does anything 'calculated to be prejudicial to the preservation of peace in Northern Ireland and not specifically provided for in the regulations'.

All of this at the discretion of one man, the Unionist Government's Minister for Home Affairs, who made full use of his powers. Internment without trial, aimed almost exclusively at nationalists and republicans, was used in each of the seven decades in which the Stormont Government existed. When the apartheid Coercion Bill was being introduced in South Africa in 1963, their Justice Minister, Balthazar Vorster, said that he would 'be willing to exchange all the legislation of this sort for one clause of the Northern Ireland Special Powers Act'. The Special Powers Act remained in force until the British Government replaced it with the Emergency Provisions Act in 1973.

The Unionist Government also controlled the Ulster Special Constabulary, the A, B and C Specials set up by the British Government in 1920, in addition to the newly formed Royal Ulster Constabulary (RUC), as the armed wing of the Unionist Party. Added together, there was one unionist police officer for every two Catholic families in the North.[9]

Nationalist compliance with the Stormont regime was sullen and defiant. The Nationalist Party did not even attend Stormont until 1927, and didn't become the official opposition until 1965.

The Unionist Government ran the North on the basis that to give something to Catholics was to take it away from Protestants, and nothing was ever willingly given to Catholics. Catholics were barred from jobs within the government's gift – according to the first Prime Minister, James Craig, they only employed 'loyal men and women' – and private employers were urged to only employ Protestants. By the 1960s, over ninety per cent of those employed in the higher ranks in the civil service and the judiciary were Protestant. Of the 332 members of public boards, less than fifty were Catholic, and the publicly owned industries – water, gas, electricity – were over eighty per cent Protestant.

They also immediately abolished proportional representation in local elections, ensuring continued Unionist rule in most local government areas. In 1920, Unionists only controlled three local authorities in the North; by 1927 they controlled fifteen.[10]

By the 1960s, the Stormont Government had refined and strengthened its sectarian rule of the North of Ireland. There had been almost forty years of deliberate neglect and electoral manipulation of the nationalist majority counties west of the

9 Jonathan Bardon, *A History of Ulster* (Blackstaff Press, 1992) p192. The A and C Specials were disbanded again in 1925, the B Specials not until 1969.
10 *A History of Ulster*, p198.

Bann, and a concentration of resources in the unionist strongholds east of the Bann.

The Unionist Government had created almost a partition within partition to protect areas where they had a natural majority. In areas where they hadn't a majority, gerrymandering, economic neglect and sectarian discrimination ensured that they retained political power. This also helped to force emigration from deprived areas, which helped to keep the population balance at partition levels.

During most of the fifty-year period of the Stormont regime, the British Government, who financed Stormont and retained ultimate responsibility for its actions, operated a policy of 'out of sight, out of mind', allowing the Stormont Government to carry on its policies of discrimination and repression as long as it did not directly affect them. It was convention that Northern Irish affairs were never discussed in Westminster. It has been reported that between 1922 and 1968 the average time spent discussing the North in Westminster was less than two hours a year.[11]

Britain's only meaningful intervention during this period was the creation of the Welfare State and the passage of the 1944 Butler Education Act. This act guaranteed free access to education and began the process where young people from areas like the Bogside and Creggan could get access to a third-level education. The ultimate outcome of this was when the first generation of university-educated working-class Catholics emerged in the early 1960s and found themselves confronting a system that had given them an education but refused to give them jobs. It was from this group that many of the leaders of the civil rights movement emerged. According to NICRA, 'Having obtained the right to free education, they were now to use that education to demand other rights.'

* * *

Derry, the largest city or town in the North with a nationalist majority, was the prime example of the result of Stormont's sectarian policies, and it was in Derry that inequality and discrimination in issues that would later make up the core demands of the civil rights movement – voting, housing and jobs – were most stark.

The Londonderry Corporation followed the lead of Stormont, immediately reinforcing its position with a new gerrymander in 1922, restoring Unionist minority rule in Derry in the 1923 election despite a 5,000 nationalist voting majority in the city.

The Derry gerrymander was repeated in 1936 when the growing Catholic population in the city was again threatening Unionist rule. Under the new gerrymander, Unionists were guaranteed twelve of the twenty seats on the Corporation. This system remained in place until the abolition of the Corporation in 1968. The Unionist Government also neutralised the fact that the Catholic majority in Derry regularly returned a Nationalist MP by dividing the city into two seats, one of which was guaranteed to return a Unionist MP to balance the Nationalist one returned by the new constituency of Foyle.

---

11   Peter Taylor, *States of Democracy* (BBC Books, 1993) p120.

Under the North's voting system, all people over twenty-one could vote in Stormont elections, but only a householder and spouse could vote in local-government elections. To vote in local elections, a person had to be over twenty-one, living in the North for at least seven years, be the tenant or spouse of a tenant or be the occupier of land or premises with a rateable value of over £10. Businesses had up to six votes, depending on their size. Under this system, around twenty-five per cent of those eligible to vote in Stormont elections – where a Unionist majority was already guaranteed – were disenfranchised for local-government elections where non-unionist votes had to be neutralised.

Therefore, to give someone a house was to give them a local-government vote. Preserving the sectarian arithmetic that ensured continued Unionist rule was then the key factor in who was housed and where. All housing allocation in Derry was in the hands of one person: the Unionist mayor. Technically, there existed a housing committee of the Corporation but it only met once in each council term to vote all its powers over to the mayor.

Nationalist voters had to be corralled into one of the three electoral wards in the city – the overcrowded South Ward, covering the Bogside, Brandywell and Creggan. Voters in the South Ward could only elect eight members of the Corporation no matter how many votes they had, while the other two wards (North and Waterside) were guaranteed to return twelve Unionist members. The 1961 census showed that Derry had a population that was sixty-seven per cent non-unionist. In 1964, there were 14,325 Catholics in Derry eligible to vote in local-government elections and 9,235 Protestants, yet the Corporation elections were still guaranteed to return the twelve-eight Unionist majority.

In 1966, the Unionist mayor of Derry, AW Anderson, declared that the electoral system in Derry was 'reasonably fair' and that it was proper that 'the person who paid the piper called the tune. The principle of one man one vote was not the law or principle at local government elections.'

When building space in the Bogside ran out, construction of Creggan began in 1947, on a high, windy hill unsuitable in all respects – except its location within the South Ward. Neither the Catholic Church nor the Nationalist Party offered vigorous opposition; the arrangement kept Catholics clustered around their 'own' schools and churches. Between 1945 and 1960, ninety-two per cent of all houses allocated to Catholics were within the South Ward. In the 1960s when space to build outwards in the South Ward had completely disappeared, the Corporation began to build upwards, and the high-rise Rossville Flats were constructed in the Bogside, cramming hundreds of nationalist families (and votes) into a few hundred square yards of ground space.

As the Catholic population in the city continued to grow – the rate of population growth in Derry was twice that of anywhere else in the North – overcrowding became more and more of a problem in the city.

Derry was the most overcrowded town in the North, with a density of twenty-five people per acre (as opposed to Coleraine with eight per acre, Lisburn with nine,

Larne with seven etc), but the Corporation refused repeated nationalist demands to expand the city boundaries, because this would have meant housing the overflow of population – mostly nationalist – in the North and Waterside Wards. The Corporation also blocked attempts by bodies such as the Derry Housing Association to build any homes outside the South Ward. Much of the Catholic population that couldn't be squeezed into the South Ward was forced to live in a run-down old army camp at Springtown, which was actually outside the city boundaries and therefore didn't affect the gerrymander.

Within the already overcrowded city, the South Ward was the most grossly overcrowded area. One house in William Street was home to seven separate families, with one family of five living in a single room. Local doctor Raymond McClean, who would later become the first SDLP mayor of the new city council, reported a case where there were twenty-six people living in 'appalling conditions' in two rooms of a house in Walker's Place.

According to Dr McClean:

The houses were old, damp, dark and dilapidated to the degree that nothing short of demolition and rehousing would really solve the problem. The people themselves were enveloped in the insidious depression and hopelessness of the area, and could not see any way forward, short of getting a house from the Corporation, which they all knew was impossible . . . The Corporation sat with a dignified silence in the Guildhall . . . I was rapidly becoming aware that any solution to the terrible environmental problems faced by those suffering people could not be achieved without significant political involvement . . .

Dr McClean went on to become deeply involved in the civil rights movement, and then in local politics in Derry.[12]

Over twenty per cent of the South Ward population lived in homes that were officially classified as overcrowded, compared to less than six per cent in the North Ward and less than eight per cent in the Waterside Ward. In the North Ward, there were 2,230 more habitable rooms than people, in the Waterside Ward 210 more rooms than people, but in the South Ward there were 4,400 more people than habitable rooms. It was a running joke that the skeleton on the city's coat of arms actually represented a Catholic waiting for a house.

Overcrowding in the South Ward caused major problems for its inhabitants. Incidence of diseases such as tuberculosis were around twice that of other parts of the North – although the Unionist mayor of Derry claimed that this fact was simply part of a Nationalist Party smear campaign and insisted it was removed from the Corporation's own Health Committee report – and created perfect conditions for 'Rachmanite' landlords to thrive, letting out substandard, and in many cases condemned, housing to tenants desperate for a home.

---

12 Raymond McClean, *The Road to Bloody Sunday* (Guildhall Press, 1997) pp37-38.

* * *

Derry also suffered from massive discrimination in employment. Unionist ministers directed industries to unionist areas.

Partition had separated Derry from its natural hinterland of Donegal, and this had immediate economic effects in the city. Many businesses closed, or moved closer to their customer bases in the South, and by 1926 unemployment in Derry had reached twenty-six per cent.

In 1932, the Derry unemployed organised a peaceful march to the Guildhall to present proposals to ease both unemployment and overcrowding in the city by embarking on a series of improvement schemes for local housing. The Corporation responded by ordering their annual clothing supply a few months early.

The Stormont Government instituted a programme of building advance factories to attract new industries to the North. Between 1945 and 1964, 224 new industries were attracted to the North, but only nine per cent of these went west of the Bann. Only six advance factories were built in Derry, where unemployment was so high. Thirteen were built in Lurgan, where unemployment averaged six per cent and ten in Bangor with four per cent.

The 1965 Wilson Plan outlined four areas that could benefit from 'rapid industrialisation' – all were unionist areas in and around Belfast. When it was decided that the North needed a major new development to absorb population increases, the investment went to the pipe dream that was the planned new city of Craigavon, in the safely unionist North Armagh, rather than into the existing second city, Derry. Craigavon, which turned out to be a truly spectacular failure in terms of town planning, was named after the first Stormont Prime Minister, James Craig, First Viscount Craigavon.

As shown, the Unionist Government had done its best to ensure that jobs within its gift were allocated on sectarian grounds. In Derry, the Unionist Corporation practised their own version of this.

In a city with such a large Catholic majority, the Corporation still managed to ensure that only eighteen per cent of its own employees were Catholic, and that none of those employed in senior positions were Catholic. In the Guildhall, the headquarters of the sectarian Corporation, they didn't, to paraphrase former Stormont Prime Minister Lord Brookeborough, 'have a Catholic about the place'.

With an average rate of over twenty per cent throughout the Stormont years, Derry had the second highest unemployment figure in the North. The average unemployment rate for the North was only eight per cent, and only Strabane had a higher unemployment rate than Derry. While there was some employment available for women in the local shirt factories, the male unemployment rate in Derry was closer to thirty per cent than twenty.

One of the few new companies that did come to Derry during the Stormont era – Monarch Electrics – had eased unemployment in Derry for a time, and one of its factories had been located in the South Ward, at Bligh's Lane in Creggan. Its closure in 1966 and the effect that this had locally was a major influence on local reaction to the obvious injustice and discrimination being practised on the majority population of the city. After its closure was announced, Nationalist Party MP Eddie McAteer described the employment situation in Derry as 'rushing back to the hungry thirties'. As a sign of things to come, workers reacted to the announcement of the closure of the factory by marching in protest through the city centre.

* * *

After partition, nationalist Derry had settled into a resigned political routine that was to last into the 1960s. Almost all non-unionist councillors and MPs came from the Nationalist Party. Fully supported by the Catholic Church, it was said that Nationalist Party representatives were not so much elected as anointed.

Republicanism in the city went underground after partition, confined to small groups of veterans of past struggles. The main, but unsuccessful, challenge to the Nationalist Party came from labour and trade union groups, although republicans also stood against the Nationalist Party in elections.

A visit to the city by Éamon de Valera in 1951 reignited nationalist sentiment. When marchers tried to carry a tricolour inside the walled city on St Patrick's Day that year, they were battered off the streets by the RUC. One local republican, Manus Canning, addressed this a few weeks later by climbing to the top of Walker's Pillar, the symbol of unionism overlooking the Bogside, and attaching the green, white and orange flag to the top. Later that summer, the IRA raided Ebrington Territorial Army base in the Waterside and escaped with almost thirty guns.

Internment without trial was introduced against republicans in the 1940s and again in the 1950s. During the Second World War, Derry Jail was used to house republican internees. In March 1943, twenty-one republican internees managed to escape from Derry Jail via a tunnel, but most were soon arrested as they fled over the border into Donegal.

One Derry man, Connie Green from Bishop Street, was killed in the short-lived *Saor Uladh* (Free Ulster) rising in 1955 that preceded the IRA 'border campaign'. He was described in death notices as 'Lieutenant Connie Green, No1 Active Service Unit, Saor Uladh, killed in action, Nov 26 1955'.

There was very little IRA action in the city during these years, even during the IRA border campaign (Operation Harvest) between 1956 and 1962, although at Easter 1957 unsuccessful attempts were made by the IRA to burn out the Customs Clearance Station on Strand Road and the Corporation electricity substation on William Street. There was much resentment against the internment of a small number of local men, but no mass protest. By the end of the border campaign, republicanism, not just in Derry but across the North, seemed to be finished. Again the movement went underground, and again republicanism was only kept alive in Derry by a small group of what many considered to be eccentric activists.

Nationalists in Derry, after four decades of oppression, entered the 1960s with no effective leadership and seemingly little hope of change. As British Premier Harold Macmillan was boasting 'We have never had it so good', in Derry, people were having it as bad as ever. But the time was coming when they were going to do something about it.

Thousands of Derry people converged on Stormont in 1965 to demand that the proposed new university
sited in the city. John Hume and Eddie McAteer MP can be seen at the front of the crowd. (*Derry Journa*

he Wilson family's caravan in a laneway off the Lecky Road, which became the centrepiece of an early civil rights protest in the summer of 1968. (Eamon Melaugh)

Dockers staging a sit-down protest on Ferryquay Street, November 1968. (Barney McMonagle)

Civil rights protesters outside the Guildhall, 1968. (Barney McMonagle)

The biggest civil rights protest in the North to that date as thousands cross Craigavon Bridge on 16 November 1968. (*Derry Journal*)

Derry Housing Action Committee protest outside the courthouse in Bishop Street, 1968. Third in line is prominent civil rights activist Eamonn McCann. (Eamon Melaugh)

50 days — NORTHERN IRELAND'S POLITICAL REVOLUTION

The stage is set

DERRY SHOUTS
and the world hears

THE FIFTY DAYS Revolution, which began with batons in Londonderry and ended with Northern Ireland's biggest ever programme of reform, was played out on three distinct arenas. While citizens took to the streets in Derry (in the manner of all true revolutionaries) the big decisions were taken at Stormont and Whitehall.

Like all revolutions, this one had been fathered by history and born of circumstances. Bad housing, unemployment, and the absence of of universal suffrage in local elections were still bitter grievances after 50 years of constitutional government. The city was ripe for an explosion.

There were straws in the wind for those who wanted to read them. Earlier a young ambitious Nationalist MP, Mr. Austin Currie, had defied authority by squatting in a Caledon house to protest about discrimination in housing.

In Dungannon a civil rights march ended up with scuffles, with police in the no-man's land between civil rights marchers and Unionist supporters. "The Unionists fear civil rights marches," Mr. Currie was reported as saying.

THE MOMENT OF CONFRONTATION . . . police and demonstrators come face to face (left) . . . later a demonstrator is tackled by three policemen.

WHEN the Government of Northern Ireland issued its statement on political reforms at the week-end 50 days had passed since the clashes in the streets of Londonderry, clashes that brought the demands of the civil rights campaigners to the attention of the world. This is the first article in a special series in which the dramatic events of those days are charted by Alf McCready, drawing on material from the "Belfast Telegraph's" political staff and our reporters resident in Derry.

Belfast Telegraph headline from 27 November 1968, looking back on a period of fifty days that had changed the course of history in the North. (MoFD collection)

Early Rising

The 1960s were to become a decade of momentous change around the world, when the oppressed began to mount a serious challenge against the oppressors. It was a decade when previously accepted authority was faced down across the world, from the southern states of the USA to Paris and Prague, and eventually from the Bogside to Belfast.

The process had already begun a number of years earlier in the USA. On 1 December 1955, Rosa Parks refused to sit at the back of a bus in Montgomery, Alabama. This small gesture, which started the Montgomery Bus Boycott, was a seminal moment for the emerging civil rights movement in the USA. The year-long boycott, led by the then relatively unknown Martin Luther King, ended segregation on buses.

In Little Rock, Arkansas, in 1957, the National Guard had to escort nine black schoolchildren past white, racist protestors who opposed the decision to desegregate schools. Just a few days earlier, the governor of Alabama had called in the same National Guard to block the integration of Little Rock Central High School but was overruled by the same government in Washington that had banned segregation in schools three years earlier. State force supporting reactionary protestors was something that the civil rights movement in the North of Ireland would soon have their own experience of.

In March 1960, black South Africans began a campaign of civil disobedience against the infamous apartheid regime. Before the first day of their campaign was over, more than sixty protesters had been killed by state forces, massacred in Sharpeville and other townships.

On 28 August 1963, around 200,000 civil rights supporters marched in Washington DC to hear civil rights leader Martin Luther King deliver his famous 'I have a dream . . .' speech.

On Sunday 7 March 1965, the Selma Voting Rights Movement organised a peaceful march from Selma to Montgomery. The 600 marchers were stopped on a bridge by a massive police blockade; one marcher was killed and many more injured. The day became known as Bloody Sunday. A week later, 2,500 marchers succeeded in crossing the bridge.

By the end of the 1960s, most racist laws had, on paper at least, been repealed in the USA.

All that was achieved by the civil rights campaign of non-violence and civil disobedience was achieved in the face of intense opposition from racists and the harassment, arrest and murder of civil rights supporters, activists and leaders.

But the perseverance of the black civil rights movement was a major inspiration for the civil rights movement in the North of Ireland.

The oppressed in the North, with ever easier access to television and radio, watched what was happening in America, and what the civil rights campaign had achieved. They recognised the connection between the position of blacks in America and nationalists in the North, between the white racists and sectarian unionism. They saw how the same tactics could be used. They even stole their main protest song, with *We Shall Overcome* becoming the anthem of the new civil rights movement in the North of Ireland.

The first organised civil rights protests in the North of Ireland took place in Dungannon in 1963. Dungannon was an average-sized town in County Tyrone, with a population of about 7,000 people at the time, divided almost equally between unionists and nationalists. But, like Derry, the town had been gerrymandered to ensure a Unionist majority on the local council, and nationalists suffered from the same problems of housing allocation and job discrimination as their counterparts in Derry. A small number of those suffering from discrimination in the town came together as the Homeless Citizens' League and began to picket the local council offices demanding fairer allocation of housing. When their demands were ignored, they took to the streets to march in protest around the town. Drawing very obvious direct inspiration from the black civil rights movement in the USA, the protesters carried placards stating 'If our religion is against us, ship us to Little Rock' and 'Racial discrimination in Alabama hits Dungannon'.

The actions of the Homeless Citizens' League created a momentum in the County Tyrone town which led to the formation of the Campaign for Social Justice in 1964, which was effectively the launch of the civil rights campaign in the North.

As civil rights protests were beginning in Dungannon in 1963, the 'liberal' Terence O'Neill replaced the more hardline Lord Brookeborough as the North's Unionist Prime Minister, and promised a new era of modernisation and greater equality. An Irish Taoiseach, Seán Lemass, visited Stormont for the first time ever[13] and the arrival of new multinational industries with no vested interest in unionism or discrimination all seemed to herald a change in the fortunes of nationalists. But all the talk of change was just that, talk, and the North under the new boss continued much the same as under the old boss. And the oppressed nationalists of Derry were just about to follow their Dungannon counterparts onto the streets.

In the early 1960s, the Stormont Government had announced plans to build a second university in the North. Nationalist politicians, supported by some Unionists and the Londonderry Corporation, called for it to be built in Derry, at Magee College, and there was widespread support for their call from across the city. The University for Derry Action Committee was set up under the leadership of a then relatively unknown local school teacher called John Hume, and the campaign culminated in a mass rally at Stormont in February 1965 when around 25,000 people travelled by motorcade from Derry to a mass rally at Stormont to demand that the university be built in the city. According to the *Derry Journal*:

> Virtually every business house in the city had at least one representative in
> the cavalcade – and there must have been few households which did not have

---

13 In an example of how the Irish Government was following the British Government's line on the North by trying to ignore what was happening here, a documentary filmed by RTÉ, the South's state-sponsored broadcaster, in 1964 on the gerrymander in Derry was deemed too politically sensitive to be shown, and was not eventually broadcast until 1989.

a representative taking part. All creeds and classes and all shades of political opinion were included . . . Clergy of all denominations joined with business and professional men, factory workers, dockers, school teachers and students in a motorcade which varied from the stately limousines to furniture vans, coal lorries and bread vans and cars of every make and size . . .[14]

It seemed an obvious choice to build the North's second university in the North's second city, but the Stormont-appointed Lockwood Committee ignored the 'unanimous' demands of the citizens of Derry and recommended that the new university be built in Coleraine, a staunchly unionist town. The Unionist Government accepted their recommendation, continuing the enforced apartheid of nationalist areas west of the Bann (in this case just about, since the new university was sited right on the east bank of the River Bann).

After the defeat of the university campaign, it was widely believed that while many unionists in Derry had publicly voiced support for the campaign, others in the background – the 'faceless men' – had plotted against the university coming to Derry, fearful of the effect it would have on the delicate balance of power and privilege in the city.

But the university campaign had laid the seeds of a new trend in Derry, and as the problems of poor housing and high unemployment continued, local reaction was beginning to take shape. According to Brian Lacey: 'The University for Derry Campaign of the mid-1960s was a form of dramatic, political, street education for the people of the city, the bitter results of which were to emerge in the tumultuous years ahead.'[15]

The Derry Unemployed Action Committee (DUAC) was formed in 1965, bringing together a small collection of republicans, socialists and others to highlight the scale of unemployment in Derry and became effectively the first civil rights organisation in the city. Among the first members of the DUAC were Gerry Mallett, James Gallagher, Bobby Campbell, Ted Bradley, Eamon Melaugh and Fionnbarra O'Dochartaigh. From picketing council meetings and holding teach-ins at the labour exchange, the DUAC soon expanded and was able to gather 600 protestors outside the Guildhall when Brian Faulkner, then Minister for Commerce, was meeting the mayor.

On 25 March 1966, the DUAC brought their message to London, with a twelve-hour picket outside the 'Ulster Office' in London with placards demanding 'Work Not Talk', 'No Industrial Apartheid' and 'Thirteen Per Cent Unemployment, Not Good Enough'. They handed in a letter demanding that industry be directed to Derry and an end to the 'shameless industrial discrimination' against the city.[16]

The year 1966 was also the fiftieth anniversary of the 1916 Easter Rising, and the Stormont Government used this as an excuse to rouse hysteria around the threat of possible republican actions in the North. In April of that year, they declared that

---

14 *Derry Journal*, quoted in Brian Lacey, *Siege City* (Blackstaff Press, 1991) p249.
15 *Siege City*, p250.
16 *Derry Journal*, 29 March 1966.

'Police and other security forces have been placed on a footing of instant readiness to meet any unlawful activity which may be mounted by the IRA.'[17] The UVF in Belfast responded to the Stormont-generated panic about a republican uprising by killing three people, two young Catholic men and a Protestant pensioner. Although ignored in many histories, these three people, John Scullion, Peter Ward and Matilda Gould, were the first victims of the Troubles.

On Sunday 10 April 1966, around 1,000 people attended a march and rally around the Bogside to mark the fiftieth anniversary of the Easter Rising. During the rally in Celtic Park, the speakers repeated traditional republican calls for unity and breaking the link with Britain but said little or nothing about the social conditions in the city.[18] Afterwards, six of the organisers – Neil Gillespie, Seán Keenan, Seán Shiels, Patrick Kirk, Michael Montgomery and Fionnbarra O'Dochartaigh – were charged in connection with the rally, and their court appearances were marked by protests outside the courthouse in Bishop Street.

As republicanism was re-emerging in Derry, so too was loyalism. It was reported in June 1966 that 'Paisley's volunteers have come to Derry' after the formation of a local division of the Ulster Protestant Volunteers, who threatened action against nationalists, republicans and 'unionists who display sympathy towards Catholicism'.[19] In December 1966, local republican Seán Keenan, who had been interned in the 1940s and 1950s (and was to be interned again in the 1970s) received a threat from the 'Londonderry Division, the Ulster Volunteer Force' telling him 'he had better go south before Christmas'.[20]

On 7 October 1966, the Derry City branch of the Young Republican Association organised one of the first 'direct action' civil rights protests in the city, occupying the house of a widow and her three children who were due to be evicted from their home in Harvey Street.

Bailiffs had arrived to evict Mrs Ellen McDonnell and her children from their home in Harvey Street on the edge of the Bogside and members of the Young Republican Association had barricaded themselves inside the house. According to the *Derry Journal*, this was the 'first time in memory an eviction in Derry City was threatened with opposition'.[21]

Mrs McDonnell, a widow, said she was willing to leave the house but only when alternative accommodation was made available. This was promised, and the protesters left her home that night.

Mrs McDonnell remained in her home until July 1967, when bailiffs again arrived to evict her. Again members of the Young Republican Association barricaded themselves inside her house and a standoff began. The republicans stayed in the house until 1 August, leaving only temporarily after 'legal advice' that a hearing was due to take place in Belfast the following day which would allocate Mrs McDonnell a new home.

17 *Derry Journal*, 8 April 1966.
18 *Derry Journal*, 12 April 1966.
19 *Derry Journal*, 28 June 1966.
20 *Derry Journal*, 9 December 1966.
21 *Derry Journal*, 11 October 1966.

But the bailiffs arrived as soon as they left. As a last stand, Mrs McDonnell pelted the bailiffs and RUC with 'crockery and other household items' but was eventually forcibly evicted from her home, along with her children, and frogmarched straight to a waiting ambulance while hundreds of people gathered to protest outside.

The protests surrounding this eviction galvanised people in Derry to take a stand against the unjust laws which allowed such evictions to take place. According to one of those involved in the protest, Fionnbarra O'Dochartaigh, the incident 'educate[d] the wider public in those previously unseen and unspoken horrors associated with the eviction process . . . her heroic stand forced evictions and other working-class issues onto the agenda of those struggling for civil rights and equality. Others benefited directly from her brave stance . . .'[22]

Protests across the North of Ireland gathered pace throughout 1966, and in January 1967 the Northern Ireland Civil Rights Association (NICRA) was formed to bring the protesters together within one group to demand changes from Stormont which, under O'Neill, still 'preached liberalism and practised sectarianism'.

In January 1967, 800 Monarch Electric Workers staged a protest march through the city at the threat of the closures of the firm's factories at Drumahoe in the Waterside and Bligh's Lane in Creggan, but within a week the factories had closed, bringing the city's jobless total to 5,000, over twenty per cent of the working-age population. The Star Factory on Foyle Road, which employed 240 people, closed a month later.

In February 1967, Nationalist Party Councillor James Doherty claimed that there were 'nine to ten thousand people living in substandard conditions in the city'[23] but the Corporation had not built one new house in the whole of the previous year.

In April 1967, the *Times* newspaper reported in England that the electoral system in Derry was deliberately weighted against nationalists and that there was widespread discrimination in housing and in government and private employment. A group of Labour MPs who visited Derry told British Prime Minister Harold Wilson that 'irrefutable evidence exists of gerrymandering in Derry in order to perpetuate minority control . . . allegations of discrimination in housing were examined and there can be little doubt that this exists on a wide scale, particularly where a dispersal of the population would result in a changed political balance . . .'[24] But still the British Government continued to ignore the problem that was festering on their doorstep.

In May 1967, local republicans protested against the ban on Republican Clubs and in July resumed their protest against the eviction of Mrs McDonnell in Harvey Street. The People's Action League organised protests against the Corporation's refusal to extend the city's boundaries, and organised tenants' groups to protest about housing conditions in their own areas.

On 15 May 1967, in what was to be the last-ever election to the Londonderry Corporation, Unionist candidates gained thirty-two per cent of the vote in Derry,

---

22 Fionnbarra O'Dochartaigh, *Ulster's White Negroes: From Civil Rights to Insurrection* (AK Press, 1994) p35.
23 *Derry Journal*, 3 February 1967.
24 *Derry Journal*, 28 April 1967.

which again translated into sixty per cent of the seats and a twelve-eight majority. The election was different to previous ones only in that a female candidate stood for the first time in forty years. Mary Harrigan, who stood for the Nationalist Party in the South Ward, was elected with over 4,000 votes.

In July, the first barricades went up in the Bogside when local pig dealer Thomas Keys objected to his premises at 99 Bogside being demolished as part of the development scheme for the area.[25] It was the only time that barricades were put up in the Bogside to keep the pigs in. The 'Bogside Siege', as it was referred to in *Derry Journal* headlines, did not end until September.

In September 1967, the People's Action League held a seven-day protest outside the Guildhall against the construction of another new factory west of the Bann, in staunchly unionist Ballymena, while the Industry for Derry Committee organised a march of the unemployed from the labour exchange in Bishop Street to the Guildhall to demand more jobs for the city. They carried banners condemning the high rate of unemployment in the city and sarcastically welcoming plans for a new labour exchange.

In March 1968, the Derry Housing Action Committee (DHAC) was formed. Another ad hoc coalition of labour and republican activists, it was formed with the intention of 'disrupting public life in the city to draw attention to the housing problem'. The DHAC made its first public appearance disrupting that month's Corporation meeting to demand extension to the city boundaries and the immediate building of new housing in the city. Before the RUC dragged protesters out of the Guildhall, Nationalist Party Councillor James Hegarty accused them of being communists after their spokesperson read out a statement that concluded:

We believe that the only long-term solution to the social cancers which beset Derry lies in the establishment of workers' power and public ownership of all land, banks and industries. The formation of this committee marks the beginning of a mass movement away from the false political leaders and against the exploiting capitalist class, who have in their wake a trail of human misery, degradation and decay that runs through many generations of working-class families in our city.[26]

The protest drew wide media attention and was repeated at the April and May meetings of the Corporation.

In May 1968, the DHAC submitted a dossier on housing cases to the Corporation. Their spokesperson, Brigid Bond, told the *Derry Journal* that it would be 'their last attempt through normal channels to have our just demands met'.[27] After the RUC again forcibly removed DHAC members from the Guildhall during a Corporation meeting

---

25 During the 1960s, much of the old Bogside was demolished and redeveloped, with new houses, maisonettes and flats replacing the old terraced housing. The current Bogside, bar the high-rise Rossville Flats which were demolished in the late 1980s, is the result of this redevelopment.

26 *Derry Journal*, 2 April 1968.

27 *Derry Journal*, 3 May 1968.

at the end of the month, the DHAC released a statement saying that:

> It is the policy of the committee to go through all existing channels to have our demands met before taking extreme action. We have made our final appeal to the Corporation yesterday. The response was totally unsatisfactory.[28]

In June 1968, the DHAC took direct action in the case of John Wilson, whose family had spent three years forced to live in a tiny caravan parked in a lane way in the Brandywell. Members of the DHAC dragged the caravan on to the Lecky Road, blocking the main road. The protest generated a lot of attention and support and was repeated the following week. Before the next week had finished, the Wilson family had been given a new home and the protest organisers charged with illegally blocking the road.[29] According to Eamonn McCann:

> Mr Wilson was living with his wife and two children in a tiny caravan up a mucky lane in the Brandywell district. The caravan was an oven in the summer, an ice-box in winter. One of the children had tuberculosis. Mr Wilson had been told by the Corporation Housing Department that he had 'no chance' of a house . . . On 22 June, a Saturday, about ten of us manhandled the Wilson's caravan on to the Lecky Road . . . parked it broadside in the middle of the road, stopping all traffic. We distributed leaflets in the surrounding streets explaining that we intended to keep the caravan there for twenty-four hours as a protest against the Wilson's living conditions . . . We then phoned the police, mayor and the newspapers . . . The mayor did not come . . . the police merely looked and left . . .
>
> On the Sunday, we hauled the caravan back to its original parking place. We had about 200 supporters with us . . . Reports of the incident were carried with some prominence . . . We announced that next weekend we would repeat the performance . . . we were visited by policemen who explained almost apologetically that if we went through with this they would 'have to take action' . . . we knew if we were arrested we would have strong support in the area . . . We lugged the caravan on to the road again the following Saturday and waited two nights for the police onslaught . . . nothing happened. We dragged it back to its lane way and resolved next week to take it into the city centre . . . before the week was out, the Wilsons had been guaranteed a house and ten of us had been summoned to appear in court . . . It was a perfect ending.[30]

At the end of that month, the Nationalist Party announced that they were considering a campaign of non-violent civil disobedience. They said:

28 *Derry Journal*, 31 May 1968.
29 Eleven of those who organised the protest appeared in court in early July charged with causing an obstruction. All were bound over to keep the peace and a number were also fined, including Eamonn McCann, Eamon Melaugh, John White, Robert Mitchell, Janet Wilcock and John Wilson, the occupant of the caravan.
30 Eamonn McCann, *War and an Irish Town* (Pluto, 1984) p34.

We have pleaded too long for our basic human rights. We must now be prepared to stand up like men and claim what is rightfully ours. If we cannot have justice, we must make a government based on injustice unworkable.[31]

But with the Nationalist Party on the verge of fading into political extinction, it would be others who would take up this challenge.

On 3 July 1968, the DHAC staged a sit-down protest on the newly opened second deck of the Craigavon Bridge. Again a number were arrested and charged and two of those – Thomas Carlin and Neil O'Donnell – chose to go to jail for a month rather than enter into bail bonds. They served the full month in prison.

On 12 July, the republican Connolly Commemoration Committee announced that it would go ahead with a planned march and rally for the city on 21 July. The march had already been banned by the RUC. About 600 people attended the rally to hear Republican Labour MP Gerry Fitt declare that 'if constitutional methods do not bring social justice, if they do not bring democracy to the North, then I am quite prepared to go outside constitutional methods.'[32]

On 18 August 1968, Eamon Melaugh told a DHAC protest meeting in the Diamond that if the housing situation was not sorted out then violence in Derry was 'not only a possibility but an inevitability'.[33]

On Saturday 24 August 1968, CSJ and NICRA organised the first major civil rights march in the North of Ireland, from Coalisland to Dungannon, in County Tyrone. Loyalists organised a counter-demonstration in an effort to get the march banned, and Stormont duly acceded. Despite this, the march took place and passed off with little incident. The publicity surrounding the march acted as an encouragement, and branches of NICRA were formed across the North. A NICRA spokesperson said that the march was 'only the beginning'.

After yet another DHAC protest in the Guildhall, on 27 August 1968, Eamon Melaugh contacted NICRA to ask them to arrange a civil rights march for Derry. The date set for the march was 5 October 1968.

After a few years of slowly escalating protest in the city, and a more rapid escalation over the previous few months, civil rights agitation was just about to move to a whole new level.

31 *Derry Journal*, 25 June 1968.
32 *Derry Journal*, 23 July 1968.
33 *Derry Journal*, 20 August 1968.

Fifty Days of Revolution

> The Fifty Days Revolution, which began with batons in Londonderry and ended with Northern Ireland's biggest-ever programme of reform, was played out over three distinct arenas. While citizens took to the streets in Derry (in the manner of all true revolutionaries) the big decisions were taken at Stormont and Whitehall.
>
> Like all revolutions, this one had been fathered by history and born of circumstances. Bad housing and unemployment, and the absence of universal suffrage in local elections were still bitter grievances after fifty years of constitutional government. The city was ripe for an explosion . . .[34]

So said the *Belfast Telegraph* in November 1968, looking back on an amazing period of fifty days that had changed the North of Ireland forever, and had set in motion a chain of events that would have repercussions for generations. And the events had centred on the city of Derry.

From the beginning of October until almost the end of November 1968 the protests that had gathered pace over the preceding months took on a whole new momentum and brought a problem that had been ignored for decades onto front pages across the world.

On 1 October 1968, the organisers of the proposed parade for 5 October said that they expected no RUC objection to their march, which would leave from the railway station in Duke Street and finish with a rally in the Diamond. They called for no flags to be carried on the march, only banners and placards demanding civil rights. They also asked Derry City FC to put back their match on that day so that it did not coincide with the march.

On the same day, the Apprentice Boys of Derry announced their intention to hold a march along the same route.

On 3 October, the march was banned by the Unionist Minister for Home Affairs, James Craig. The march organisers responded by announcing that they would go ahead with the march as planned. The decision and counter-decision started the fifty-day countdown.

On 5 October, about 400 people turned up in Duke Street to take part in the march. The RUC, batons drawn, blocked Duke Street and the side streets and hemmed the marchers in. Some in the crowd tried unsuccessfully to break through police lines, and a number of those in the front line were batoned and arrested, including MP Gerry Fitt. There were attempts to hold a sit-down protest and rally in Duke Street. But then:

> At the conclusion of the meeting, the crowd surged forward and once again police drew their batons . . . the police water cannon was then brought into action and it drove through the crowd with both jets spraying at full pressure. It was

---

34 *Belfast Telegraph*, 27 November 1968.

followed into the crowd by a large number of steel helmeted police with batons swinging. The police charged from both ends of the street as the marchers broke up in a bid to find a way through the barricades.

The water cannon swept both sides of the street and at one stage on its way back elevated its line of fire to direct a jet through an open window of the first floor of a house where a television cameraman was filming.

It then continued over Craigavon Bridge with its jets hosing both footpaths. Hundreds of afternoon shoppers, many of them women and some accompanied by young children, were caught in the deluge as the water carrier travelled to the Derry side of the bridge and continued round the roundabout at the foot of Carlisle Road, more than a quarter of a mile from the scene of the trouble.[35]

The single cameraman in the window filming all of this as it happened was Gay O'Brien from Irish national broadcaster RTÉ. The water-cannon attack didn't work and his footage was broadcast around the world, ensuring that what could well have passed off as just another small protest in Derry became headline news.

As marchers fled back towards the safety of the city centre and the police continued to attack them, young people came out from the Bogside to attack back. The situation 'erupted into a riot which convulsed a large area of the city'.[36] That night there were clashes between the police and Bogside youths in Fahan Street, William Street, Little James Street and Great James Street, with twenty people ending up in hospital.

Trouble flared again the following day as nationalist youths tried to get to the Diamond, the proposed setting for the previous day's rally, and were beaten back by police. Around 1,000 young people gathered in Rossville Street and William Street, and clashed with police on the edges of the city centre. A barricade was set up in Rossville Street to try to keep the police out of the Bogside. A police vehicle smashed the barricade and they stormed through, only to be beaten back by stones.

On the same day, twenty-nine people were charged with offences relating to the previous day's attempted march. Among them were three of the march organisers, Eamonn McCann, Eamon Melaugh and Fionnbarra O'Dochartaigh.

Clashes between the police and Bogside youths continued well into the Sunday night, and by Monday morning almost 100 people had been hospitalised.

Even the British Government had to take notice of this, and Stormont Prime Minister Terence O'Neill was 'invited' to London to explain the situation to British Prime Minister Harold Wilson.

The events of that weekend in October were investigated by the Cameron Commission, set up by the Stormont Government in January 1969 to investigate the causes of the trouble that erupted in October 1968 and continued until the end of the year. Its report, published in September 1969, found the causes for the trouble to include:

---

35 *Derry Journal*, 8 October 1968.
36 *Derry Journal*, 8 October 1968.

- A rising sense of continuing injustice and grievance among large sections of the Catholic population, particularly because of the housing provision of some local authorities and unfair methods of allocation of houses to perpetuate Unionist control;
- Religious discrimination in appointments by some Unionist-controlled authorities;
- Deliberate manipulation of local-government electoral boundaries to achieve or maintain Unionist control of some local authorities;
- A growing and powerful sense of resentment and frustration among the Catholic population at the failure of the government to investigate complaints and provide a remedy for them;
- Resentment, particularly among Catholics, at the existence of the USC as a partisan paramilitary force recruited exclusively from Protestants;
- Widespread resentment, among Catholics in particular, about the Special Powers Act.

In other words, according to the Stormont-appointed Cameron Commission, the cause of the trouble was the Stormont Government's policies that the marchers were protesting against.

The report also condemned the ban on the 5 October march – 'whether to impose the prohibition was wise or not, and in the circumstances we are of the opinion it was not' – and the police action in enforcing the ban, saying that it:

> . . . appeared excessive and unnecessary, produced an even more serious and widespread reaction against both Minister and police . . . if the objective of this operation was to drive the Civil Rights movement into the ground by a display of force and firmness in the enforcement of the ministerial order, it signally failed. The principal result of the operation, widely publicised at the time, was the opposite.

The result was indeed the opposite. Instead of being 'driven into the ground', the revolution continued.

On 9 October, the Derry Citizens' Action Committee (DCAC) was formed, bringing together many of those who had been involved in organising the 5 October march and earlier radical protests with mainstream nationalist politicians and businessmen. The elected officers of the DCAC were Ivan Cooper (Chair), Michael Canavan (Secretary), Campbell Austin (Press Officer), John Hume (Vice-Chair) and James Doherty (Treasurer). The DCAC immediately called for calm in the city, and cancelled a march planned for Saturday 12 October. This prompted one of the more radical organisers of civil rights protests in the city, Eamonn McCann, to refuse an invitation to join the DCAC, which he described as 'middle-class, middle-aged and middle-of-the-road'. He criticised the make-up and membership of the new organisation:

It was significant that the five officers elected at the meeting did not contain among them one working man . . .

The ad hoc Civil Rights Committee succeeded in provoking a militant mass response precisely because it was not tainted with the 'liberalism' which has propped up the system in N Ireland for half a century. The substantial citizens who attended the meeting leaped adroitly on to another band wagon with the intention of guiding it away from 'dangerous territory' . . .

. . . the civil rights movement is now in danger of being suffocated and only a total rejection of old ideas and old men gives any hope of real success . . .[37]

Another organisation was also formed on 9 October. Around 2,000 students from Queen's University in Belfast had tried to march to Belfast City Hall to protest against the police brutality in Derry. The march was blocked by a loyalist counter-demonstration, and a three-hour sit-down demonstration ensued. From this, People's Democracy (PD), a radical student organisation who would play a major role in the coming months, was formed.

Back in Derry, around 4,000 people attended a DCAC organised sit-down protest in Guildhall Square on 19 October. The protest passed off peacefully and the organisers claimed that this was proof that there would have been no violence on 5 October if it hadn't been for the actions of the RUC.

On 24 October, the DCAC announced that their full fifteen-member committee would march the route planned for 5 October and called on the citizens of Derry to line the route in silent support. Ian Paisley immediately announced a march for the same date, route and time.

On 26 October, twelve civil rights supporters attempted to march the fourteen miles from Strabane to Derry in protest at RUC actions on 5 October. They were attacked by loyalists in the villages of Bready and Magheramason, a few miles outside Derry. The DCAC claimed that the RUC knew of the planned attacks but did nothing to prevent them, and marchers said that the RUC were seen talking to the loyalists just a few minutes before the march was attacked.

At the end of October, members of the DHAC occupied the Guildhall during the monthly Corporation meeting. During the occupation, Eamon Melaugh of the DHAC took over the mayor's chair and Unionist members of the Corporation were warned that 'not many more, if any, minority mayors will occupy the mayoral chair in this Guildhall.'[38] He was right.

On 30 October, about two dozen unemployed men burned their signing-on cards at Derry labour exchange in protest at the lack of jobs available in the city.

On Saturday 2 November, the fifteen-man board of the DCAC successfully completed their planned route, while about 4,000 supporters lined the footpaths along their way. A small number of loyalists, led by Paisley's right-hand man, Major Ronald Bunting, gathered in Duke Street when the march was due to start. He advised his

---

37 *Derry Journal*, 11 October 1968.
38 *Derry Journal*, 1 November 1968.

followers to follow the civil rights marchers but to 'keep out of the way if you want to avoid the stench [of the civil rights marchers]'.[39] Despite the loyalist protests, which continued on Carlisle Road and Ferryquay Street, the march passed off peacefully and 'the right of the citizens of Derry to parade peacefully through the streets of the city was established . . .'[40]

On 7 November, the DCAC announced plans for a major civil rights march from Duke Street to Guildhall Square, to be held on Saturday 16 November. When announcing the march, they called on 'the people who supported civil rights' to ignore a march planned by Ian Paisley for Saturday 9 November. Paisley had announced a march to the Diamond for the Saturday afternoon, at the same time as the DUAC were intending to hold a teach-in in Guildhall Square. The DUAC invited Paisley to come along:

As Mr Paisley will be in Derry on Saturday, we thought it appropriate to extend an invitation to him to speak at our teach-in, since we believe that many of the homeless and unemployed of all creeds, and indeed the working class in general, would be curious to hear his views on the misery and hopelessness which affects so many of our citizens.[41]

Paisley's march went ahead on the Saturday, with about 700 of his supporters following him across Craigavon Bridge. There were minor scuffles around the Diamond as nationalist youths protested at the presence of the Paisleyites, but they weren't the only ones not enamoured of his presence in the city. The Church of Ireland Bishop of Derry and Raphoe, the Reverend Dr Charles Tyndall, also condemned the inflammatory presence of Paisley and his men. Speaking at a Remembrance Sunday ceremony the following day, he said:

Did I see yesterday on Craigavon Bridge in Derry something sinister? Did I see the march of men dedicated to religious genocide? Did I see the rising of an ideological force based on cultivating hatred and invective? Did I see the sign once again of the Swastika?[42]

Speaking at the DUAC teach-in in Guildhall Square, Eamon Melaugh said that Paisley's presence in Derry brought much-needed attention to the situation in the city.

The following week saw the first real signs of a constructive response to the demands of the civil rights marchers when the Londonderry Corporation accepted Nationalist Party motions for a points system for housing allocation and the return of decision making on housing from the mayor to the housing committee, where it was

---

39 *Derry Journal*, 5 November 1968.
40 *Derry Journal*, 5 November 1968.
41 *Derry Journal*, 8 November 1968.
42 *Derry Journal*, 12 November 1968.

always supposed to have been anyway. Housing was now to be allocated by a three-man committee comprising the mayor and two aldermen (councillors).

The Unionist Government redressed the balance by banning all parades inside Derry's Walls for a month, apart from 'customary' (loyal-order) ones, and the RUC served a notice rerouting the proposed march for 16 November away from the city centre.

The DCAC defied the ban, and around 15,000 civil rights supporters marched across Craigavon Bridge and into the Diamond, the largest civil rights march in the North to date. The leaders of the march made a symbolic breach in the RUC lines at the end of the bridge while thousands of others just walked around the barriers and into the Diamond, despite coming under attack from stone throwers along Carlisle Road.

On the following Monday, Derry reacted to Craig's ban on marches inside the Walls by basically making a joke of it. Marchers emerged from the shirt factories and docks and from anywhere where large groups of people were gathered, and seven separate civil rights marches made their way through the city centre on that one afternoon, Monday 18 November 1968.

According to the *Derry Journal*:

The ban imposed by Home Affairs Minister William Craig on parades and assemblies within the Walls of Derry was defied yesterday no less than seven times as spontaneous demonstrations in support of civil rights brought the city's dockers, girls from the city's shirt factories and unemployed teenagers onto the streets of the banned centre of the city.

It was a day on which chanting demonstrators made the banned area within the city's Walls their own . . .

400 Derry dockers [who] left their work and staged a march through the city centre to their union headquarters . . .

1,000 shirt factory girls drawn from about half a dozen of the city's factories marched through Shipquay Gate to the Diamond . . . immediately they had dispersed, a group of about 100 unemployed teenagers marched the one-mile circuit of Derry's Walls chanting 'We want work' . . .

. . . the police took no action as the ban was defied on seven separate occasions . . .[43]

The following day, around 1,500 people attended a meeting in the Guildhall, with thousands more outside, to endorse the work of the DCAC. However, it was pointed out to the committee that it did not actually contain any women, a point which was reinforced in a letter to the local press which said that:

Since the women of this city have had to bear most of the hardships brought on by unemployment and bad housing conditions, surely there should be at least

43 *Derry Journal*, 19 November 1968.

two ladies on the committee. I feel quite sure there must be hundreds of women who hold this view, so let their voices be heard.[44]

Sheila McClean, who had designed the oak leaf logo for the civil rights movement in Derry, was invited to join the committee.

DCAC Secretary Michael Canavan gave a lengthy report to the meeting, outlining all that they had achieved in the previous few weeks:

If the Citizens' Action Committee was born on October 9th, it was surely conceived on the 5th October, the offspring on one side of the indomitable spirit of the people of Derry and on the other of their suffering on that memorable day. For on that day, a group of no more than 500-strong set out to march in Duke Street for Civil Rights. The Government of Northern Ireland had them surrounded in the streets of their own city, beaten to the ground with truncheons and humiliated with water cannon. But when those batons rose, they fell not only on the homeless, jobless few, but upon the minds and hearts of every thinking person in this city. October 5th is but six short weeks ago and on Saturday last those few in number had become thousands strong and the might that humbled them lay outmanoeuvred, defeated and disgraced before the world . . .

The savage rupture of the October 5th march had burned deeply into the conscience of the citizens and their establishment of the rights of all citizens to peacefully assemble and march in their own city was an immediate objective. It was tackled symbolically by the march of the fifteen-man committee on November 2nd, in the name of all citizens, from the Waterside station, via Ferryquay Street, to the Diamond, where the Universal Declaration of Human Rights was read by 11-year-old Eamon Melaugh [Junior]. Only the committee marched – followed by many thousands . . .

The ultimate success of our campaign can only be achieved finally when our demands for equality of citizenship for all are granted and when a proportionate share of economic and educational development for the stricken area west of the Bann is attained . . .

On the political scene, the events of October 5th and subsequently have resulted in the visits of the Prime Minister of Northern Ireland and the Ministers of Commerce and Home Affairs to Westminster for consultation with the Premier of the Mother of Parliaments . . . It is obvious again for the first time that to satisfy the requirements of Westminster a timetable of reform will have to be drawn up and adhered to. And as we make this report, the first indications of these desperately needed reforms are issuing from Stormont . . .

For our part, we know full well that these momentous events have been set in

---

44 Eilis Heaney, *Derry Journal*, 22 November 1968. Feminism, and the realisation that the equal in 'equal rights' referred to men and women as well as unionists and nationalists, hadn't really reached Derry at this stage, and, whatever the motive, the chant and demand was 'one *man* one vote' and the majority of the marches, apart from those from the shirt factories, were very much male dominated.

train only by events here in Derry and we are firmly resolved that the campaign for civil rights in this city shall not fail or falter until all our objectives have been achieved – come what may . . .[45]

By the end of the week, there had been many more spontaneous marches through the city but, with expectations of a major announcement on reforms from the Unionist Government rising, the DCAC called for calm and an end to spontaneous marches not endorsed or organised by the DCAC until they had time to properly consider any reforms proposed by the government.

On Friday 22 November 1968, fifty days after his Home Affairs Minister had banned the 5 October march, Unionist Prime Minister Terence O'Neill, under pressure from the British Government in London, announced his reforms. His proposals included:

- A Development Commission to replace the Londonderry Corporation;
- An ombudsman to investigate complaints against government departments;
- The allocation of houses by local authorities to be based solely on need;
- A review of the Special Powers Act;
- Reform of the local-government electoral system, to include the abolition of company votes.

After fifty days of protest, it would seem that many of the demands of the civil rights marchers were about to be met, with the most momentous changes the North of Ireland had seen in its short history. The Nationalist Party welcomed the proposals as a 'momentous moment'.

The DCAC said that their 'struggle will go on' because the proposals did not do enough to tackle the issues of voting rights and democracy in the city, although in hindsight this was a bit of a moot point, since the Londonderry Corporation was about to be replaced by an unelected commission and, although the DCAC didn't know it at the time, there wouldn't be a local-government election in the city for almost five years, by which time even the Stormont Government would be gone.

But the DCAC did feel that there was enough in the proposals to make it worth giving them a chance, and after O'Neill made his famous 'Ulster at the crossroads' speech calling on the population to step back from the brink of disaster, they called for a moratorium on marches.

Derry settled back into a quieter routine after the 'fifty-days revolution', although sporadic protests continued, including a hunger strike in the Guildhall as Ambrose Moore, a father of three, demanded that his family, split because of homelessness, be re-united and rehoused.

But for many, O'Neill's reforms, which had already been met with opposition from loyalist quarters for being too much of a sop to nationalists, were seen as 'too little,

---

45 Secretary's report to DCAC, 19 November 1968. (MoFD collection)

too late'. Before the end of the month, the student group People's Democracy announced a four-day march from Belfast to Derry, to start on 1 January 1969.

Along its route, the march would pass through a little country area a few miles from Derry known as Burntollet.

You Are Now Entering Free Derry

On the morning of 1 January 1969, a group of about forty young people, mainly student members of People's Democracy (PD), gathered outside the City Hall in Belfast to begin their planned march to Derry. They carried placards calling for equal voting rights for all, fair allocation of housing and the repeal of the hated Special Powers Act. A group of loyalist opponents gathered on the pavement opposite. They were led by Paisley's aide, Major Bunting, who had vowed to do everything he could to obstruct the march.

The jostling began as soon as the march moved off and the marchers were met with loyalist protests all along the early part of their route out of Belfast, with marchers claiming that the police were either assisting or ignoring the loyalists, and even attacking marchers themselves.

The marchers spent their first night on the road in a community hall at Whitehill, outside Antrim. During the night, the police burst into the hall to claim there was a bomb scare and the students had to leave immediately. The students refused to leave and the 'bomb' was not mentioned again.

On the second day, the march left Antrim for the mainly nationalist village of Toome. The march was diverted past the village of Randalstown and there were again accusations that the police were deliberately misdirecting the marchers and trying to lead them into, and not away from, loyalist protests. On the night before the marchers arrived in Toome, a monument in the village to Roddy McCorley, who was hanged in the village during the 1798 rebellion and seen by many as a republican hero, was damaged by explosives. Five months later, the Minister for Home Affairs said that 'police enquiries were continuing' into the bomb attack.[46]

As the march arrived in Toome, Bunting and his supporters followed by car. One marcher threw a flowerpot at Bunting's car and became the first person convicted for violence on the march, despite two days of ongoing loyalist attacks on the marchers.

After lunch, the march left Toome for Maghera. The police ordered the marchers to take the road towards Bellaghy, but within two miles, the marchers again met Bunting and his supporters, who knew exactly where they were going to be despite their 'last-minute' change of route. Witnesses claimed that there were no loyalist protesters along the original planned route.

On this occasion, the police did move the loyalist protesters, but only into a better position to attack the marchers:

> Bunting's men and their local supporters were allowed to form a semicircular band from the right-hand side of the road the marchers came, across the two routes opposite, to the right and down the further side of the road into which the march turned. A quite inadequate string of police kept the groups apart, but this allowed the hostile people every opportunity to toss abuse and objects at

---

46 Bowes Egan & Vincent McCormack, *Burntollet* (LRS, 1969) p10.

the passers-by. Showers of nails, and nuts and bolts, rained down as men openly pulled handfuls out of bags. A shower of six-inch nails rained on me. No attempt was made to stop them. And no-one was arrested.[47]

As the march approached Gulladuff, near Maghera, more large groups of loyalists were seen waiting for the marchers outside Maghera, with the police making no moves to disperse them. The marchers made the decision to stop in Gulladuff, where they were warmly welcomed. Because of the large numbers of loyalists around Maghera, the decision was made to move the marchers on by car past the town to their sleeping place for the night. Many of the cars were attacked and damaged along the way. The loyalists also expressed their disappointment at missing out on attacking the march by rioting in Maghera.

The following morning, 3 January, the PD march set out for Dungiven, on the other side of the Glenshane Pass, and then onto Claudy, their planned stopping point for the night. The police again attempted to stop the march outside Dungiven, claiming in the face of eyewitness evidence that there was a loyalist protest blocking the road. The marchers ignored their orders and walked peacefully on, reaching Claudy with little incident.

In Derry, Ian Paisley and his supporters held a rally in the Guildhall. Around 1,000 nationalists gathered outside to protest and Major Bunting's car was taken and burned.

On the fourth and final day of their march, the members of PD and their supporters planned to complete the final leg from Claudy to Derry. During the night, a bus and a number of lorries had been seen delivering bottles and stones to a field a few miles outside the village. At the same time, the emergency telephone service in the area suffered a 'fault' so no outside communication was possible.

Speaking as the march was getting ready to leave, Eamonn McCann said:

In the last three days we have come more than sixty miles. I will not remind you why we embarked on this activity. We knew from the beginning that this was a protest of a most serious sort. We decided to march as a gesture of solidarity with the deprived . . . we cannot even consider abandoning our protest now, in face of opposition, which may be strong . . . Let us be clear about our policy today. For three days we have been harassed and abused without any retaliation on our part. Today we may face provocation beyond anything yet seen. We said at the outset that we would march non-violently. Today will see the test of that pious declaration . . . I am afraid that this is a policy we must support to a lunatic extreme. We must agree that not one single person will retaliate even to save himself from injury . . . Comrades this may sound insane and absurd. But it is necessary. We will be opposed, make no mistake of that. And any trust you may still have in the RUC is, in my opinion, quite misplaced. We are on our own and our only weapons are the principles we have adopted . . .[48]

47 *Burntollet*, p14.
48 *Burntollet*, pp25-26.

At just after 10.00AM, the march, now numbering about 300 people, set off. The road ahead was strangely quiet, and areas where opposition may have been expected were deserted. As it joined the main Dungiven–Derry road, it was stopped by police, who warned them of a protest ahead on their chosen route. Although there were a number of alternative routes available, this time the police didn't redirect the march but instead said they could lead them past the protesters. The police took the lead, but for the first time were prepared for major trouble or rather, as it turned out, to protect themselves, with tin hats and riot shields at the ready.

Seven miles from Derry, the march progressed along the side of a steep hill, with the River Faughan below. A high hedge obscured the marchers' view of the hill above, while a small group of loyalists walked in front of the march, unimpeded by police, singing sectarian songs loud enough for anyone on the hills above to hear. Their songs gave clear notice of the progress of the march.

Through the occasional gap in the hedge marchers could see men gathered on the hills above, with police doing nothing about them. The men were all wearing white armbands. Armed with sticks spiked with nails and stones, they formed up into groups and began to shadow the march. Soon stones began to rain down on the marchers. Many of those involved were later identified as members of the B Specials, the notoriously sectarian police reserve force. Photographs show the police making no moves to stop the attack.

As the marchers tried to flee the stones, they were forced towards another group of loyalists waiting ahead. One witness, a school teacher, said:

> I saw the police moving through the fields, and then I saw the first attacker wearing a white armband. Then I began to see other men wearing similar armbands standing in groups on high ground above the road. I remember then dismissing the idea that the attackers would simply be angry groups of locals annoyed at demonstrators passing through their village. My impression now was that the attack was well organised and the armbands were for recognition purposes.
>
> By now the field seemed crowded with men and youths, perhaps 100 or 150. I saw some women and girls, too, among the people in the field. I saw the police marshalling a girl along in the field. She carried two milk bottles in her hands. Then I saw the first stone come whizzing through the air and remember shouting to the people near me to get in against the hedge. In a second the air was thick with missiles. I pulled my coat up around my head and crouched down, stumbling forward. There was utter confusion as girls screamed, and stones and bottles crashed around. I kept my head down but on once looking up, I saw another large group of men with cudgels and sticks running onto the road ahead of us. There was tremendous confusion as people stumbled and grabbed each other for cover and protection.[49]

Another Belfast school teacher, Judith McGuffin, recounted:

49 *Burntollet*, pp32-33.

Showers of rocks crashed around us. I was in the middle of the fourth row and bent double in an attempt to avoid the hail of missiles, when a middle-aged man in a tweed coat, brandishing what seemed to be a chair leg, dashed from the left-hand side of the road, hit me on the back, then pulled down the hood of my anorak and struck me on the head. I then tried to crawl away but, teeth bared, he hit me again on the spot on my skull . . .[50]

Many other witnesses gave similar accounts of the attacks continuing as the marchers fled towards the bridge over the river at Burntollet, with the police doing little or nothing to stop them. Some of the marchers were forced into the freezing river and stoned while they were trapped there, with eyewitness accounts and press reports of one young woman who was being clubbed as she lay unconscious in the water, and who would have drowned if other marchers hadn't managed to drag her clear.

The attack lasted for about thirty minutes before the marchers were able to get clear and regroup along the road. Over seventy of their number needed hospital treatment. This was despite the presence of two county inspectors, two district inspectors, seven head constables, seventeen sergeants and 116 constables there, in riot gear, to do their job and 'keep the peace'.[51]

As those marchers who could still walk staggered on towards Derry, a number of petrol bombs were thrown at them from ditches along the road. They were met by supporters on the outskirts of the city who joined the march and warned of further trouble ahead. The march was attacked again as it passed the loyalist Irish Street estate in the Waterside, with bricks, bottles and even petrol bombs raining down on the marchers, and again at the quarry near the bottom of Spencer Road, where the police held the march up.

But the march eventually made it onto Craigavon Bridge and over to the city side, where a crowd of around 3,000 was waiting for them in Guildhall Square.

This four-day series of events, known ever since simply as 'Burntollet', was the most extreme example yet of how far the police, government and loyalists would go to oppose demands for civil rights, but worse was to come.

* * *

As the crowd in Guildhall Square were greeting the arrival of the marchers, a crowd of around 500 loyalists came down Shipquay Street, and although separated from the civil rights supporters by a line of police, there was a brief flurry of stone throwing between the two crowds. As the main crowd dispersed, a police water cannon arrived on the scene, with sirens blaring, and clashes broke out between police and nationalists. The police baton charged the crowd, who were forced back into the Bogside.

Rioting continued on the edges of the Bogside until the early hours of the morning and over 150 people ended up in hospital. Afterwards, there were reports of upwards

---

50 *Burntollet*, p33.
51 *Burntollet*, p41.

of 200 policemen making indiscriminate raids into St Columb's Wells and the Lecky Road. Residents of these areas were adamant that they were quiet at the time, and that there was no trouble at all until the police arrived. One resident, an American citizen who was staying in her old home in Wellington Street while her husband was fighting in Vietnam, told the *Derry Journal*:

> I went to the window and saw the police give a man an awful beating. A policeman came over and smashed my window with his baton. My mother had to leave the house because she was so upset. I went to the door and was challenged by the police. One of them said, 'You f**king Fenians will have no windows left before the night is over. We are authorised to do anything we please tonight.' He took up his baton and hit me. I told him I was an American citizen and he said, 'You are a f**king Fenian.'[52]

Many other residents reported similar incidents, and alleged that many of the police officers involved were obviously drunk at the time. The following morning, around 1,000 men gathered to march to the police station at Victoria Barracks to protest about the police actions, but they were dissuaded by members of the DCAC. It was agreed that women from the area should make a peaceful protest there instead. The women marched to the barracks in the form of a 'funeral procession'. The women were told that the police would not return to the area that night if it was peaceful. They replied, 'It was peaceful last night and look what happened.'[53] The DCAC announced that the moratorium on public demonstrations they had called in November was now over. Barricades went up around the Bogside and residents undertook to look after the area themselves. The first Free Derry was born.

When the Cameron Commission report was published in September, it referred to the police actions of the night of 4/5 January in the Bogside. It reported that:

> Our investigations have led us to the unhesitating conclusion that on the night of 4th/5th January a number of policemen were guilty of misconduct which involved assault and battery, malicious damage to property in streets in the predominantly Catholic Bogside area, giving reasonable cause for apprehension of personal injury among innocent inhabitants, and the use of provocative sectarian and political slogans . . . we are afraid that not only do we find the allegations of misconduct substantial, but that for such conduct among members of a disciplined and well-led force there can be no acceptable justification or excuse. We have also considered the full and careful report of County Inspector Baillie and we note with some satisfaction though with regret that his independent investigation has led him to reach the same conclusions as to the gravity and nature of the misconduct . . .[54]

---

52 *Derry Journal*, 7 January 1969.
53 *Derry Journal*, 7 January 1969.
54 *Derry Journal*, 12 September 1969.

* * *

In the early hours of 5 January 1969 as youths gathered in the Bogside preparing for more police attacks, one group waited at the junction of the Lecky Road and St Columb's Street. Standing around in the cold with nothing better to do, they decided on a piece of graffiti. After various suggestions were put forward, Eamonn McCann suggested a slogan inspired by one he had read about in Berkeley College in California, where 'You Are now Entering Free Berkeley' had been painted on a college wall during a free-speech protest. He amended it to 'You Are Now Entering Free Derry'. The slogan was then painted on the gable end of 33 Lecky Road. Handwritten on a dirty grey wall at the time, it was replaced by the more familiar black block lettering on a white background in August 1969, after the Battle of the Bogside.

The area around the gable wall had already become an ad hoc meeting place, as the area in front of it had been cleared during the ongoing renovations of the Bogside, but now the slogan gave it an added focal point, and it became, and remains, the centre for public meetings in the Bogside. The street has long since gone, finally demolished in the mid-1970s, but the original gable end remains, Free Derry Wall, the enduring symbol of the civil rights movement in Derry and an inspiration for civil rights struggles across the world.[55]

* * *

On 9 January, Radio Free Derry broadcast for the first time on 240m medium wave. The original broadcasts were from the Bogside, from the McClenaghan home in Wellington Street, but the equipment moved to Creggan to get a stronger signal. The station broadcast for two nights, and then went off-air over the weekend, returning on the Monday evening, 13 January.

By the end of the following week, 116 people had lodged complaints about police brutality with the DCAC, which were delivered to County Inspector Harry Baillie. Baillie said he was 'conducting general inquiries' about police actions in the Bogside the previous weekend. As he visited the Bogside with members of the DCAC, he was photographed walking past Free Derry Wall. This is the first known mention of the slogan in the media.

On Saturday 11 January, the DCAC removed the barricades which had gone up around the Bogside the previous week to keep the police out. According to the *Derry Journal*:

The barricades erected in the Lecky Road/St Columb's Wells district of Derry after the residents of the area, incensed by allegations that riot police had run amok in the area in the early hours of Sunday week, had taken over the policing of the district, came down on Saturday morning.

---

55   For further reading on Free Derry Wall see Jim Collins & Adrian Kerr (Eds), *Free Derry Wall* (Guildhall Press, 2009).

Those at Fahan Street, Hamilton Street and Eglinton Place were quickly removed by men who, during the week, had taken part in dusk-to-dawn patrols of the area.

But the barricades at Bogside, which had been made by a bigger excavator-digger and a dumper from the nearby building site, proved a much more difficult proposition . . .

The decision to call off the citizen patrols and remove the barricades was made by the DCAC and approved at two public meetings held in the area. The patrols had been operating since the previous Sunday night. They were started after allegations that riot police had stormed into the Lecky Road and St Columb's Wells in the early hours of the morning, breaking windows and threatening and terrorising residents.

The DCAC in a statement early on Saturday said they had decided to formally call of their protest in the area since they felt that their point had been very powerfully made in their most potent protest to date.

'We warn the RUC that we will never allow a repetition of last Sunday morning and we call on the government to take serious note of the strength of the people's feelings on the civil rights issue and if they wish to maintain a stable community then they must speedily introduce the remaining reforms.

'Our confidence in the forces of law and order was shattered when the ravage of people's homes took place in the early hours of Sunday morning. We were left with no alternative in the face of such partiality by the forces of law and order but to lend assistance to the people in defence of their area – an action which we took for several reasons.

'Firstly, we wished to ensure the protection of the people of the area against a repetition of the savage events of Sunday morning; secondly, we were concerned about maintaining peace, law and order throughout the city, and thirdly, by taking over the policing of a whole district we were making the strongest possible protest against the partiality of law in Northern Ireland . . .

'We congratulate the residents of that area on their wonderful performance under very great strain for the past week . . .'[56]

Thus ended the first phase of Free Derry, 5 January 1969 to 11 January 1969.

---

56 *Derry Journal*, 14 January 1969.

Public Disorder and Division

By the middle of January, there were signs that the delicate coalition that was the civil rights movement in Derry, as represented by the DCAC, was beginning to split as the differing motives of those involved – left, centre and republican – began to come to the fore.

Representing the centre ground, Ivan Cooper released a DCAC statement condemning those he said were using the civil rights movement for their own ends, or had different tactics in mind:

> We are going to adopt a tough line. These people are jumping on the civil rights platform and are using it to further aims that are not embraced by the civil rights programme. They seem to have no scruples about how they are going to achieve their aims.[57]

He included a thinly disguised attack on the left and republicans: '. . . the committee's function was not to unite Ireland or the working class.'

Eamonn McCann, one of the more radical left-wing activists in Derry, rejected this sort of reasoning:

> There has already been talk of purging the movement of 'extremists'. I think that it is people who talk like this that are falling into a trap, because they are accepting [the] analysis of the Civil Rights movement as being composed of 'nice' moderates and 'nasty' militants.
>
> I do not see any crucial division between moderates and militants . . . the basic division is between those who wish to see a more liberal unionism entrenched and those who hold that the achievement of social justice is quite incompatible with the maintenance of Unionist rule and the maintenance of the Tory system itself . . .[58]

The divisions became even more obvious when Stormont Prime Minister Terence O'Neill announced the dissolution of the Stormont parliament at the beginning of February. His move was seen as a challenge to the hardliners in his own party to test themselves at the ballot box,[59] but for Derry it created the opportunity for three supporters of the civil rights movement to stand against each other. Eamonn McCann, John Hume and Eddie McAteer all announced their intention to stand for the Foyle constituency seat. McCann was standing as Derry Labour, Hume as an Independent and McAteer as Nationalist Party.

---

57 *Derry Journal*, 17 January 1969.
58 *Derry Journal*, 17 January 1969.
59 One of those who opposed O'Neill was Derry MP and former mayor Albert Anderson, who caused outrage at the announcement of the election when he told rowing Unionists to 'not get down to the level of the Lecky Road. Let us be the decent Protestants we are.'

John Hume released a statement saying that his entry into the political arena was not incompatible with his membership of the DCAC, stating that every member had the right to their own political views, but prominent committee member Eamon Melaugh resigned in response to Hume's decision to stand in Foyle, and that of Ivan Cooper to stand in Mid-Derry. Melaugh claimed that:

> Certain members of the committee – those who had projected themselves as protagonists of the civil rights movement in Derry – have decided to foist themselves on the public as political candidates at the forthcoming general election in preference to working as a committee for the benefit of the working class.[60]

Melaugh admitted that his remarks were aimed directly at Hume and Cooper, and called on McCann, who was not a member of the DCAC, to 'get out of this murky contest and leave the constituency of Foyle to the place-seekers'. He also argued that the DCAC should have consulted the people of Derry about what they wanted from the election before any members should decide whether or not to stand.

Within a week, all three candidates were accusing the others of smear campaigns against each other. McCann's supporters accused Hume's of trying to smear him by calling him a communist while Hume claimed that the Nationalist Party were 'trying to drag this election into the gutter with personal attacks' and McAteer said he was 'getting a little tired of the insinuations being whispered by canvassers for one of the opposing candidates'.[61]

When the election was held on 24 February, with an eighty-five per cent poll in Derry, Hume got a record vote and began a political career that was to last for decades. His election also signalled the end of the road for the Nationalist Party, which would never again be a prominent player in Irish politics.

Across the North, the future of the Unionist Party was the major issue, but twenty-seven of the thirty-nine Unionist candidates returned were supporters of Terence O'Neill, who was re-elected as Prime Minister, and his programme of 'reforms' continued.

One of the first acts of the new government was to resume plans for amendments to the Public Order Act.[62] The Derry Labour Party attacked the plans, saying that they would be 'back on the streets' if they were ever passed, and criticised John Hume and Ivan Cooper for being complicit by their presence in Stormont and their support for the continued 'liberal unionism' espoused by O'Neill and his supporters.

The Public Order Bill was an example of how the government were trying appeasement in regard to some civil rights demands on voting and housing, at the same time exacerbating the situation by increasing resentment in other areas – in this case, repressive legislation. While removing some of the reasons for people to protest with one

---

60 *Derry Journal*, 11 February 1969.
61 *Derry Journal*, 18 February 1969.
62 The Public Order Act had been passed in 1951 and gave the police and government additional repressive powers in respect of public meetings and parades on top of those already covered by the Special Powers Act.

hand, O'Neill was giving back reasons with the other. The Derry Labour Party called for people across the North to stage a sit-down protest against a proposed amendment in the Public Order Act which would outlaw any such protest. They said that:

> Captain O'Neill has learned nothing from recent months. He thinks that he has deceived the people of Northern Ireland by his 'liberal' prattle. It is up to those who see through his deception to have a massive province-wide sit-down protest on the day this bill has its final reading at Stormont.
>
> This will at least show our PM that all those who take part in such a protest despise his 'liberal' mouthings and his jackboot actions.[63]

Speaking at a DHAC protest in Derry on St Patrick's Day, Bernadette Devlin also called for people to take to the streets again in opposition to the Public Order Bill. She said O'Neill had been given enough time for his promised reforms and all he had produced was this new repressive bill. 'It is time we were on the streets again,' she said. 'We have been off the streets too long. We are sick, sore and tired of it. We are finished with it, and if Captain O'Neill has not got the message by now, it is time we were rid of him.'[64]

Protests against the Public Order Bill gathered pace in Derry throughout the rest of the month and opposition MPs at Stormont even staged a sit-down protest in parliament buildings against the bill. Three thousand people took part in a sit-down protest outside the police headquarters at Victoria Barracks, which ended with coins and stones being thrown at the barracks' windows.

The North Derry Civil Rights Association then announced plans to retrace the route from Burntollet to Derry on Saturday 29 March to link up with another march being planned for the city for that day. While approximately 8,000 people took part in the Derry march, which passed off peacefully, the proposed Burntollet march was postponed.

The James Connolly Republican Club also announced an extended route for that year's Easter parade, which would now finish at Guildhall Square. The march was always led by someone carrying a tricolour, which was banned from the city centre. Five men were arrested after the march for defying the ban, and three tricolours were carried through the city centre in protest on the day they appeared in court.

On 17 April, Bernadette Devlin was elected MP for Mid-Ulster at Westminster. She was the youngest-ever woman to be elected to the British parliament.

The following weekend, the proposed march from Burntollet to Derry was banned, and the resentment that had been building again in Derry over the previous few months erupted into violence.

The ban, justified by the threat of 'bloody and violent opposition' by loyalists, was announced on the Friday night. Although there was no attempt to defy the ban, around 200 loyalists gathered at Burntollet Bridge to attack anyone who tried. But

---

63 *Derry Journal*, 11 March 1969.
64 *Derry Journal*, 18 March 1969.

there were a number of spontaneous protests in Derry which ended in clashes between civil rights supporters and loyalists, and eventually with the police. According to the *Derry Journal*:

> The violence which erupted on Saturday afternoon following a clash between civil rights sympathisers and Paisleyites who had earlier gathered at Burntollet Bridge, the announced assembly point for the banned civil rights march, swept through the city centre, with a strong force of riot police fighting running battles with Civil Rights supporters.
>
> The trail of violence ran through the Diamond, Waterloo Place and Strand Road as police, supported by an armoured water cannon, drove the crowd back into the Bogside area of the city. There, a massive and bitter confrontation went on into the early hours of Sunday morning, with casualties mounting steadily.
>
> On Sunday morning, the riot-torn and devastated Rossville Street/William Street junction resembled a battlefield, the street littered with stones, rocks, pieces of metal and broken glass with overturned, and in one case burned, vehicles forming barricades behind which police and Civil Rights sympathisers had faced each other for nearly five hours the previous night.[65]

Over 160 people were hospitalised on the Saturday evening, and police admitted that an officer had opened fire with live rounds in Hamilton Street, the first shots of the conflict fired in the city.

The police remained in the area, and at 2.00PM on the Sunday afternoon, there was a 'mass evacuation' of families from the Bogside to the safety of Creggan. After a meeting in Creggan, an ultimatum was issued to the police: either the riot police withdrew from the Bogside by 5.00PM or the residents would return and they 'would not be responsible for the consequences'. With just fifteen minutes to go to the deadline, it was announced that the riot police would leave the area. Ten minutes after the police left, about 3,000 men, armed with sticks, iron bars and other weapons, marched back into the Bogside.

But during the trouble on the Saturday night, police action had irrevocably changed the situation in Derry when they stormed into the home of the Devenny family in William Street.

Sammy Devenny

On the evening of Saturday 19 April, Sammy Devenny, a 42-year-old father of nine, was standing at the front door of his family home in William Street on the edge of the Bogside as riot police chased youths up the street. Several of the youths ran through his home to escape the police, but the police battered down the door and followed them in. When they couldn't catch their intended targets, the police attacked the residents of the house with batons. Mr Devenny and two other men, Freddie Budd and Patrick Harkin, were batoned by the police and seriously

---

65 *Derry Journal*, 22 April 1969.

injured. Mr Devenny's 16-year-old daughter Cathy, who had just been released from hospital following an operation, also needed hospital treatment after being kicked unconscious during the attack. Seven more of the young Devenny children witnessed the attack on their father, a number of whom were also injured.

One member of the Devenny family recounted how Mr Budd 'lay across two of the children to protect them . . . the police batoned him and his blood flowed over the children'. Mr Devenny was taken to hospital with 'head and stomach injuries and smashed teeth'.[66] He also suffered a severe heart attack. He was released from hospital after three days, but readmitted and treated for almost another month.

He died on 17 July, and the inquest reported that he had died from natural causes, but his family, and the people of Derry, never accepted this finding, and to them the RUC had now become killers. It was the final breach in any trust the nationalist people of Derry had in the RUC. He had become the second man in the North West to die at the hands of the RUC; just three days earlier, 67-year-old Francis McCloskey, from nearby Dungiven, had died after the RUC baton charged a crowd protesting in the town.

A team of detectives from London were brought in to investigate Sammy Devenny's death, but they announced there was a lack of evidence due to a 'conspiracy of silence' from the RUC. No charges were ever brought against those RUC officers responsible for the attack on the Devenny family or their neighbours.

Mr Devenny's family never accepted the 'official' version of events put out about their father's death, and in 2001 they achieved a measure of success with the release of a report by the Office of the Police Ombudsman of Northern Ireland (OPONI) into the investigation of their father's death.

Among the findings released by OPONI were that there were differences of opinion in the medical evidence at the time that Mr Devenny's death had not been a direct result of the attack and that it was reasonable for the family to hold the view that the two were directly connected; that the original RUC investigation into the attack was completely inadequate; that the Metropolitan Police investigation had been obstructed and that it was wrong that its findings were never shared with the Devenny family.[67]

On the Monday after the weekend of violence, Derry was again brought to a halt by a series of spontaneous demonstrations against the police brutality of that weekend; there were also demonstrations in many other towns across the North.

By now, the mood in the city and elsewhere was darkening, and the period for reforms to be enough to settle the situation seemed to be drawing to a close. By the end of April, Terence O'Neill had resigned as Unionist Prime Minister, to be replaced by James Chichester-Clark. One of his first acts was to order an amnesty for those convicted of 'political' offences since October 1968. The amnesty covered Ian

---

66 *Derry Journal*, 22 April 1969.
67 Report of the Office of the Police Ombudsman of Northern Ireland, 27 September 2001. OPONI was set up in 2000 to investigate complaints about the RUC, and then the Police Service of Northern Ireland (PSNI) after it was renamed in 2001.

Paisley, who was released from prison, where he was serving six months for unlawful assembly, and any RUC officers who had been involved in any attacks on civil rights marches. Many regarded this latter result as the main reason for the amnesty, because most of the charges against civil rights supporters had already been dealt with.

The civil rights movement in Derry was split even further when a new organisation, the Derry Civil Rights Committee (DCRC), was formed. Two leading members of the DHAC resigned because they claimed the DHAC now supported the new body instead of the already established DCAC.

At the end of May 1969, the Independent Organisation was formed to support the work of Independent MP John Hume. The Independent Organisation was a direct forerunner of the Social Democratic and Labour Party (SDLP), which was to take over the Nationalist Party's role as the North's main constitutional nationalist party.

As the summer, and the annual loyalist marching season, approached, tensions rose in Derry and across the North.

The Twelfth of July, the biggest day in the loyalist marching calendar, saw another major outbreak of prolonged rioting in Derry, with trouble across the city lasting for two nights and a day. Under the headline 'Derry is rocked by weekend of violence', the *Derry Journal* reported:

> A massive mop-up operation got underway in Derry yesterday as the business community in the city centre got down to the task of assessing the damage after two nights and a day of violent disturbances . . .
>
> Of the eighty-nine people taken to Altnagelvin Hospital between Saturday night and early yesterday morning, forty-five were policemen and forty-four civilians . . .
>
> The rioting, in which a crowd of youths and young children ranging in numbers from about 100 to 300 were involved, was sparked off late on Saturday night after the return to the city of about 1,000 Orangemen . . .
>
> Violence raced through the centre of the city and finally centred on William Street, close to the Bogside area of the city, the scene of violent disturbances earlier this year.
>
> It reached a peak on Sunday night when riot police drew their revolvers and fired warning shots over the heads of a hostile crowd which had cut off a detachment of eight police in a cul-de-sac in Prince Arthur Street off little James Street . . . One man was taken to hospital with a bullet wound . . .[68]
>
> The rioting, which was on a fairly widespread scale throughout the Diamond, Butcher Street, Waterloo Place and William Street areas of the city, was the most vicious the city has seen in the past nine months . . .
>
> About 300 riot police were engaged in the thirty-hour-long battle with the crowd during which sticks, bricks, bottles and petrol bombs were thrown at police and their vehicles . . .[69]

---

68 Other reports state two men were injured by police gunfire.
69 *Derry Journal*, 15 July 1969.

The *Derry Journal* went on to report that the source of the violence could be traced to skirmishes between rival gangs of nationalists and unionists both before and after the Orangemen had paraded in the city. Some moderates in the city, mostly linked to the DCAC, called for the formation of a Citizens' Council to bring an end to such trouble in the city.

Many histories of the conflict in the North trace its starting date to 14 August 1969, the date when British soldiers returned to the streets of Derry. But it was confirmed by the British Army that they were on stand-by in Derry on the weekend of 12 July.[70] If the rioting had lasted a little longer and the army had been called in as prepared for, the Troubles would have started a month earlier.

The city was just getting over the weekend of violence when Sammy Devenny died. His funeral was the largest that the Bogside had ever seen, with close on 20,000 people there to pay their respects. His widow called for peace in the city and for no resentment to be caused by the death of her husband who was, she said, a 'peaceful man' who hated violence and would not want any committed in his name.

Meanwhile, Derry prepared itself for the next major event of the marching season – the annual Apprentice Boys' parade due to pass through the city on 12 August.

The DCAC called for calm in the city ahead of the parade, while a newly formed body, the Derry Citizens' Defence Association (DCDA)[71] called for a register of 'volunteer guards' for the Bogside, stressing that their emphasis was on peacekeeping in the city. The Derry Labour Party called for a United Nations peacekeeping force to be sent to Derry ahead of the Apprentice Boys' parade.[72]

As the day of the parade approached, the Derry Development Commission, which had replaced the old Londonderry Corporation, called for calm (while continuing the Corporation's practice of erecting bunting for the parade) and Eamonn McCann claimed that the sectarian situation in the city had never been 'more dangerous', citing instances of sectarian attacks on homes across the city belonging to people of all religions. At a public meeting in Celtic Park on 10 August, calls for calm were repeated, but there were also warnings of the need for defence. Seán Keenan, a leading republican in the city, said that:

> If all our efforts [to ensure peace] fail, and please God they will not fail, the next thing for us to do is to provide the best defence we can to defend our people should they be attacked from any quarter . . .[73]

The people of Free Derry hoped for the best but prepared for the worst. The barricades went up again around the Bogside.

---

70   *Derry Journal*, 15 July 1969.
71   By this stage the 'united' civil rights movement in Derry was being led by the DCAC, DHAC, DUAC, DCRC and the DCDA. Unity was dead.
72   *Derry Journal*, 29 July 1969.
73   *Derry Journal*, 12 August 1969.

Mural highlighting the drunkenness of the RUC officers who had attacked the Bogside on 4 January 1969. (George Sweeney)

One of the barricades that went up after the RUC attack on the Bogside, satirising the burning of Major Ronald Bunting's car during a protest outside the Guildhall a few days earlier. (MoFD collection)

The original slogan painted on the wall of 33 Lecky Road in the early hours of 5 January 1969. (Jim Davies)

Civil rights activist Eamon Melaugh broadcasts for Radio Free Derry, August 1969.

Protesters clash with the RUC in Waterloo Place, 12 August 1969. (Barney McMonagle)

Bernadette Devlin addresses the Bogside from a barricade in Rossville Street, 12 August 1969. (Barney McMonagle)

Barricade at the junction of Anne Street and Hamilton Street in the Brandywell, August 1969. (George Sweeney)

Rossville Street, 13 August 1969. (Robert White)

The RUC try to fight their way along Rossville Street, 13 August 1969. (Barney McMonagle)

```
DERRY CITIZENS DEFENSE ASSOCIATION

PRESS BULLETIN  NO. 1.

         1am AUGUST 1969

DERRY CITIZENS DEFENSE ASSOCIATION.

       PRESS BULLETIN NO.1.

       1am B4 : 8: 69.

     THE COURAGEOUS FIGHT PUT UP BY THE MEN, WOMEN, BOYS
AND GIRLS OF OUR CITY AGAINST SUCH HEAVY ODDS HAS WON THE
ADMIRATION AND WHOLE - HEARTED SYMPATHY OF, NOT ONLY THE
IRISH NATION, BUT ALL PEOPLES WHO ADMIRE COURAGE IN A
FIGHT AGAINST GLARING INJUSTICES.

     WE ARE RESOLVED THAT THE FIGHT SHALL CONTINUE AS IT
BEGAN AND THAT THOUGH GUNS AND NERVE GAS ARE BEING USED
AGAINST US WE WILL NOT HAVE ANY RECOURSE TO FIREARMS.

     WE ARE IN FIRST FLUSH OF VICTORY TO-DAY AND TOMORROW
             WE SHALL OVERCOME.

     WE WISH TO PAY A SPECIAL TRIBUTE TO THE YOUTH OF
DERRY WHO HAVE DISPLAYED A COURAGE AND INTEGRITY NEVER
EXCELLED IN THE HISTORY OF OUR NATION.

       STAND FIRM UNTIL VICTORY IS ASSURED.
```

DCDA press bulletin praising the defenders of the Bogside, 14 August 1969. (MoFD collection)

Petrol-bomb 'factory' in Nelson Street in the Bogside, 14 August 1969. (George Sweeney)

DCDA receipt for petrol during
the Battle of the Bogside.
(MoFD collection)

The British Army return to the streets of Derry on the afternoon of 14 August 1969. (Barney McMonagle)

BRITISH TROOPS IN DERRY

THIS IS A GREAT DEFEAT FOR THE UNIONIST GOVERNMENT. WE DO NOT YET
KNOW WHETHER IT IS A VICTORY FOR US. A GOVERNMENT WHICH CAN ONLY
BE MAINTAINED BY THE USE OF ARMED TROOPS IS NO LONGER A LEGAL
GOVERNMENT. WHAT WE HAVE TO WAIT AND SEE IS WHETHER WESTMINSTER
IS PREPARED TO ADMIT THIS. FOR THE MOMENT THE FIRST PRIORITY IS
THE SAFETY OF THE PEOPLE OF DERRY. IT IS ESSENTIAL THAT NO-ONE
SHOULD ATTACK THE SOLDIERS. IN THE PRESENT STATE OF TENSION IT
COULD LEAD TO A BLOODBATH. DO NOT LISTEN TO RUMOURS.

AT the moment the situation is fluid. It is clear thatthe
official news reports and comments are not reliable. These are
the FACTS as we know them:

300 SOLDIERS of the Prince of Wales Regiment moved
into the streets of Derry at about 5p.m. today.

They are under the command of the army C.O. At the
moment they are stationed at: the end of the bridge, Guildhall Square,
Waterloo Place, bottom of Great James's Street; they are armed with
sub-machine guns and CS anti riot gas. There is a machine gun nest
on the Ulster Bank building directed at William Street. Barbed
wire barricades have been erected at most of these points.

MEETING WITH THEIR C.O.

The C.O. has seen a deputation and told them that the army is
waiting for reinforcements, that the police have been withdrawn,
the specials have been disarmed. There are no orders for the army
to enter the area.

THE SOUTH

The Irish Army has announced that troops are being moved to the
border to guarantee the field hospitals.

LONDON

The British Home Office has said that the troops were brought in
at the request of the Inspector General of the R.U.C. They make it
clear that the army's presence is a short time operation to restore
law and order. When this is achieved they will be withdrawn. The
British Govt. has also reaffirmed its support for the Government of
Ireland Act 1949 and said that there can be no reconsideration of
the constitutional position unless this is approved by a majority of
the people in both parts of the country.

IMPORTANT

The presence of the troops solves nothing. We must not be fooled
by anyone into taking down the barricades. WE DO NOT GO BACK TO
pA gT ONE.

It is good that we have a rest from fighting, but at least a token
force must man the barricades tonight. Others must hold themselves
ready to come out if necessary. We do not know what is going to happen.

The barricades must only come down on our terms. The first thing
we must demand is the release of all prisoners taken over the past
four days and a clear and unequivocal statement that there will be
no prosecutions. It would be disastrous tactics for anyone to go out
with the idea of attacking the troops. Anyone setting out on such a
venture should be stopped. But, we stress again WE DEFEND OUR AREA
AGAINST ANYONE.

'BB' is produced by members of the Derry Labour Party

Barricade Bulletin No2, produced by the DCDA, the first printed reaction to the arrival of British soldiers
the city, urging a cautious reaction. (Frankie McMenamin)

itish Home Secretary James Callaghan is greeted by John Hume as he visits the Bogside on 28 August 1969.
(Barney McMonagle)

YOU ARE NOW ENTERING FREE DERRY

Bunting goes up as the Bogside prepares for the Liberation Fleadh at the end of August 1969.
(Barney McMonagle)

The British Army strengthens its barricades around the Bogside: Waterloo Place, August 1969. (George Sweene

Members of the DCDA Peace Corps preparing to patrol Free Derry. (Barney McMonagle)

Derry Citizens' Defence Committee

Name...

Address..

Phone No....................................

(Please Complete Above)

TRANSPORT:

Loan of Car-   Hours available-

....to............

Is Driver Required?...

MANPOWER AVAILABLE:

(A) Police Patrol Work ☐   (B) Defence ☐

(C) Ex-Service Experience ☐

Accommodation for Visiting Helpers:

(A) No. of Guests? ☐   Can you supply if required-

(A) Canned food ☐.   (B) Bedding, Blankets Etc. ☐

TICK WHERE APPROPRIATE

Cash Donations gratefully Received by:

Mr. P. L. Doherty,
10 Westland Street,

or The Munster & Leinster Bank, Ltd., Shipquay Street, Derry.

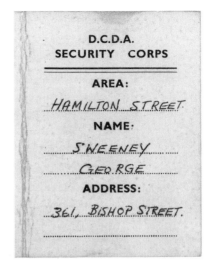

D.C.D.A.
SECURITY CORPS

AREA:

HAMILTON STREET

NAME:

SWEENEY

GEORGE

ADDRESS:

361, BISHOP STREET.

Above: Membership card for DCDA Security Corps. (George Sweeney)

Left: Rota for DCDC [DCDA] patrols of Free Derry. (MoFD collection)

Below: Meeting at Free Derry Corner in September 1969, when residents of Free Derry voted to take down the barricades surrounding their area. (George Sweeney)

INVOICE

B   05027

W. & J. McMONAGLE & CO., LTD

Furniture Removers and Motor Haulage Contractors · Manufacturers of Concrete Brick and Blocks
Sand and Gravel Merchants · Plant Hirers

153 STRAND ROAD, DERRY

M̲r̲.̲ P̲.̲ D̲o̲h̲e̲r̲t̲y̲
c̲/o̲ D̲e̲r̲r̲y̲ D̲e̲f̲e̲n̲c̲e̲ C̲o̲m̲m̲i̲t̲t̲e̲e̲
1̲0̲,̲ W̲e̲s̲t̲l̲a̲n̲d̲ S̲t̲,̲ D̲e̲r̲r̲y̲.̲

Works at
MABUOY and CAMPSIE, Co. Derry and DUNAMANAGH, Co. Tyrone
Telephones : DERRY 3575 and 4083 ;   CAMPSIE 286 ;   DUNAMANAGH 211

Date O̲c̲t̲o̲b̲e̲r̲ 1̲9̲6̲9̲

DATE	GOODS	Docket No.	FROM	TO	Wt. Tons	Cu. Yds.	Hrs.	Rate	£	s.	d.
Oct 6	CAT 944 Heel	PH 3964	d-	Barricades			6½		17	1	3
	Lorry Hire 49281						4½		6	15	=
	― ― 31130						2		4	10	=
6	DB Tractor Hire PH						1¾		2	5	=
									£ 33	11	3

Date 5/11/69

W. & J. McMonagle & Co. Ltd
153 STRAND ROAD, DERRY

Received of :
M/S DERRY DEFENCE COMMITTEE
10 WESTLAND STREET – DERRY
Thirty Three .... POUNDS
Eleven Shillings Three .... PENCE

Signed ....

R   02164

	£	s.	d.
CHEQUE	33	11	3
CASH			
DISCOUNT			
ALLOWANCE			
TOTAL £	33	11	3

Removing barricades

Invoice from W&J McMonagle and Co for the removal of barricades in October 1969. The materials were s[old] for scrap and all monies received were donated to the children's home at Termonbacca. (MoFD collection)

…e physical barricades were replaced by symbolic white lines which the British Army and RUC agreed not to cross. Holding the outline board is prominent activist Paddy 'Bogside' Doherty. (Willie Carson)

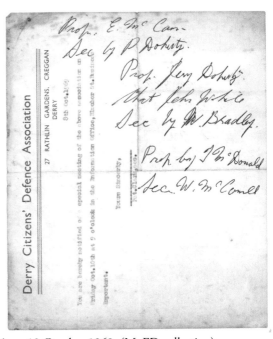

Handwritten proposal to terminate the DCDA on 10 October 1969. (MoFD collection)

The Battle of the Bogside

On Tuesday 12 August 1969, thousands of Apprentice Boys prepared to march through a Derry seething with anxiety and discontent after the events of the previous few months. The RUC attacks on the Bogside in January, the death of Sammy Devenny, the riots in July, all had contributed to the sense of foreboding in the city.

It was reported that the Apprentice Boys' parade would be marshalled by the largest force of RUC ever gathered in one place, while DCAC stewards and DCDA 'volunteer guards' would patrol the edges of the Bogside. Shops in the city centre had erected shutters.

As the march passed the Bogside around 2.30PM, stones were thrown at marchers from behind the barricades erected at the end of William Street. The RUC turned to face the nationalist crowd, with batons drawn, and loyalists gathered behind the police. The RUC and loyalist crowd grew in numbers as the stone throwing continued.

At just after 4.00PM, the first petrol bombs were thrown, and the police charged the Bogsiders, hurling the stones that had been previously thrown at them. The loyalists followed them. The Bogsiders were forced back as far as Chamberlain Street, but unlike during previous incursions, this time they were ready. Existing barricades had been strengthened and new ones erected. Stockpiles of petrol bombs and stones were waiting.

The RUC brought in armoured vehicles and water cannon as back-up. As they advanced towards Rossville Street, they were met with a hail of petrol bombs, and burning drums of oil were rolled out onto the road.

At 7.00PM, the RUC attempted their first big push into Rossville Street. Forming up in lines and banging their riot shields, they moved towards Rossville Street, followed by their loyalist supporters, who broke windows in buildings as they passed. But the first push into Rossville Street failed as the RUC were forced to retreat 'at hot pace from the concentrated opposition which they met'.[74]

Later that evening, the RUC upped the ante and CS gas (tear gas) was brought into the Bogside. Over the next two days or so, over 1,000 CS gas canisters would be fired into the small area at the edge of the Bogside. They also opened fire with live ammunition and two local men were injured. Volunteer first-aid workers in the Bogside treated over 100 people for injuries on the first day.

A few people in the Bogside had access to WWII vintage gas masks found in attics and cupboards across the area where they had lain since the end of the war. Some friendly US soldiers, who were based in the Waterside, also supplied some gas masks and field medical equipment, especially to the volunteer medics.

Some Bogsiders had taken up a defensive position on the roof of the high-rise Rossville Flats from where they were able to keep up a steady rain of petrol bombs to keep the RUC back, largely untroubled by the CS gas which was diluted by the time it reached their high position.

---

74 *Derry Journal*, 15 August 1969.

A leaflet was circulated in the Bogside advising on how to deal with CS gas:

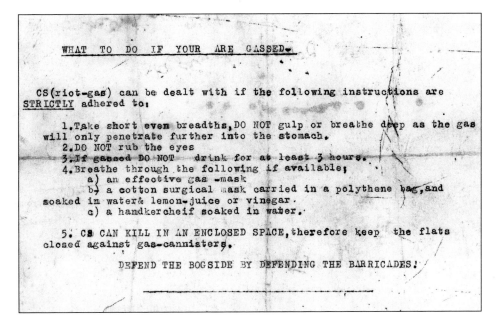

```
        WHAT  TO  DO  IF  YOUR  ARE  GASSED.


    CS(riot-gas) can be dealt with if the following instructions are
    STRICTLY adhered to:
        1.Take short even breadths,DO NOT gulp or breathe deep as the gas
    will only penetrate further into the stomach.
        2.DO NOT rub the eyes
        3.If gassed DO NOT  drink for at least 3 hours.
        4.Breathe through the following if available;
            a) an effective gas -mask
            b) a cotton surgical mask carried in a polythene bag,and
    soaked in water& lemon-juice or vinegar.
            c) a handkercheif soaked in water.

        5. CS CAN KILL IN AN ENCLOSED SPACE,therefore keep  the flats
    closed against gas-cannisters.

            DEFEND THE BOGSIDE BY DEFENDING THE BARRICADES!
```

The trouble lessened slightly during the early hours of the morning, but by 5.00AM, crowds were already gathering for the second day. Radio Free Derry was also back on the airwaves.

Rioting and attacks on the Bogside continued throughout the following day and into the following night, with the RUC never being able to pass the defensive position of the top of the Rossville Flats. An Irish tricolour, a Starry Plough and, briefly, a Stars and Stripes flew from the roof of the flats. Rioting spread to other parts of the city nearby, and Rosemount RUC Barracks ended up under siege, which only ended when an agreement was reached that the attack would stop if no more RUC were brought into the area.

As evening approached and the RUC had temporarily retreated from Rossville Street, Bernadette Devlin, using a loud hailer, urged the Bogsiders to strengthen their barricades, and a crowd of about 400 people gathered behind them and waited, confronting the RUC who were positioned at William Street, and loyalists who had gathered in Little James Street.

Around 9.00PM, the loyalist crowd attacked the barricade and there were exchanges of missiles before they were beaten back to Little James Street.

The ferocity of the rioting increased again as darkness approached and three more men were shot and injured by the RUC. The shootings occurred as the police, followed again by loyalists, charged up Great James Street, where nationalists had erected a barricade of a lorry and burning tyres.

DCDA leaders in the Bogside had debated the possibilities of how to get petrol for the petrol bombs to keep the defence going and an alternative to siphoning it from locally owned cars. Some small amounts of money had been donated to the DCDA to help in the defence of the Bogside and it was decided to use some of this to buy petrol from stations still open outside the area. They even kept the receipt for £65.[75]

As the fighting raged, the DCDA appealed for support, asking on the evening of 13 August for 'every able-bodied man in Ireland' to come to Derry to defend the Bogside – 'we need you, we'll feed you' – and calling for protests across the North to 'take the pressure off Derry'.

In response to the DCDA appeal, protests were organised in Newry, Strabane, Belfast and other towns. Many ended in violence, stretching RUC resources to breaking point and preventing reinforcements reaching Derry. The worst rioting was in Belfast, where simmering sectarian resentments burst onto the streets.

In two days, seven people were killed in Belfast, including nine-year-old Patrick Rooney, shot dead in his bed as the RUC opened fire with heavy-calibre machine guns. Thousands of people were made homeless and entire streets in Catholic areas – Bombay Street, Hooker Street and others – burnt to the ground by mobs. Four Catholics were killed by the police; two Protestants were killed by the IRA; one republican was killed by loyalists.

The Battle of the Bogside continued through a second night, and Derry awoke on 14 August to 'a battlefield, the streets littered with debris from fired buildings and still smoking ruins of property lining the streets.'[76]

The DCDA released the following statement in the early hours of the morning:

The courageous fight put up by the men, women, boys and girls of our city against such heavy odds has won the admiration and wholehearted sympathy of not only the Irish nation, but all peoples who admire courage in a fight against glaring injustices.

We are resolved that the fight shall continue as it began and that though gun and nerve gas are being used against us we will not have any recourse to firearms.

We are in first flush of victory today and tomorrow we shall overcome.

We wish to pay a special tribute to the youth of Derry who have displayed a courage and integrity never excelled in the history of our nation.

Stand firm until victory is assured.[77]

Trouble continued throughout Thursday 14 August with the RUC still unable to get past the defensive position of the Rossville Flats. At one point, they made it onto the roof of the maisonettes opposite and tried to fire CS gas onto the roof but were again forced to retreat before they could dislodge the defenders from the roof of the high-rise flats.

Throughout the day, rumours abounded of intervention coming from either London or Dublin to end the battle. The Irish Army were known to be setting up field

---

75 Original receipt in MoFD collection.
76 *Derry Journal*, 15 August 1969.
77 *DCDA Press Bulletin No 1*, 14 August 1969. (MoFD collection)

hospitals just across the border in Donegal at Muff, Killea and Carrigans, just a few miles from the beleaguered Bogside, and with Taoiseach Jack Lynch's statement that the Irish Government 'could no longer stand by' there was a genuine belief that the Irish Army were going to directly intervene. Over 500 people had already been evacuated from Free Derry to Donegal, where local committees had arranged accommodation for almost 5,000 expected refugees from Derry and Belfast.[78]

But the first new force to appear was the hated sectarian police reserve force, the B Specials, who were seen to be gathering in the city centre during the afternoon. As the RUC were being pushed back out of the Bogside, again, it looked like they were about to be replaced by something even worse.

At 4.00PM as the people of the Bogside prepared for what would have undoubtedly been the most violent confrontation so far, soldiers of the Prince of Wales Regiment of the British Army were deployed around the area. The RUC and B Specials were moved back – in some cases almost forcibly – and the British Army now stood between the Bogside and the beaten police.

As the *Derry Journal* reported:

Amazing scenes were witnessed at Magazine Gate and Butcher Gate last night as the taking over of the two gates from the police by British troops was greeted with wild enthusiasm from a large crowd of Catholics.

The start of the extraordinary train of events was in William Street when Eddie McAteer, leader of the Nationalist Party, conferred with the officer in charge. An assurance was received that as soon as the troops could be put in position, the police and B Specials would be withdrawn from the streets and all strategic points taken over by army personnel.

The police first withdrew from William Street to the accompaniment of derisive cheers and then the crowd moved up toward Magazine Gate where a considerable force of riot police were astride the gate. Until the military arrived, the police were verbally abused but stood stolidly and sullenly and silently. On the arrival of an officer and two soldiers, a cheer went up and after the officer had spoken to the police, the police moved back to the mouth of the gate.

This did not satisfy the crowd, however, who demanded the complete removal and to more cheers, the police moved off, leaving the gate guarded by military . . .

First contact between the Catholic civilians who have fought for four days and the military came at the junction of battle-scarred William Street and Rossville Street. The civilians advanced towards the troops with arms upraised saying 'We have no quarrel with the military, only with the police.'

The officer in charge gave a friendly acknowledgement and this began the course of events resulting in the evacuation of the gates and Walls by the police.[79]

---

78 *Derry Journal*, 5 September 1969.
79 *Derry Journal*, 15 August 1969.

The Battle of the Bogside was over; the community felt victorious. Over three days and two nights of fighting, they had held the barricades despite sustained attack from the RUC and loyalists. One hundred and fifty civilians and almost 140 police officers had been hospitalised, and scores more treated in the volunteer first-aid centres. The Bogside had defended itself against the forces of the Stormont Government and Free Derry had been reborn. Hundreds of young defenders, with the active backing of the entire community, had secured their area and defended it against all that could be thrown at them.

According to Bernadette Devlin:

> . . . Ordinary, peaceful people, who had no desire to spend fifty hours throwing stones and petrol bombs, had realised the harm that had been done to them for half a century and were learning how to fight in self-defence. We threw up barricades of rubble, pipe and paving stones – anything we could get our hands on – to prevent the police coming straight into the area . . .
>
> We got medical supplies from the South, but gas masks we had to go without. So we made do with wet blankets, with cotton wool steeped in vinegar, with handkerchiefs soaked in sodium bicarbonate, and we fought on through the night, all through the next day and the following night, and into the third day . . .
>
> We had an influx of foreign revolutionary journalists searching for illumination on the Theory of Petrol Bomb Fighting. The people of the Bogside thought it was fantastic; they didn't know how to spell revolution, never mind work it out, but they were really delighted with themselves, that people should come from the Sorbonne to ask the unemployed of the Bogside where they learned to fight so well . . .[80]

But now a new force was in to do the job and the people were glad of the respite. Eddie McAteer heralded their arrival as a defeat for the Stormont Government, and their presence was welcomed by many.

But for how long would the welcome last? It was the British Army, after all, an enemy centuries older than the RUC or B Specials. Time would soon tell.

The Scarman Tribunal and the Battle of the Bogside

In late September, yet another tribunal of inquiry into the recent trouble in the North opened in Derry – the Scarman Tribunal. Over the following few months, the Tribunal would hear a lot of eyewitness evidence on the recent trouble in the city and on the Battle of the Bogside.

Fr Anthony Mulvey from St Eugene's Cathedral testified that when he complained to an RUC officer on 12 August about loyalist mobs trying to get into the Bogside, in full view of the watching police, that the sergeant said that he would 'go

---

80 Bernadette Devlin, quoted in *Siege City*, p261.

into the Bogside and lead the people [loyalists] myself'. A reporter for the London *Times* also stated that he witnessed loyalist mobs attacking nationalist homes in William Street while the RUC looked on. Kevin McNamara, who went on to become the Labour Party's Shadow Secretary of State for Northern Ireland in the 1980s and 1990s testified that it was his opinion that the people of the Bogside had only acted in self-defence.[81]

Graham Shillington, Deputy Inspector General of the RUC, revealed that the RUC had fired 1,147 units of CS gas during the forty-one hours of the Battle of the Bogside, which worked out at an average of one unit every two minutes. He claimed that the RUC needed to use such quantities in 'self-defence'. Another RUC witness, County Inspector Gerald Mahon, denied that his men had entered the Bogside 'in a militaristic manner to achieve victory over the people' and claimed that if they had wanted to invade the Bogside they would have found an easier way in than along Rossville Street.[82] Referring to the loyalists who followed the RUC to the Bogside, District Inspector Francis Armstrong said that he 'had quite a feeling that the police were glad to see somebody giving them a hand'.[83]

Seán Keenan of the DCDA denied that any defensive plans were put in motion before the RUC tried to enter the Bogside on 12 August, and claimed that barricades and petrol bombs hadn't been prepared in advance. He said that the DCDA had only responded after the RUC attacked. Referring to the arrival of the British Army, he said:

I think the people of the Bogside were delighted to see the military because they had heard there were B Specials on the streets with arms and batons and the Bogside would have been invaded by these people.

Keenan also denied that he and five other members of the DCDA were members of the IRA.[84] After the questioning about Keenan's membership of the IRA, and the possibility of witnesses being charged under the Special Powers Act after giving evidence to the Tribunal, the Tribunal said that it would deplore any attempt by Stormont to take action against anyone on the basis of evidence given to the Tribunal.[85]

Bernadette Devlin told the Tribunal of disagreements within the DCDA about the arrival of the British Army, and that she had been called an 'agitator' because she disagreed with some of the others in the Association. As she arrived to give her evidence, she was handed thirteen summonses relating to the Battle of the Bogside. Among the charges were incitement to riot, riotous behaviour and assault on police.[86]

Eamonn McCann told the Tribunal that while he had done everything he could do to keep the peace, he had thrown two petrol bombs at the RUC in Great James Street.

---

81 *Derry Journal*, 26 September 1969.
82 *Derry Journal*, 3 October 1969.
83 *Derry Journal*, 7 October 1969.
84 *Derry Journal*, 28 October 1969.
85 *Derry Journal*, 31 October 1969.
86 *Derry Journal*, 31 October 1969.

He said he did not regret his actions, but rather that the situation demanded them.[87]

A number of garage owners testified that over 3,200 gallons of petrol were stolen on 13 August.[88] The DCDA retained a receipt that showed a large amount of petrol – £65 worth – bought and paid for from one of the garages in question on this date.[89] In a related court appearance in May 1970, the RUC claimed that 21,600 milk bottles had been stolen for use as petrol bombs during the Battle of the Bogside.[90]

Paddy Doherty, vice-chair of the DCDA, gave evidence that there were no guns in the Bogside in August, and that an offer from a man, who 'was not a local person', to provide guns was refused.[91]

The Scarman Tribunal eventually reported in April 1972, by which time the situation in the North had irrevocably changed. It stated that there had been no central plot to overthrow the Stormont Government or mount an armed insurrection, as unionist politicians had often accused the civil rights movement of promoting, but rather that the disturbances had arisen out of the social, political and economic situation that had existed in the North at the time. The report found the RUC to be at fault on a number of occasions, including on 12 August in Derry and during the widespread burning of nationalist homes in Belfast, but said that this had been due to circumstances beyond their control. While clearing the RUC of acting in a partisan way with loyalist mobs, the report was clear that the perception of this had resulted in a complete loss of confidence in the RUC from within the nationalist community.

---

87 *Derry Journal*, 4 November 1969.
88 *Derry Journal*, 14 November 1969.
89 MoFD collection.
90 *Derry Journal*, 22 May 1970.
91 *Derry Journal*, 2 December 1969.

Free Derry and Brits In

In the common narrative of the Troubles, the British Army were widely welcomed when they arrived on the streets of Derry and Belfast in August 1969, and were greeted with tea and biscuits by grateful nationalists who regarded them as their new defenders.

This was broadly true, at least for a short time, but not everyone welcomed their arrival. Republicans certainly still viewed the British Army as the enemy, but caution was urged from other quarters as well. In the first published reaction to the arrival of the troops, the Derry Labour Party warned that:

> The presence of the troops solves nothing. We must not be fooled by anyone into taking down the barricades. WE DO NOT GO BACK TO SQUARE ONE.
>
> It is good that we have a rest from fighting, but at least a token force must man the barricades tonight. Others must hold themselves ready to come out if necessary. <u>We do not know what is going to happen.</u>
>
> The barricades must only come down on our terms . . . It would be disastrous tactics for anyone to go out with the idea of attacking the troops. Anyone setting out on such a venture should be stopped. But, we stress again, WE DEFEND OUR AREA AGAINST ANYONE. [Emphasis as in original document][92]

The appearance of British troops was viewed as a victory over the RUC and unionism, but the people of Free Derry were cautious and not only remained behind the barricades but began to rebuild and strengthen them. In the few days after the arrival of the British Army, barricades were erected on Creggan Street, High Street and Harvey Street, and youths wearing white armbands patrolled behind the barricades.

The DCDA stated that the RUC would never again be allowed to operate in the Bogside, Brandywell or Creggan, and called on all residents of the area to co-operate fully with the 'peacekeeping corps' that had been set up to patrol the streets from 8.00PM to 8.00AM. They also set out their demands for, in the short term: the provision of protective military patrols on the edges of the Bogside; the removal of all B Specials from the Derry City area; the release of all those arrested in the past week other than those arrested for normal criminal offences and that no RUC or British Army try to enter the Bogside, Brandywell or Creggan. Their longer-term demands were for the abolition of Stormont, the disbandment of the B Specials and an assurance that there would be no prosecutions arising from the events of the past few days.

The IRA also announced that it was now on full alert and that 'fully equipped units' had been moved up to the border. They also claimed that members had already

---

92 *Barricade Bulletin Special Edition No 2*, 14 August 1969. The Barricade Bulletins were produced by different factions under the umbrella of the DCDA during August, September and October 1969, the period of the second Free Derry. This particular one was signed by the Derry Labour Party. (MoFD collection)

been in action in the Bogside and Belfast in 'defensive operations.'[93]

The Officer Commanding the British Army in Derry, Lieutenant-Colonel Charles Millman, said that he had no intention of sending any of his soldiers into the Bogside and that they would stay in the positions they had taken up when they arrived. He also revealed that they were in contact with the DCDA and that any residents who wished to make contact with him could do so via them.[94]

Meanwhile, one of the Derry doctors who had taken part in the voluntary first-aid operation during the Battle of the Bogside expressed serious concern about the use of CS gas, saying that the RUC had little or no knowledge of the toxic properties of the gas. Dr Raymond McClean was concerned about the possible short- and long-term effects of exposure to such high levels of the gas. By the end of the month, the Himsworth Enquiry had been set up to investigate the use of CS gas in the Bogside. Dr McClean attended the Enquiry and, basing his questions on a secret research document from Porton Down[95] that had been leaked to him by a friendly journalist, raised his concerns. When the Enquiry reported, although Dr McClean was less than happy with its findings, he did welcome its recommendation that more study was needed into the effects of CS gas.[96] It didn't stop the British Army from using it, however.

On 21 August, the British Army made their first joint-raids with the RUC, searching the homes of two Catholic ex-servicemen on the outskirts of the city. The DCDA demanded a clear statement from the British Army on whether or not this raid was carried out under the hated Special Powers Act, but the British refused to answer.

The cycle of demand and counter-demand continued. Stormont Prime Minister James Chichester-Clark demanded that the barricades come down; the DCDA said they were staying up. The British Army reiterated their statement that they had no intention of trying to move into the Bogside but made a proposal to the DCDA that it should agree to take the barricades down. The British offered: that no male member of the RUC would enter the Bogside or Creggan areas; that the army would remain in place to guarantee the safety of Free Derry and ensure free access in and out of the area; engineering assistance to remove the barricades; military patrols inside Free Derry if requested and the provision of military police and an assurance that the B Specials would not be allowed into any area west of the Foyle. The DCDA refused the offer, stating:

> The Defence Association refused for a number of reasons. Among these were:
> The fact that [unclear] with Belfast and take their situation into account before making a decision. The people of Belfast have suffered more than us and we cannot climb down now from our position while they need us.
> The fact that our holding this area is a symbol of our continuing struggle against the Unionist Government.

---

93 *Derry Journal*, 19 August 1969.
94 *Derry Journal*, 22 August 1969.
95 Controversial British Army chemical weapons research facility.
96 *The Road to Bloody Sunday*, pp80-89.

That fact that the barricades are protecting against attack from any quarter.

That fact that the barricades mark our frontiers. We hold 888 acres and two roods. Within this area, we have 25,000 people. This indicates the extent of our strength and the massive nature of our protest.[97]

On Thursday 28 August, British Home Secretary James Callaghan – referred to in a DCDA bulletin by the Gaelicised version Mr Seamus O'Callaghan[98] – visited the Bogside. After making his way through crowds of hundreds who were determined to have their voices heard – albeit in a mostly friendly way – Callaghan stopped at the home of Mrs Ellen Diver on Lecky Road, where he met with local representatives and spoke to the crowd gathered outside from an upstairs window. Seán Keenan demanded the release of all 'political prisoners' and the abolition of Stormont, which Callaghan said he would not do, but promised that he would 'bind Stormont hand and foot'[99] so that it could never again act in such a discriminatory way. Keenan also told him that the provision of 4,000 jobs and 2,000 homes for Derry would go a long way towards ending the problems in the city. Callaghan refused to answer many of the DCDA's questions on the recent trouble and who had given the order for the use of CS gas, saying he 'had not come to be cross-examined'. The DCDA threatened a campaign of civil disobedience if their demands were not met.[100]

At a public meeting in the Bogside, the DCDA welcomed those that had come into the area to help during the Battle of the Bogside, but demanded that those who were there simply to cause trouble should leave. They stated that the area was peaceful and crime free and should stay that way. Referring to the reported fears of Protestant residents in the area, Seán Keenan said that:

I can assure anyone that inside the barricades not one finger will be lifted against anyone on account of his religion. We shall not stand for any person who would dare to intimidate anyone.[101]

The meeting was also told of an incident where an off-duty British soldier had assaulted a man in the Bogside. The soldier was 'arrested' and handed back to the British Army for punishment.

Free Derry decided to go ahead and celebrate its victory over the RUC with a 'manifestation of mass happiness' and hold a liberation fleadh. The newly formed Bogside Relief Fund Entertainments Committee announced that:

A Liberation Fleadh will be held in the Bogside this Saturday, 30th August. It will start at noon and continue until midnight on Sunday. It will be a manifestation of mass happiness . . .

---

97 *DCDA Newsletter*, 27 August 1969. (MoFD collection)
98 *DCDA Newsletter*, 28 August 1969. (MoFD collection)
99 *Derry Journal*, 9 September 1969.
100 *Derry Journal*, 29 August 1969.
101 *Derry Journal*, 2 September 1969.

Most performances will be in the open air. Children will dance in the streets, fiddlers will fiddle, whistlers will whistle, singers will sing. The people of Free Derry will celebrate their freedom [from] unionism and their determination never to return to the grey days of the pre-barricade age. Unionism was a miserable thing. The depression it produced was not only economic, it was spiritual. Like a damp blanket thrown across the city, it bid to snuff out light and life and create a dull existence in which the mass of the people dumbly accepted the edicts of their masters.

Now within these 888 acres and 2 roods of free territory, we the people shall celebrate our liberation by putting song in place of strife to symbolise the free future we shall build on the ruins of tyranny.

To promote the feeling of happiness, all residents are asked to hang buntings and flags from their windows.[102]

Among the acts announced for the fleadh were the Dubliners, Tommy Makem and the hit RTÉ children's show *Wanderley Wagon*.

Over the following weekend, thousands attended the Liberation Fleadh, which was regarded as a 'tremendous success' and it was announced it may become an annual event. In advance of the fleadh, Free Derry Wall, as it was now being referred to in the press, had been painted white so that films could be projected against it. This was the beginning of the wall's transformation into the now world-famous landmark. It was also reported that the DCDA had ensured that all bars in the area restricted themselves to normal opening hours to ensure that there was no drunken trouble during the fleadh.

At the beginning of September, the DCDA again announced that the barricades would remain up, but that they would be modified to allow freer movement of buses and other traffic in and out of the Free Derry area. They also said that some of those inside the perimeter ring of barricades would be removed because they no longer served any useful purpose. A public vote left the future of the barricades in the hands of the thirty-strong committee of the Association. The Derry Labour Party opposed the decision to open the barricades. The British Army reiterated their earlier proposal for joint military police and female RUC officers to patrol Free Derry on an on-call basis, but it was again rejected by the DCDA. Meanwhile, the DCDA persuaded the British Army to move three of its guard posts to make life easier for residents of Free Derry.[103]

However, within the next week, the DCDA announced that the British Army would be allowed into the Free Derry area. Following a series of meetings on Sunday 14 September, the DCDA agreed that unarmed military police would be allowed in to 'assist' the DCDA. The following Thursday, 18 September, the DCDA, after a day of negotiations, announced that all of the barricades surrounding Free Derry would now come down, to be replaced by painted white lines. The three-point plan outlined was that:

---

102   MoFD collection.
103   *Derry Journal*, 12 September 1969.

94

1 The DCDA will remove the barricades.

2 The military authorities guarantee the security of the people living in the present barricaded area in conjunction with the Defence Association as far as humanly possible.

3 Neither the RUC nor the USC will enter the barricaded area.

Paddy Doherty, one of the key figures of the DCDA, said that the British Army had agreed that they would only cross the white lines on invitation from the DCDA, and that under no circumstances would the RUC or B Specials be allowed to cross. He said that the existing 'peace corps' would remain active in Free Derry and that if the outcome of the Hunt Report[104] into policing in the North was not acceptable then 'the barricades can very quickly go up again.'[105] He said that he believed the decision would be accepted by the majority of those behind the barricades and would only be opposed by a tiny minority of 'malcontents'.

On 20 September, three summonses had been served on Bernadette Devlin for her role in the Battle of the Bogside (another thirteen would be served on her at the end of October). The Derry Labour Party said that this was evidence that the 'normality' of Stormont justice had been restored and that it was 'incredibly stupid . . . to press for prosecutions of those who prevented the RUC from entering the Bogside' when there was so much evidence piling up against the actions of the police. The Derry Labour Party also condemned others for not supporting her enough, naming specifically Eddie McAteer, John Hume and Paddy Doherty:

Bernadette Devlin acted as they had indicated the people of Free Derry should act. They have been noticeably silent in her defence hitherto. Perhaps when the other defenders of Free Derry are also summonsed, these leaders of the community will speak out? [106]

The first of the main barricades came down on Monday 22 September, with the remainder removed and replaced by the white lines by the following evening.

But on 24 September, the situation in Derry again turned violent. During sectarian clashes in the city centre, a middle-aged Protestant father of four from the Fountain estate, William King, died after being injured during the disturbances. It was reported that he had been injured while trying to help his son, who had also been injured. Although the official cause of his death was quickly announced as a heart attack, his death had a similar effect on the people of the Fountain as Sammy Devenny's had had on the Bogside.

---

104 The Hunt Committee was set up to investigate the actions of the RUC and B Specials throughout 1968 and 1969. It reported on 10 October 1969 and recommended that the RUC be disarmed and the B Specials disbanded and replaced by a part-time force under the command of the British Army. The new force – the Ulster Defence Regiment (UDR) – soon came to be regarded as being as biased and sectarian as its predecessor.

105 *Derry Journal*, 19 September 1969.

106 *Derry Journal*, 23 September 1969.

Residents of the Fountain put up barricades to protect their area, and some barricades went back up around the Bogside.

During the disturbances, nationalist youths clashed with the British Army for the first time, and there were also more clashes with the RUC in the city centre. Extra British soldiers were brought in and British Army barricades were erected around the edges of the Bogside. This time, it seemed to the people of the Bogside, the barriers were there to keep them in, not to protect them. A British Army spokesman said that restrictions on movement would remain in operation for the 'time being' around the city's 'ghettoes' and their removal would depend on the 'continuation of orderliness'. The British Army barricades meant that there was only one way for cars to enter the Bogside – through Hamilton Street in the Brandywell, a long detour from the city centre. The restrictions on movement for pedestrians, which operated from 8.00PM to 6.00AM, meant that Mass times in St Eugene's Cathedral had to be brought forward to allow people to attend. The situation was described in the local press as a 'near curfew'.[107]

The DUAC and James Connolly Republican Club called for a march to be held from Duke Street on the first anniversary of the previous year's march on 5 October. Within twenty-four hours, the Minister for Home Affairs at Stormont had banned all marches.

On 29 September, four men were sent to prison after being convicted of disorderly behaviour. The four were the first Derry citizens to be arrested by the British Army.

On Wednesday 8 October, the first British military policemen entered the Bogside at the invitation of the DCDA. They had been asked to complete investigations into the death of a man who had died after a fall in his Southend Park home five weeks earlier. The DCDA were also considering asking the military police to cover Derry City's home matches in the Brandywell, which had all been postponed since the RUC had been refused entry to the area to steward matches.[108]

On the same day, members of the DCDA received an invitation to a 'special meeting' in the Information Office, Blucher Street, to discuss 'important information'. The important information was the proposed termination of the DCDA. The proposal, put forward by Eamonn McCann and seconded by Paddy Doherty, read:

> That this committee having fulfilled the purposes for which it was introduced, now as from this Friday October 10 wishes to relinquish its authority in this area leaving such matters as law and order to be attended to by such forces as now seem agreeable to us, leaving a select body to terminate the affairs of this Association.[109]

---

107 *Derry Journal*, 30 September 1969.
108 Derry City FC were forced to play their 'home' matches in Coleraine from September 1971 until October 1972 because of security concerns about teams visiting the Brandywell. When the Irish League refused to lift this sanction, the club left the league, playing in a junior league until they entered the League of Ireland in 1985. The police still do not steward matches in the Brandywell.
109 Handwritten note. (MoFD collection)

On the day of the meeting, it was reported that the DCDA had been administering Free Derry at a cost of around £500 a week, which had come from donations from private individuals and organisations. The organisation also had a 'security force' of some 200 volunteers, which had reportedly been led by an American journalist named James Gibson O'Boyle.

The DCDA was duly stood down at the meeting on 10 October, and among the duties of the 'select body' left to terminate its affairs was the removal of the last of the barricades. Documents kept by the DCDA treasurer, Johnny McDevitt, show that local firm WJ McMonagle and Company, from Strand Road, were paid just over £33 by the DCDA to remove the remaining barricades and debris. Anything that could be sold for scrap was sold to John Doherty & Son, Iron, Metal and Machinery Merchants for just over £19. From the sale, the DCDA made a donation of £20 to the local children's home at Termonbacca, between the Bogside and Creggan.[110]

The following day, the British Army began a formal, unarmed, policing role in the Bogside. Photographs appeared in the *Derry Journal* of 'Redcaps' on patrol in Creggan, with enthusiastic children tagging along. The military police, supported by a detachment of Grenadier Guards, took over a six-classroom wing at St Cecilia's Secondary School in Creggan as their headquarters for the area. They even had their own telephone line for public calls – Derry 4141.[111]

On the same day, the new Chief Constable of the RUC, Sir Arthur Young, became the first RUC officer to enter the Bogside since August, when he accompanied James Callaghan on his second visit to the area. While in the Bogside, Young said that the RUC, now unarmed since the publication of the Hunt Report, would soon be back in the Bogside, 'firmly but with tact'. The first move, he said, was to get the RUC in, and then the second to move the British Army out. With the DCDA's security force having already been stood down, their chairman, Seán Keenan, said there would be no problem with the RUC returning:

There is virtually no obstacle to the reorganised RUC coming back into the Bogside. Probably their first appearance will be with the military. I have no idea how soon they will come in but I suggested myself that they should wait at least a week before they enter the area. Our duty is finished to all intents and purposes and whatever happens now is a matter for the military commander.[112]

The Independent Organisation said that they had no objection to the re-entry of the RUC into the Bogside, and the Nationalist Party called for support for the unarmed RUC. The Derry Labour Party said that the Hunt Report's reforms of the RUC pointed the way towards normal policing for the North.

On Friday 17 October, two unarmed RUC officers, Constables Edmund Dolan

---

110 DCDA internal documents. (MoFD collection)
111 *Derry Journal*, 14 October 1969.
112 *Derry Journal*, 14 October 1969.

and William Hetherington, joined a military police patrol into the Bogside; a second patrol entered Creggan.

Thus ended the second phase of Free Derry, 12 August 1969 to 17 October 1969.

* * *

After the barricades came down and the RUC were allowed back in, Free Derry returned to a fairly normal routine. According to the history books yet to be written, the Troubles had started, but for the rest of 1969, Free Derry was basically dealing with the hangover from the long, hot summer just past.

By the end of the second Free Derry period on 17 October 1969, fourteen people had already lost their lives across the North so far in 1969, but ten of those had been in Belfast and only two in Derry – Sammy Devenny and William King. So far, the police had killed six people, the British Army one, republicans three and loyalists two.[113] The first policeman to die in the conflict had been shot by loyalists, and the first soldier by the RUC.

A week after the barricades came down, the British Army found a number of weapons in Creggan. Although old, the army said the guns were still usable, and were thought to be some of a number of weapons stolen from a van in the city centre in June.

An organisation calling itself the Committee Against Injustice in Derry handed out 300 'confession forms' for people to sign stating that, 'I . . . hereby certify that I actively participated in the defence of the area known as the Bogside on the following dates . . .' The forms were to be handed to the 'appropriate authorities'. There is no indication of where this group came from or how many, if any, of their 'confession forms' were ever signed, though it is doubtful if too many people signed a form that would automatically earn them a six-month prison sentence.[114] The group later claimed that they represented the DUAC, Young Socialists, Republican Party and Derry Labour Party.[115]

Throughout November and December, local people continued to pass through Derry Courthouse, charged with offences arising from the trouble of the summer months. Many of them were jailed.

In the middle of November, John Hume accused the Stormont Government of actively recruiting former B Specials into their replacement, the Ulster Defence Regiment (UDR). The government claimed that they had only been sent information, not application forms. On the same day that this argument was taking place in Belfast, Santa Claus arrived in Derry in a British Army helicopter.[116]

At the beginning of December 1969, John Hume released a statement calling for Free Derry Corner and the streets surrounding it to be preserved because of their potential as a tourist attraction. He said:

---

113 Figures exclude William King, who was not killed by an armed organisation.
114 *Derry Journal*, 14 November 1969.
115 *Derry Journal*, 2 December 1969.
116 *Derry Journal*, 18 November 1969.

I believe that the Bogside will in future become a major tourist attraction and that some idea of the old Bogside should be maintained in the redevelopment scheme. The ideal choice would be this particular row of houses because of the number of historic events that have taken place there . . . I think any community should have the foresight to realise the historic and tourist potential that is there.[117]

Hume's prediction turned out to be true, and although it took a few decades to happen, Free Derry Corner, although not the street it once stood on, did survive the redevelopment of the area and became one of the main tourist attractions in the city, visited every year by thousands of people keen to have their photograph taken there.

On 16 December, the same day that the inquest into the death of Sammy Devenny reached a verdict of natural causes, Bernadette Devlin appeared in Derry Courthouse to face charges arising from the Battle of the Bogside. On 22 December, she was sentenced to six months in prison, but released on bail pending an appeal scheduled for the following February. The appeal was eventually completed in June 1970. Devlin lost and served almost four months in prison.

Before the decade could limp quietly to a close, however, one event occurred that would have a major impact on the decades to follow – the Irish Republican Army split. The movement had been divided throughout the latter part of the 1960s, with the Dublin-based leadership's desire to take a more political path frustrating a lot of Northern members who saw the movement's politicisation as the main reason it could not play any effective role in the trouble that erupted in Belfast and Derry in the summer of 1969. Despite grandiose statements about IRA units being deployed along the border and ready for active service, they had played little role as an organisation in the events in August, and the taunting slogan 'IRA = I Ran Away' had appeared on walls in their traditional strongholds in Belfast. At a special IRA convention in the middle of December 1969, the Army Council[118] voted to accept the proposal that republicans recognise the governments in Belfast, Dublin and London, and take seats if elected. A minority of those at the meeting opposed the ending of the traditional abstentionist policy. This group elected a new 'Provisional' Army Council a few days before Christmas 1969 and the Provisional IRA (PIRA) was born. Those that remained supportive of the old leadership were thereafter known as the Official IRA (OIRA). The Provisional IRA went on to become the most active paramilitary organisation during the conflict in the North, and are officially recorded as having killed 1,771 people by the end of 1999. The Official IRA, who called a ceasefire in the middle of 1972, were responsible for 54 deaths.[119] The republican movement's political wing, Sinn Féin, which was at that time a very small and ineffective support organisation, followed suit, splitting in January 1970.

---

117 *Derry Journal*, 5 December 1969.
118 Leadership of the IRA.
119 McKittrick, Kelters, Feeney & Thornton (Eds), *Lost Lives* (Mainstream Publishing, 1999) p1475. Throughout the book, PIRA and OIRA are used whenever possible. IRA is used where it is not clear which of the two organisations is being referred to.

Petrol Bombs and CS Storms

So Free Derry entered the 1970s with two IRAs in existence but with very little action from either of them, there or anywhere else in the North.

But both groups had benefited from events since 1968. Recruits were easily found from among the ranks of teenage rioters who had been fighting on the streets since October of that year, and subsequent events had generated a level of support for republicanism that was greater than it had been for decades. Both IRAs were growing in numbers and beginning to make ready for an armed campaign, but it would take some time to become evident.

What was immediately apparent, however, was that the British Army had replaced the RUC as the target and/or cause of unrest on the streets of the city. The barricades around the Bogside were a particular cause of ill feeling, especially one on William Street which operated a one-way system at nights, whereby citizens of the city could get into the Bogside but not out of it. This effectively imprisoned the entire community during the hours of darkness. It was the only barrier in the city to operate in such a way, and local representatives described it as discrimination. The British Army said it was because of the actions of 'hooligan elements'.

As the DUAC continued to protest against the high levels of unemployment in the city, and PD formed a Derry branch and continued to campaign against the Public Order Bill, which became law in early February, trouble following such protests was slowly becoming the norm. In the first week of February 1970, there were disturbances in the city centre after Ian Paisley held a meeting in the Guildhall and local nationalists protested outside. British Army snatch squads moved into William Street and a number of local men were arrested and jailed. In early March, there were further skirmishes after a DUAC protest.

In the midst of the growing unrest on the streets, a young Bogside girl, Rosemary Brown, who performed under the name of Dana, won the Eurovision song contest with *All Kinds of Everything*, bringing some much-needed light relief to the city. Thousands turned out to greet her return in Guildhall Square at the end of March, without rioting afterwards (although there had been three days of rioting over the preceding weekend).

By Easter 1970, when republicans commemorated the 1916 rising, small-scale clashes between young people and the British Army in Derry had become an almost daily occurrence, but after almost 6,000 people had taken part in an Easter commemoration, what the *Derry Journal* described as 'another battle of the Bogside' and 'the first serious confrontation between British troops and people in Derry' broke out.

The parade organisers claim that the trouble started because missiles were thrown from Victoria RUC Barracks at the parade as it passed along the Strand Road from where they said a Union Jack was also being flown to provoke the marchers. The RUC denied this. Marchers attacked the barracks, and running battles around the city centre and the edges of the Bogside followed. One rioter was reported to have told a local priest that 'the army were as bad today as the police were in August and they will get the same treatment from us as the police did then.'[120] Prominent civil rights activist Eamon Melaugh was arrested for trying to photograph a soldier who he claimed had assaulted a march steward. He was released without charge after a protest outside the barracks.

As a number of local youths were being jailed for their part in these riots, the 'Derry City Command' of the IRA released a statement saying that 'action will be taken against collaborators with the British occupation forces in the Bogside.' This was, they said, in response to the heavy sentences being handed out to rioters. According to the statement: 'The first action will be the daubing of doors and if the collaboration persists, severe action will be taken against these people.'[121]

Following the Easter riots in Derry and in other parts of the North, the General Officer Commanding of the British Army in the North, Ian Freeland, said that petrol bombers could now be shot dead if they did not heed warnings to stop.

On 22 June, Bernadette Devlin lost her appeal against her conviction for her part in the Battle of the Bogside. Seen as a heroine by many in Derry for her role the previous August, her arrest and jailing on 26 June led to another serious outbreak of rioting in the city, which was to have even more tragic consequences.

Devlin was travelling to the city on 26 June after an agreement had been reached between her solicitor and the RUC that she would hand herself in to the police in the city that night after addressing a rally in the Bogside. As her car reached Drumahoe, on the outskirts of the city, it was surrounded by up to thirty RUC officers and British soldiers and Devlin was arrested.

Several thousand people had already gathered at Free Derry Corner to hear her speak, and when news of her arrest came through, a large section of the crowd moved towards the edges of the Bogside and started throwing stones and bottles at British soldiers. Barricades were quickly erected as the soldiers tried to move into Rossville Street and petrol bombs were thrown from side streets in the Bogside. The British Army responded with CS gas.

The rioting ebbed back and forth along the edges of the Bogside, the British being pushed back towards the town centre a number of times. It continued through the Friday night and into Saturday, and a number of shops and other business premises on the edge of the city centre were burned to the ground. It was reported that almost 10,000 bottles of beer were taken from one of the destroyed businesses, JJ McGinley Wholesale Spirit Merchants in William Street.[122]

On the Sunday, petrol bombs were thrown at the Royal Mail sorting office in Sackville Street but were extinguished by postal workers, who stayed on the roof throughout most of the day. Later that evening, a combination of a concentrated British push into Rossville Street, the efforts of local community leaders and the outbreak of heavy rain spelled the end of the weekend's disturbances. Two armoured

---

120 *Derry Journal*, 31 March 1970.
121 *Derry Journal*, 3 April 1970.
122 *Derry Journal*, 30 June 1970.

vehicles, followed by around sixty soldiers, broke through the barricades in Rossville Street. A number of civil rights activists, including John Hume and Eamon Melaugh approached the officer in charge and asked to be allowed to try to speak to the rioters to calm the situation down. They tried to approach the rioters but were stoned and called 'Lundies' (traitors), but within an hour or so, the riot had fizzled out, leaving a trail of devastation in its wake.

During the weekend of rioting, the British Army fired 1,258 CS cartridges and 59 CS gas grenades, more than the RUC had fired during the Battle of the Bogside the previous August. Over the weekend, twenty-eight civilians, twenty-nine British soldiers and one RUC officer had been taken to hospital, and eighty-nine people had been arrested.[123]

But during the trouble, another event had occurred that dwarfed all of the statistics about the damage done and the numbers injured.

Tommy, Bernadette and Carol McCool, Joe Coyle and Tommy Carlin

On Friday 26 June, the night that Devlin was arrested, three veteran republicans, Tommy McCool (43), Tommy Carlin (55) and Joe Coyle (45), said to be the core of the newly formed Provisional IRA (in Derry, were preparing an explosive device of some sort in McCool's home in Dunree Gardens, Creggan. Just after midnight, it exploded prematurely, engulfing the house in flames.

McCool and one of his five children, four-year-old Carol, died in the fire, while his nine-year-old daughter Bernadette and Joe Coyle, a married father of two, died within hours in hospital. McCool's wife and three other children were able to escape from the house. Tommy Carlin survived for almost two weeks before dying of his wounds on 7 July. The three men were the first republicans to die in the conflict in the city.

Almost 1,000 people attended the funeral of the three members of the McCool family, where members of the PIRA provided an honour guard and the last post was played by a member of *Fianna na hÉireann,* the youth wing of the IRA. Joe Coyle was buried the following day, again with full military honours. He was described in death notices as a Staff Captain in the IRA.

A number of witnesses to the inquest described the intensity of the blaze that engulfed the house, and an RUC witness testified that bomb-making equipment had been found in the gutted house. Verdicts of misadventure were returned in all five cases.

The Provisional Sinn Féin Cumann (association) in Creggan was named after the three deceased volunteers.

On the Sunday evening, as the weekend of violence was coming to an end, a meeting was held at Free Derry Corner to form a 'Law and Order' organisation to 'bring

---

123 *Derry Journal,* 30 June 1970.

peace to the Bogside'. The organisers in the DCCC (Derry Citizens' Central Council, basically a successor to the moderate DCAC of 1968 and 1969) called for volunteers and set up an office in an old garage near the top of William Street. Their spokesperson, John Hume, said:

> It is surely clear to everyone that such an organisation is absolutely essential and not the responsibility of any one organisation or even several organisations to do this. It is the responsibility of all citizens who want law and order restored to the Bogside.[124]

The following night, around seventy volunteer stewards were out on the edges of the Bogside, where around 200 youths had gathered and were throwing stones at British soldiers. The volunteer stewards attempted to persuade the stone throwers to stop.

Hume also told the meeting that an agreement had been reached with the British Army, whereby it would stay out of the Bogside for two weeks to allow local representatives a chance to try to calm the area down, and that only military police would enter the area during that period, with the RUC only coming in when necessary to investigate serious crimes. The British Army denied the existence of any such agreement. The DCCC withdrew from street patrols after the initial two-week period when, they said, the British Army refused to extend the agreement, even though the DCCC claimed it had been working well and keeping the Bogside free from rioting.

Perhaps surprisingly, 12 July passed off relatively peacefully in Derry in 1970, and two weeks later, the Stormont Government announced a ban on all parades, which meant there would be no Apprentice Boys' parade that year on the first anniversary of the Battle of the Bogside. At the same time, it was announced that the RUC would return to normal policing duties in the Bogside, Brandywell and Creggan, and that a permanent police presence would be set up in Bligh's Lane, on the edge of Creggan. Moderates in Derry welcomed both announcements, saying that the ban would prevent any further rioting and that the people of the area had always been law-abiding and would welcome the return of the police as long as they acted in an impartial way. The Apprentice Boys of Derry opposed the ban, and there were rumours that they would go ahead with their parade, banned or not.[125]

But rioting erupted again before the annual marching date had even been reached. On Sunday 1 August, a crowd gathered at Free Derry Corner in the afternoon in the mistaken belief that a meeting had been called following the death of Daniel O'Hagan, a 19-year-old Belfast youth shot dead by the British Army the day before. As the British Army drove slowly past the assembled crowd, stones were thrown at their jeeps. The stone throwing soon escalated into a full-scale riot that lasted for almost the next week, with petrol bombing, burning of vehicles and firing of CS gas across the Free Derry area.

---

124 *Derry Journal*, 30 June 1970.
125 *Derry Journal*, 28 July 1970.

During this phase of rioting, the first shots were fired at the British Army in Derry, six in Bishop Street in the early hours of the Wednesday morning, 5 August, and three more in the early hours of the following morning. This was the first instance of armed offensive action being taken by republicans in the city.

As 12 August approached, there were calls for calm from the usual sources in the Bogside, with the DCCC announcing that its offices would be open twenty-four hours a day until the Twelfth period had passed. They also called for volunteers to come forward again to patrol the area. It was announced that movement around the city would be severely restricted and that all pubs, clubs and hotels would be banned, under the Special Powers Act, from selling alcohol anywhere in the city on the day.[126]

But all the precautions didn't work, and the day was far from peaceful. The first signs of trouble came when Apprentice Boys attempted to march across Craigavon Bridge after a rally in St Columb's Park in the Waterside and were forced back by British soldiers using CS gas. Conor Cruise O'Brien, a pro-unionist member of the Irish Government, was attacked and beaten up at the rally and had to be treated in hospital. Two local press photographers had their cameras taken and smashed while taking pictures at the rally. The Apprentice Boys also took part in a series of mini-parades in direct defiance of the ban, clashing with soldiers and police who were put in place to stop them marching.

By the middle of the afternoon, a large crowd of nationalist youths had gathered in William Street and began to throw stones at some of the 3,000 British soldiers who were on duty in the city that day. Soon after the stone throwing started, the first rubber bullets were fired by British soldiers in the city.[127] The rioting continued into the early hours of the following morning, with running battles in William Street and Rossville Street.

On 21 August, a number of prominent moderates from Derry and across the North came together to form the Social Democratic and Labour Party (SDLP). The SDLP, under its first leader Gerry Fitt, and subsequently under the leadership of John Hume, would remain the largest nationalist party in the North for more than the next thirty years.

There were further outbreaks of serious rioting in Derry in October. Although a rally to mark the second anniversary of the 5 October march in 1968 passed off with only minor trouble, the following weekend saw another sustained outbreak of trouble, which started when nationalist youths, protesting against a unionist meeting in the Diamond on the Saturday afternoon, were forced back towards the Bogside by

---

126 *Derry Journal*, 11 August 1970.

127 At the beginning of August 1970, the British Army introduced the baton round (rubber bullet) into the North of Ireland. These supposedly non-lethal weapons were to be used in riot situations, but over the next five years, during which time the British Army fired over 50,000 rubber bullets, three people were killed by them, including Thomas Friel in Creggan, and hundreds seriously injured. The rubber bullets were replaced by plastic bullets in 1975, and a further fourteen people were killed by the replacement, including 11-year-old Stephen McConomy, 15-year-old Paul Whitters and 44-year-old Henry Duffy in or near the Bogside. Nine of those killed by rubber or plastic bullets were aged eighteen or under.

soldiers. During the subsequent riot, four civilians, six RUC officers and forty British soldiers were injured. The disturbances continued into the following Monday.

But there were also two incidents during this particular weekend of rioting that highlighted a change in the nature of violence in the city. As well as the usual stones and petrol bombs, a new weapon was used: a gelignite bomb was thrown at soldiers in Chamberlain Street, injuring one of them. In another incident, in the early hours of Monday 12 October, the offices of the Derry Gaslight Company, on Lecky Road, were completely destroyed in an explosion. These two incidents, following the shootings in July, were evidence of the re-emergence of armed republican groups in the city, which had been largely dormant until then.

They marked the beginning of an IRA bombing campaign that, after a slow start, would greatly increase in intensity over the coming months and years. By the end of 1970, there had been seven separate IRA bomb attacks, including the destruction of a car showroom on the Foyle Road and major damage caused to the British Customs Station on Strand Road. If 1970 had begun with two separate IRAs in the city but both staying relatively quiet, 1971 would be the year when they would really begin to make their presence known.

Local youths clash with the British Army on the edge of the Bogside, 1970. (George Sweeney)

Former servicemen burning their army discharge papers in protest at the actions of the British Army in Derry. Kneeling at the back is Vincent Coyle, an ever-present and influential figure at civil rights protests in the city. (Eamon Melaugh)

Soldiers in riot gear attempt to advance into Rossville Street, Easter 1970. (Barney McMonagle)

Rioting at St Eugene's Cathedral, June 1970. (George Sweeney)

The 'New Road' (Eastway), Creggan, summer 1971. (Barney McMonagle)

The British Army truck that crushed nine-year-old Damian Harkin on 24 July 1971, taken and burned by enraged locals. (George Sweeney)

Residents of Free Derry march in the city centre against internment. (Willie Carson)

Residents of Free Derry march against internment. (Eamon Melaugh)

113

Members of the OIRA training in Cregga
during the third incarnation of Free Derry
1971. (Eamon Melaugh)

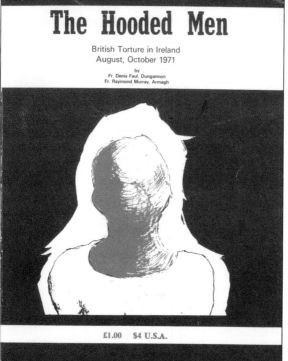

Book produced in 1971
by Revs Murray and Faul,
highlighting the ill-treatment
of internees. (MoFD
collection)

Children pose with an IRA volunteer in Creggan, 1971. (Eamon Melaugh)

Graffiti in Chamberlain Street, December 1971. 'Buy early while shops last' was a reference to the growing intensity of the IRA's bombing campaign in the city centre. (Peter Moloney)

Towards War

The year 1971 saw a steady escalation in violence in Derry and across the North. In 1970, five people had died in Derry and twenty-eight across the North. During 1971, seventeen people were killed in Derry City (including two children that are not officially listed as victims of the conflict) and 180 in total across the North, the majority after the introduction of internment without trial in August that year. All but one of those who died in Derry did so in, or on the edges of, Free Derry.

After a fairly quiet start to the year, rioting around the edges of the Bogside and the city centre became such a common occurrence that it was known as the 'matinee', and the corner of William Street and Rossville Street became known as 'Aggro [Aggravation] Corner' because of the amount of rioting that centred on it. As the IRA's bombing campaign in the city centre began to gather momentum, five stores in the city centre were damaged in one night in early February by incendiary devices.

In March 1971, the more hardline Brian Faulkner replaced James Chichester-Clark as Stormont Prime Minister.

The first British soldier to die in Derry perished during a petrol bomb attack in Westland Street on 1 March.

Lance Corporal William Jolliffe

William Jolliffe (18), a lance corporal in the Royal Military Police, died after a petrol bomb attack on the Land Rover he was travelling in at the junction of Westland Street and Cable Street in the Bogside.

As the jeep reached the junction, up to ten petrol bombs were thrown by a crowd of youths. Four hit the vehicle, which went out of control and crashed into a wall. The driver of the vehicle managed to get out straightaway, but it took some time for local residents to get the other two soldiers out of the badly damaged Land Rover. The soldiers were taken to a nearby house to wait for an ambulance, but Jolliffe died soon after admission to hospital.

At the inquest into his death, the front-seat passenger gave evidence of how both he and William Jolliffe were using fire-extinguishers to try to put out the flames inside the vehicle, and that at one point, thinking Jolliffe was on fire, he had doused him with the fire-extinguisher.

The medical evidence was that William Jolliffe had died from inhaling a high concentration of chemicals from the fire-extinguishers, and a verdict of misadventure was returned, though his family was later awarded criminal-injury compensation.

The RUC set up a twenty-four-strong team to investigate the incident.[128]

The Easter commemoration in Derry that year heard a statement from the

---

128 *Derry Journal*, 2 March 1971; *Lost Lives* 63. All references to deaths from *Lost Lives* use the book reference number rather than the page number.

Provisional IRA that while IRA volunteers had to date been involved in operations in defence and support of their communities, this would inevitably lead to offensive actions if equal rights were not given by peaceful means and the British Government did not recognise its responsibility for the current problems and respect 'the wishes of the vast majority of the people of Ireland and withdraw her troops to garrisons in England where they belong'.[129]

The commemoration was inevitably followed by an outbreak of intense rioting in the Bogside.

With republicans resuming their traditional stance of violent opposition to the British presence in the North, and with the youth of Free Derry in almost constant conflict with the British Army on the streets of the city, whatever lingering relationship there was with British soldiers was certainly coming to an end. Events in July 1971 would prove to be the final and permanent split.

Seamus Cusack, Dessie Beattie and Damian Harkin

In the early hours of 8 July 1971, during a period of sustained rioting in the Bogside, 28-year-old Creggan man Seamus Cusack became the first person to be shot dead by the British Army in Derry.

According to eyewitnesses, the rioting on the night Cusack was shot was no more serious than normal, and they had not seen any petrol bombs, nail bombs or guns being used against the soldiers that night.

A detachment from the 1st Battalion of the Royal Anglian Regiment were positioned between Fahan Street (Bog Road) and the Little Diamond, where a small group of youths were throwing stones at them, at one point knocking the helmet off the head of a soldier who was a bit of a distance from the rest. As a 17-year-old boy ran out to get the helmet for a trophy, he was hit by a rubber bullet. He later claimed that Cusack came out to help him to safety, and then the two had tried again a number of times to get the helmet. During the last attempt, the soldier opened fire, missing the boy and hitting Cusack in the thigh.

Cusack was carried to safety, but it was decided to take him over the border to Letterkenny Hospital for treatment instead of to the local Altnagelvin Hospital, where he would almost certainly have been arrested and sentenced to the mandatory six months for rioting. No-one thought his injury – a bullet wound in the leg – could be so dangerous that it was risking his life to take him on the half-hour car journey to Letterkenny. But by the time they reached hospital, Cusack had lost so much blood he died within minutes of admission.

All of the civilian eyewitnesses were adamant that Cusack had done no more than throw a few stones that night, but the British Army and Government immediately labelled him a gunman, with the official statement to the House of Commons stating that the soldiers had shot a gunman after a clear warning had been given. None of the civilian witnesses heard any warning being given. The soldier who shot Cusack was later acquitted in court, with the judge saying that Cusack

129 *Derry Journal*, 13 April 1971.

was as much to blame for his own death as the soldier who shot him.

As the news of Cusack's death spread around the city, rioting in the Bogside intensified. At about 4.00PM that afternoon, near the junction of Westland Street and Lecky Road, a group of youths were throwing stones at members of the same British Army regiment who had killed Cusack.

The British later claimed that nail bombs had been thrown at the soldiers and that they had shot a nail bomber just as he was about to throw another bomb. Civilian witnesses were adamant that Desmond Beattie (18) from Rosemount was unarmed when he was shot dead. There was also a discrepancy in the accounts of exactly where Beattie was when he was shot, with the soldiers' versions placing him much closer to their positions, and therefore more of a danger to themselves, but civilian witnesses placing him much further away, where he posed no threat to the soldiers. It was also claimed that he had actually been shot by soldiers from McKeown's Lane, a side street off Lecky Road, rather than by the soldiers who claimed to have shot him from the junction of Westland Street and Lecky Road. One witness, a local priest, claimed to have seen three soldiers opening fire from this position at a group of youths running away. One fell and the priest ran over to him, giving him the last rites even though he already appeared to be dead. The crucial issue here is that there was no claim that the soldiers in McKeown's Lane were under any sort of attack and therefore had even less justification for opening fire than the soldiers at the bottom of Westland Street.

Local politicians immediately called for a judicial inquiry into the shootings and the SDLP withdrew from Stormont when this was refused.

An unofficial inquiry was set up in the Guildhall to look into the killings, chaired by English barrister Lord Gifford QC (who later played a part representing some of the Bloody Sunday families in the second inquiry into the events of that day), assisted by an American lawyer, Paul O'Dwyer, and Albie Sachs, a South African lawyer.

The inquiry studied all the available statements from the British, who refused to take any part in the inquiry, and questioned civilian eyewitnesses to both shootings. They came to the conclusion that Cusack was definitely unarmed when he was shot and that it was most likely that he was a random victim, shot dead in retaliation for the ongoing attacks on soldiers (shots had been fired at soldiers on the preceding three nights). They also found that there was no evidence that Beattie had a nail bomb when he was shot – no traces of explosive were found on his body or clothing when he was examined by the Forensic Science Department – and that he had been shot where the civilians claimed, not where the soldiers claimed, and that he was running away from the soldiers' positions when he was killed.

The shootings and their aftermath set the precedent for later British Army killings in the North, with the victims immediately being labelled as gunmen or bombers and anonymous 'alphabet' soldiers giving evidence at the subsequent inquests (military witnesses routinely appeared at inquests, court hearings etc as Soldier A, Soldier B etc). It is only recently that in a number of cases from this era, dealt with below, the British Government has been forced to admit that their claims at the time were false and that the victims were, in fact, innocent, as the civilian witnesses had claimed at the time. At the time of writing, no such admissions have been made in the cases of Seamus Cusack and Desmond Beattie.[130]

The shootings proved to be the final break in any sort of relations between the local population and the British, a break that lasted for the duration of the conflict. The days of negotiations between community representatives and British officers were over; the British Army were seen as killers now. The Nationalist Party claimed that the British Army had now 'declared war' on the nationalist population of the city and had 'embarked on a campaign of terror'. The Republican Clubs said that the soldiers were engaged in 'selective murder'.

Just over two weeks later, the British Army were responsible for another death in the Bogside.

On 24 July, nine-year-old Damian Harkin was making his way home from a children's show in the local cinema. As he passed the junction of Westland Street and Blucher Street, in the heart of the Bogside and about fifty yards from his home in Gartan Square, he was struck by an armoured vehicle that, according to eyewitnesses, had skidded and mounted the pavement, crushing him against a wall. One eyewitness said that there had been a convoy of three armoured vehicles travelling very fast down Westland Street and the leading one had hit the boy as he walked along the pavement with a companion.

The soldiers immediately left the scene, leaving the damaged lorry and the dead boy behind. When the RUC arrived, they were allowed to examine the scene, take measurements and drive the armoured vehicle back onto the road to test its brakes. Local people followed the RUC, and when the tests were completed, the vehicle was looted and burned.[131] The inevitable riot followed.

Despite the circumstances and the people and vehicles involved, the death of Damian Harkin was treated as a simple traffic accident and he is not officially recorded as a victim of the conflict.

The three deaths in July 1971 contributed greatly to the increase in violence across the city in the summer of 1971 as Derry, and the rest of the North, spiralled downwards towards all-out war.

The Unionist Government at Stormont decided to resort to a familiar tactic in an attempt to combat the rising tide of republican violence, one they had used in every decade of their existence so far.

On 9 August 1971, they reintroduced internment without trial.

---

130 *Derry Journal*, 9 July 1971; *Lost Lives* 76, 77; Gifford, O'Dwyer & Sachs, *Inquiry into the Circumstances Surrounding the Deaths of Seamus Cusack and George Desmond Beattie* (1971).
131 *Derry Journal*, 27 July 1971.

Internment and Free Derry

In the early hours of 9 August 1971, the British Army launched Operation Demetrius, raiding nationalist homes across the North and arresting 342 men. Sixteen of these arrests on the first morning were in Derry City, and included prominent local republicans such as Seán Keenan (about to be interned for the third time in his life) and John White. Internment allowed for the men to be imprisoned indefinitely without charge, trial, proof or evidence.

The order for internment was officially given by the Stormont Government but had to have the backing of the British Government, who retained control over their army.

All of those arrested were from a perceived republican background (the only two Protestants in the first wave of internees, including John McGuffin, a radical civil rights activist, would have been regarded by the authorities as republicans). Despite repeated claims at the time, and since, that internment was not being used in a sectarian way, it was not until the end of 1972, after the Stormont Government had been dismantled, that the British Government began to discuss an 'arrest policy for Protestants' and 1973 before the first suspected loyalist paramilitaries were interned. They felt that 'there was no serious Protestant threat in that period of a kind which led to death and serious injuries.'[132] This was despite the fact that in 1971 loyalist paramilitaries killed twenty-two people and fifty in 1972.

But the operation was not the success for which the Stormont Government and British Army had hoped. Much of their intelligence, provided by RUC Special Branch, was outdated and they ended up arresting many men who had last been active in the republican movement in the 1950s or early 1960s, or relatives of their targets who just happened to be in the wrong house at the wrong time. Within two days, over a third of those arrested were released, and it is not believed that the first wave of internment arrests did any particular damage to either the Official or Provisional IRA, who had gone underground after a series of army raids a fortnight beforehand.

The reaction to the raids in Derry was predictable. Riots raged from the early morning as the soldiers poured in to raid homes. Barricades were erected and Free Derry resurrected. Within hours, six British soldiers were wounded by republican gunfire, one seriously, and both wings of the IRA began to patrol openly in Free Derry. The third Free Derry period would differ radically from the first two, which had been relatively peaceful after riotous beginnings. This time, Free Derry was at war, and the barricades would remain for the next eleven months.

Violence escalated across the North after the introduction of internment. In the

---

132 Note of a meeting held in the Northern Ireland Office, 13 November 1974. The document, discovered in the Public Records Office by the Pat Finucane Centre, is marked confidential. Other documents discovered at the same time show an ongoing discussion within the British Government and Army about how to balance the obviously one-sided nature of the internment policy. At the time of writing, a number of former loyalist internees are taking legal action for wrongful imprisonment, on the grounds that they were only interned as a political gesture to answer those who criticised the sectarian aspect of internment.

first seven months of 1971, thirty-four people had lost their lives. From the introduction of internment until the end of August, 1971 thirty-five people were killed, and a total of 139 between the beginning of internment and the end of the year.

The first person to die in Derry after the introduction was also the first British soldier to be shot dead by the IRA in the city, and the hundredth person to die since the UVF began the current spate of killings in 1966.

Bombardier Paul Challenor

The 22-year-old soldier in the Royal Horse Artillery, who was married with a one-month-old child, was shot by a sniper while on duty in an observation post in Bligh's Lane[133] in Creggan on 10 August. One witness stated that the shots were fired from a car that had pulled up outside the base and flashed its lights to warn a passing civilian to get out of the way.

Challenor, from Leicester, died an hour and a half after the shooting, in Altnagelvin Hospital.[134]

The days that followed the introduction of internment were violent ones in Derry, with ongoing shooting and rioting across the city. Republicans and nationalists across the North reacted with anger as the arrests continued. There were widespread reports of ill-treatment and abuse of those arrested, but it soon became clear that a number of them – who became known as the 'Hooded Men' – had been selected for special treatment.

According to an Amnesty International report, which also outlined the abuse suffered by most of those arrested, twelve others suffered a much worse fate:

Apparently pre-designated persons were arrested and not maltreated until processed and transferred to a special interrogation centre, where they were subjected to severe beatings and physical tortures in the nature of being forced to stand in a 'search position' (legs apart, hands against wall) for hours at a time. When they would collapse, severe beatings were again administered. This pattern was followed by prolonged interrogation, often over several hours. The prisoners were offered money to give information relating to Irish Republican Army activities in Northern Ireland. During these tortures, the prisoners were first stripped naked, their heads covered with an opaque cloth bag with no ventilation. They were then dressed in large boiler suits (one-piece overall garments). They were forced into the search position in a room filled with the high-pitched whining sound of an air compressor or similar device. This went on in some cases for six to seven days. Many prisoners felt they were on the brink of insanity – one alleges he prayed for death, another that he tried to kill himself by banging his head against some metal piping in the room.

---

133 The British Army post in Bligh's Lane was also known locally as Fort Essex, after a factory that had previously occupied the site.
134 *Lost Lives* 100.

In short, the allegations are of such a nature as to provide a *prima facie* case of brutality and torture in contravention of Article Five of the Universal Declaration of Human Rights and Article Three of the European Convention on Human Rights.[135]

Among these twelve were two Derry men, Mickey Montgomery and Mickey Donnelly.

The British Government launched an inquiry into these allegations, the Compton Commission, that found that there had been no 'physical brutality' against internees but that the so called 'five techniques' used – sleep deprivation, white noise, making the subject stand in a painful position for hours, hooding of the subject and starvation – had amounted to 'physical ill-treatment'. In a later case, brought to the European Court by the Irish Government, it was decreed that the five techniques amounted to inhuman and degrading treatment but were not technically torture. The British Government promised not to use them again.

In protest at internment and the abuse of internees, a massive campaign of civil disobedience was launched. There was widespread support for a rent and rates strike, with protestors refusing to pay either to their local authorities until internment was stopped. Upwards of ninety per cent of households in some nationalist areas took part in the strike, with ninety-three per cent being reported in Creggan.[136] NICRA launched a five-point civil disobedience plan calling for anyone who opposed internment to withdraw their support from all government institutions, and more than 130 non-unionist councillors resigned their positions on councils across the North. The SDLP actively promoted the rent and rates strike but were later heavily criticised for supporting measures to recoup the lost monies when they entered the new Northern Ireland Executive set up under the Sunningdale Agreement in 1973.[137] Thirty-two 'prominent Catholics' who held public posts in the city, including members of the Derry Development Commission, the Derry Police Liaison Committee, the Board of Governors of Derry Technical College and the Port and Harbour Commissioners, among others, also resigned their posts in protest.[138]

The second fatality in Free Derry came just four days after the internment raids.

Hugh Herron

On 13 August 1971, at just after midnight, Hugh Herron, a 31-year-old married father of two, was shot dead in Henrietta Street, off Long Tower Street, by a British soldier stationed in an observation post on Bishop Street Without.

Soldier C told the inquest that he saw a car pulling up on Long Tower Street and

135 Amnesty International, *A report on allegations of ill-treatment made by persons arrested under the Special Powers Act after 8th August 1971*, 30 October 1971.
136 *Derry Journal*, 27 August 1971.
137 A British Government attempt to set up a power-sharing executive in the North after talks at Sunningdale in England in 1973. The executive collapsed again under intense loyalist opposition in 1974.
138 *Derry Journal*, 20 August 1971.

two figures emerge. Soon afterwards, he claimed shots were fired at his position and that he fired two shots in return but was not sure if he had hit anybody. Other soldiers testified that they had seen two gunmen firing on the observation post, and Soldier E claimed that he had hit one of them.

About ten minutes later, a small group of soldiers were sent into the area on foot, and they stated that they had found Hugh Herron lying on his back with a revolver lying at his side. One of the soldiers also claimed that he had seen the same man earlier that night, armed and with two other men behind the Bogside Inn.

This became the officially accepted version of events surrounding the death of Hugh Herron and there was no further investigation.

However, his family have always claimed that he had no connection to any para-military organisation. There were no paramilitary trappings at his funeral, as would have been customary if he had been a member of any organisation, and his name does not appear on any of the IRA's rolls of honour, which list all dead volunteers.

It was believed locally that Hugh Herron's death was the result of drunken reck-lessness, when in a state of intoxication he had got a gun from somewhere and fired off a few wild shots in the general direction of the observation post before being shot dead. His autopsy revealed a high concentration of alcohol in his bloodstream.

But just two days after the death of Hugh Herron, an extraordinary incident oc-curred that harked back to earlier, more innocent incarnations of Free Derry.

On 16 August, at a time when violence across the North from all sides was spiral-ling out of control, RUC Constable Daniel Barr decided to visit some family mem-bers inside Free Derry. He was recognised as an RUC officer and attacked and beaten by a number of men.

Barr was taken, injured, to a house in Laburnum Terrace, where a large crowd gathered outside. Two local priests and a British Army chaplain pleaded with the crowd to leave the young constable alone, and they eventually were able to move him up to St Mary's Secondary School in Creggan, where he could be treated by a doctor.

After they had left Laburnum Terrace, the British Army arrived and a riot started.

But up at St Mary's, seven masked men appeared, members of one of the wings of the IRA. They agreed that the RUC officer needed hospital treatment but demanded that he be sent to Letterkenny Hospital in Donegal rather than Altnagelvin Hospital in the city. Negotiations between the IRA and British Army followed, with the priests acting as intermediaries, and it was agreed that an Order of Malta[139] ambulance could take him across the border unhindered, where a Garda[140] patrol escorted the ambu-lance to Letterkenny.

It was reported that the IRA had planned to take Barr, the grandson of a former Nationalist Party councillor, hostage for the release of two internees but that they had changed their mind when they realised how bad his injuries were. Barr was later

139 Order or Knights of Malta – a volunteer first-aid group that played a hugely important role in providing medical aid to all sides during the early years of the conflict in the North.
140 An Garda Síochána, police force of the Republic of Ireland.

transferred to a Northern hospital, but if the same incident had happened just a few months later as the conflict deepened further and all members of the security forces became automatic targets for the IRA, it is unlikely that he would have been allowed to leave the area alive.[141]

The first major British Army response to the reborn Free Derry came on 18 August. Over 1,300 soldiers, backed up by helicopters, armoured cars and mechanical equipment, poured into the area to try to destroy the barricades. The IRA responded, and there were twenty-three separate reported incidents of republican gunfire in the two hours following the entry of British soldiers into the area. The British Army managed to destroy a number of barricades, but by later that day they were already being rebuilt.

During one of the many shooting incidents during the raid, Eamonn Lafferty became the first Provisional IRA volunteer to die in action in the city.

Óglach[142] Eamonn Lafferty

Eamonn Lafferty (19), from Creggan Road, was involved in a gun battle with British soldiers at Kildrum Gardens in the city when he was shot dead. It was reported that his body was found in a car at a British Army checkpoint in the Diamond in the city centre, and four others in the car, who had been trying to get him to hospital, were arrested.

A PIRA statement referred to Lafferty as a lieutenant in their organisation, and said that he had:

. . . led a section of volunteers in defence of the Kildrum Gardens area and after a long battle, during which the British forces suffered many casualties, the section was ordered to withdraw. During the withdrawal Lt Lafferty was wounded and, as he fell, the enemy moved in and continued to fire. It was at this stage that Lt Lafferty received the fatal wounds.[143]

Eamonn Lafferty was the second eldest in a family of eleven, and had four brothers and six sisters. At the time of his death, he was working as a baker at the Milanda Bakery.

The British Army pulled out of Free Derry again a few hours later.

Republicans were not the only ones who protested against the British raids, and the more moderate SDLP also came out onto the streets in response. Two hundred people staged a sit-down protest on Laburnum Terrace, where a major barricade had just been destroyed. British soldiers responded to the peaceful protest with tear gas, rubber bullets and water cannon. SDLP MPs John Hume and Ivan Cooper were arrested during the protest and taken to the RUC headquarters at Victoria Barracks, where a deputation of over 300 women marched to demand their release. Both men were charged under the Special Powers Act with failing to disperse when an order was

---

141 *Derry Journal*, 17 August 1971.
142 Irish, literally soldier or warrior, used to denote a volunteer by Irish republican organisations.
143 *Derry Journal*, 20 August 1971.

given, and were released to appear in court on 6 September.

On 19 August, James O'Hagan (16) was killed in an apparently accidental shooting at the Waterside home of the sister of Unionist MP Albert Anderson. Weapons and explosives were found at the scene, and O'Hagan is listed as a volunteer in the PIRA roll of honour.

On Saturday 21 August, the 'biggest outdoor rally since the early days of the civil rights movement' was held in the Brandywell football ground. Over 7,000 people gathered to pledge their support to the passive resistance campaign against internment. Republicans and those on the left claimed that they were not invited to the rally and labelled it an SDLP attempt at taking control of all opposition to internment.[144]

On 6 September, as the two SDLP MPs were due in court to face charges arising from the sit-down protest on 18 August, small-scale stone throwing soon degenerated into full-scale rioting as the British Army moved in to disperse a crowd who had gathered outside the courthouse in support of the two MPs and were returning towards the Bogside after the cases were adjourned.

As the rioting spread across the Bogside, a 14-year-old schoolgirl was shot dead by a British soldier.

Annette McGavigan

Annette McGavigan lived with her family – her parents, four brothers and two sisters – in Drumcliffe Avenue in the Bogside. She was a pupil at St Cecilia's Secondary School. According to her family, she was a bright and cheerful girl who loved music and art.

On the early evening of 6 September, Annette was at Eglinton Place in the Bogside, where there had been some rioting earlier and two nail bombs had been thrown at soldiers. Annette, who was with a crowd of girls, was looking for a rubber bullet for a souvenir, a common pastime for young people in Derry at the time. A soldier from 2nd Battalion the Royal Green Jackets opened fire from the grounds of the old post office near the Little Diamond and Annette, still in her school uniform, was hit in the back of the head. She died instantly.

The British Army immediately released a statement claiming that they had been involved in a gun battle with republicans and that at least nine shots had been fired at their position, implying that Annette had been killed in crossfire by a republican bullet. But all of the civilian eyewitnesses were adamant that there were no shots being fired at the soldiers around the time Annette was killed. Neither the British Army nor the RUC were able to produce any evidence of incoming fire, in the shape of bullet strikes around the soldiers' positions or any spent bullets in the area.

In what was becoming typical fashion, three soldiers – A, B and C – gave evidence to Annette McGavigan's inquest, and all gave differing versions of events surrounding the shooting, describing different types of gunfire they claimed was being aimed at their position, and claiming to have hit and seriously injured a

---

144 *Barricade Bulletin*, 21 August 1971.

gunman when there was no evidence whatsoever of any other casualties in the area at the time.

There was no proper investigation carried out into the shooting of Annette Mc-Gavigan, with the soldiers involved only being interviewed by other soldiers – a practice that was later condemned by the European Court of Human Rights. Based on this purely internal 'investigation' of the British Army by the British Army, the Northern Ireland Attorney General ruled that 'there was no evidence available in the file to justify any criminal prosecution.'

Some light was shed on this sort of internal investigation in documents that came to light during the Bloody Sunday Inquiry, where it was revealed that the army and RUC had agreed in 1970 that the Royal Military Police and not the RUC would conduct investigations into soldiers' actions and the RUC would deal only with civilian witnesses. It was felt that 'with both RMP and RUC sympathetic to the soldier, who after all was doing an incredibly difficult job, he was highly unlikely to make a statement incriminating himself . . .' The investigations were described by one army officer as 'tea and biscuits' affairs. Other information would also emerge later of how all involved, including politicians, senior army and RUC officers and the prosecution service would do everything in their power to keep soldiers out of court, even when they had killed clearly innocent people in the most questionable of circumstances.[145]

To date, the British Army have never clearly stated that they shot Annette Mc-Gavigan, and her family have never received any sort of apology or explanation from them.

Annette was the hundredth civilian to die in the conflict, and the fortieth to be killed by the security forces.

As anti-internment protests and violence continued across Derry, the City of Derry and Foyle Unionist Association called for the formation of a 'third force' of local loyalists to help defeat the IRA.

The British Army continued with regular large-scale incursions into Free Derry, which were routinely met with a violent reaction. Within two weeks of the death of Annette McGavigan, another three people, including a three-year-old child, were killed in Free Derry, and a fourth, a soldier shot by the IRA, would die of the wounds he received.

Major Robin Nigel Alers-Hankey, Gary Gormley, Sergeant Martin McCarroll and William McGreanery

On 2 September, Robin Nigel Alers-Hankey (35), a major in the Royal Green Jackets, was shot and wounded in Abbey Street in the Bogside. The married father of two was part of a squad protecting firemen who had come under attack from

---

145 Pat Finucane Centre fact file on the death of Annette McGavigan. The Pat Finucane Centre works with the families of many of those killed during this period and has prepared detailed fact files in many of the cases which have been used here as a source.

stone throwers as they tackled a blaze in a timber yard.

He was initially treated in Altnagelvin Hospital before being moved to hospital in England, where he was expected to make a full recovery. He was released from hospital but readmitted following complications. He died from his wounds on Bloody Sunday, 30 January 1972, the day that fourteen civil rights marchers were killed by the British Army in the Bogside, just yards from where Major Hankey was shot.[146]

Gary Gormley, one of a family of six children, became the third child to die in the Free Derry area in the summer of 1971. The three-year-old was knocked down by a British Army armoured vehicle near his home in Carrigans Lane, off Foyle Road, on 9 September 1971.

According to eyewitnesses, the armoured personnel carrier (APC) was travelling at 'powerful speed' when it hit the child, and it failed to stop after the accident. A second APC did stop at the scene, but two soldiers just got out, looked at the child, and got back in their vehicle and left again. A taxi driver who was following managed to get the number of the vehicle that killed the child and passed in on to John Hume, who passed it on to the RUC.

Gary Gormley was taken to Altnagelvin Hospital, but was pronounced dead on arrival.

After his death, a group of men attacked the army observation post in nearby Hamilton Street, while a crowd of over 100 women marched from Rossville Street to the British Army post in the Diamond chanting 'Hey, hey, British Army, how many children have you killed today?'

As in the case of Damian Harkin earlier in the summer, and again despite the clear circumstances, the death of Gary Gormley was officially treated as a road accident, and he is not recorded as a victim of the conflict in the North.

Over 2,000 people attended his funeral, during which rioting in the area stopped for a short time. It resumed immediately after the burial ceremony ended.[147]

Sergeant Martin McCarroll (23), a sergeant in the Royal Artillery, who was married with a pregnant wife, was on duty in Bligh's Lane army post when he was shot by an IRA sniper on 14 September 1971. According to a colleague, he had just left the secure sandbag emplacement to fire CS gas at a crowd of rioters when the shot was fired.

Carroll's half-brother, a sergeant major, was on duty in the same army post at the time he was shot and witnessed the shooting. He said, 'Suddenly I heard my brother shout, "I've been shot." I was twenty yards away. I rushed over. He lost consciousness immediately and I helped to get him into an armoured car. My brother was a popular kid with all the boys. He was a great mimic, always livening up duties.' Martin McCarroll was from Merioneth in Wales. The OIRA later claimed responsibility for his death.[148]

---

146 *Lost Lives* 256.
147 *Derry Journal*, 10 September 1971 & 14 September 1971.
148 *Lost Lives* 124; *Derry Journal*, 17 September 1971 & 21 September 1971.

William McGreanery (41), a single man who worked as a shop assistant, was walking past the junction of Eastway and Lone Moor Road in the early hours of the morning on 15 September 1971 when he was shot dead by a British soldier firing from the same Bligh's Lane army post where Martin Carroll had been shot dead by the IRA just hours earlier.

The British Army immediately released a statement claiming that the soldier had opened fire on and hit a man armed with a rifle, a claim denied by six civilian eyewitnesses who were with McGreanery at the time he was shot.

In the aftermath of his death, William McGreanery's family issued a statement calling for no retaliation:

> We ask everyone not to use Billy's death in any way to arouse hatred or revenge. Billy lived quietly. He was not in any political organisation. The statement that he had a rifle when he was shot is not true.

After an investigation, the RUC, unusually, recommended that the soldier who shot William McGreanery be charged with murder, but the Attorney General over-ruled their recommendation, stating that whether the soldier had acted wrongly or not, he was acting 'in the course of his duty'.

The British Army claim that William McGreanery was armed when he was shot dead persisted for over forty years, until a report by the Historical Enquiries Team (HET)[149] in June 2010 found that he was unarmed and innocent when he was shot and forced the Ministry of Defence to finally acknowledge the truth and apologise to his family. Writing to the family in July 2011, the Chief of the General Staff of the Ministry of Defence, General Sir Peter Wall acknowledged that:

> In the light of what it [HET report] says, it is clear to me that such an apology is right and proper . . . it is evident that the soldier who shot him was mistaken in his belief that he had a weapon and this error, tragically, resulted in the death of an innocent man . . .[150]

On 20 September, a corporal from the Royal Anglian Regiment was shot and seriously wounded while on duty in an army observation post in the Mex Garage on Foyle Road. The British Army released a statement claiming that he had been hit by an illegal dumdum bullet. The OIRA, who claimed responsibility for the shooting, denied this.[151]

---

149 The Historical Enquiries Team is a police investigation unit, answerable to the Chief Constable of the Police Service of Northern Ireland, set up to re-examine killings from the conflict in the North.
150 Letter from Ministry of Defence to McGreanery family, 14 July 2011; *Lost Lives* 123; *Derry Journal*, 17 September 1971; *Derry Journal*, 13 September 2011.
151 *Derry Journal*, 21 September 1971. A dumdum bullet is one that has been illegally tampered with to cause maximum damage on impact. The use of such bullets was banned by The Hague Convention in 1899.

Private Roger Wilkins

Roger Wilkins (31), a private in the 1st Battalion Royal Anglian Regiment and a married father of five, was shot by a republican sniper while on duty in an army observation post in Bishop Street on 27 September 1971. He was using binoculars to search the area after a shot had been fired at his position when he was hit by a burst of machine-gun fire coming from the direction of the Lone Moor Road.

Wilkins, from Hastings in Sussex, was airlifted to the Royal Victoria Hospital in Belfast, where he was treated in intensive care, but he died from his injuries on 11 October.[152]

On 3 October 1971, a five-year-old girl was shot and seriously wounded as she travelled with her mother and brother in their car on Bishop Street. The child's mother and brother were also injured.

It was reported that as their car approached Bishop's Gate, there was an explosion nearby and a soldier opened fire from an observation post, hitting their car twice. The army at first claimed that they had shot at a car from which a bomb had been thrown, and then changed their story to claim that there were two cars and that they had hit the wrong one. There were no other cars in the area at the time.

After the shooting, SDLP MP Ivan Cooper said:

Now will the British Government believe that the army shoots first and ascertains the facts later? This proves what we have been alleging for a long time, that the army shoots on suspicion.

What difference is there between this incident and the shooting of Eamonn McDevitt [a deaf and mute man shot dead by the British Army in Strabane on 18 August], Seamus Cusack, Desmond Beattie and Billy McGreanery? This incident shows that several innocent people have been shot down by the British Army in their 'shoot-on-suspicion' campaign . . .

The brigade commander of the soldier who had shot the child apologised for the shooting, but tempered the apology by repeating the claim that the soldier had believed he was firing at a bomber.

It was later reported that the injured child was making a good recovery and that her mother believed the soldier's version of events and did not blame him for what had happened to her child.[153]

In response to fears that the Stormont Government would deliberately run down essential services, such as the collection of rubbish, in areas that were participating in the rent and rates strike, the Socialist Resistance Group (which was made up of members of the James Connolly Republican Clubs, Derry Young Socialists and People's Democracy) proposed the creation of street committees to help fulfil the needs of the communities 'behind the barricades'. They claimed that proposed legislation

---

152 *Lost Lives* 140.
153 *Derry Journal*, 5 October 1971 & 8 October 1971.

to recover money being withheld during the strike was a 'blatant attempt to coerce' people into giving up the strike.[154]

Rifleman Joseph Hill

The 24-year-old married man, who was serving with the Royal Green Jackets, was shot dead by an IRA sniper during rioting in the Bogside on 16 October 1971.

Hill was part of a unit that had moved in to occupy side streets off William Street to try to force the rioters back into the Bogside, and as they entered Columbcille Court, he was hit by a single shot in the head.

Joseph Hill, who came from the Isle of Sheppey in Kent, was based in Ballykelly, a few miles outside Derry, at the time of his death.

The Provisional IRA claimed responsibility for his death, and for the wounding of four other soldiers in the days preceding his death.[155]

In the same statement in which they claimed responsibility for the death of Joseph Hill, the Provisional IRA also claimed responsibility for the tarring and feathering of three young men who they claimed had been involved in criminal activities. They also warned local girls against fraternising with British soldiers. According to the report:

> The intelligence unit of the Women's Action Group of the Provisional IRA in Derry claimed yesterday that they have information that a ten-man unit is operating in the Derry area 'whose job is to seek out young girls from areas such as the Creggan and Bogside, to give them a good time and to find out about barricades and the whereabouts of men on the army's wanted list'.
>
> The unit, in a statement last night, said their information was confirmed when the unit questioned a young girl regarding the lifting of five men in the Creggan last Friday. They claimed that the girl told them that an army sergeant whom she had met in the Viking Club and with whom she had been going out for three months told her that he had been sent specially to Derry to get information about no-go areas and that he was paid a special allowance every week to take girls out. 'He said,' according to the statement 'that there were eight or nine other chaps and he pointed them out to me in the club'.

The statement said that the girl had nothing to do with the recent arrests. It added, 'We now issue a final warning to the girls still going to the Viking Club and Ballykelly. Your selfishness for a few hours' entertainment is directly contributing to the internment of local innocent men. Wives and children are suffering. This must stop. We will stop you.'[156]

Within the next few weeks, three girls were tarred and feathered and had their hair shaved off in the Bogside and Creggan. One of the girls had been just about to marry

---

154 *Derry Journal*, 8 October 1971.
155 *Lost Lives* 145; *Derry Journal*, 26 October 1971.
156 *Derry Journal*, 26 October 1971.

a British soldier. A fourth girl was reported to have fled to England after the words 'Soldier Dolly Beware' had been painted outside her home. Both wings of the IRA denied any involvement. The Official IRA claimed that their earlier warning about local girls fraternising with British soldiers was not aimed at all local girls who had got engaged to soldiers, but only to those who were passing on information, and warned that they would take action against anyone using their name in such an attack.[157] The Provisional IRA released a statement that anyone involved in such attacks on local girls would be 'dealt with'. It was later reported that the girl had married the soldier in a ceremony at Ebrington Barracks.[158]

The British Army approach to Free Derry continued for the time being to be one of containment, making sporadic entries into the area in force but otherwise remaining on the edges. At the time, they considered three main options:

> Course 1. Continuing as we are, controlling the rest of Derry and raiding the [Creggan and Bogside] area for gunmen as our intelligence allows us. We would hope, though without great confidence, that progress in the political field would produce a gradual return to normality.
>
> Course 2. Show our ability to go into the area when we want by establishing regular patrol patterns. This will achieve little except to please the Protestants. It is a practical course but it will not achieve the removal of the obstructions and certainly will not re-establish law and order throughout the areas. But it could be done with our present force levels.
>
> Course 3. To occupy and dominate the areas, take down the barricades, and, we hope, eventually persuade the RUC to play their full part. This is a practical military operation although it will involve casualties and, most important, stir up Catholic opposition as much as it will satisfy the Protestants. It is difficult to estimate how great the political reaction would be. This must be a political and not a military decision. However, there is one significant military factor. We could only occupy and dominate these areas by an increase in our force levels by three battalions.

For the time being, the British decided to stick with 'Course 1'. They considered Creggan and the Bogside to be virtual No Go areas, where about '200 extremists and a number of hardcore hooligans operated unchecked'.[159]

On 27 October, two British soldiers were killed just outside Free Derry when the Provisional IRA bombed an army observation post in Rosemount. Lance Bombardier David Tilbury (29) and Gunner Angus Stevens (18), both single men and members of the 45 Medium Regiment Royal Artillery, died instantly when a bomb was thrown into their post from Brooke Park. On the same day, the Provisional IRA fired around

---

157 *Derry Journal*, 12 November 1971.
158 *Derry Journal*, 16 November 1971.
159 Chief of the General Staff, General Sir Michael Carver, *Northern Ireland – An Appreciation of the Security Situation as at 4th October 1971*, quoted in the *Report of the Bloody Sunday Inquiry* (BSI), (TSO 2010), Volume 1, 8.80.

twenty shots at the Mex Garage army post on Foyle Road, while shots were also fired at the British Army in Bligh's Lane, Lone Moor Road and Fahan Street. No other casualties were reported.[160] By this stage, IRA attacks on British soldiers were becoming an almost daily occurrence.

On 4 November 1971, the British Army launched their biggest raids into Free Derry since internment, arresting seventeen men. The raids resulted in widespread protests that brought the city centre to a standstill and ended in major rioting.[161]

The following night, they raided Free Derry again, with 200 members of the Royal Green Jackets moving into Creggan to search a house in Rathlin Drive and arrest any males they found there. As they were leaving the area, empty-handed after a fruitless search, a soldier opened fire, killing a 47-year-old mother of six in the back garden of her own home.

Kathleen Thompson

As the Royal Green Jackets were leaving Creggan, they claimed that two shots were fired at them, though all civilian witnesses claim that no shots were fired. Soldier D responded with eight shots, two of which he claimed were at a figure he could see behind a fence from where he said a shot had been fired, and the others at two alleged bombers.

The only figure behind the fence was Kathleen Thompson, who was holding nothing more deadly than a dustbin lid, which was commonly banged on the ground to warn of incursions by the British Army. She was hit by a single shot in the chest and died instantly.

The 'investigation' into the death of Kathleen Thompson was carried out by the British Army, and the soldiers who gave statements, listed at her inquest as A, B, C and D, were only questioned by other soldiers, not by the RUC. They all gave conflicting accounts of the events of that night, which amounted to an impossible description of the events surrounding her death. According to their statements, the shot that killed her was supposedly fired from a position that could not possibly give the clear view into the back garden of the Thompson home that Soldier D claimed to have had when he opened fire.

Despite the obvious issues arising from the internal army investigation, the RUC did not become involved in any sort of investigation into Mrs Thompson's death until ten months afterwards when they were preparing paperwork for the inquest. Their lack of investigation, as noted above, was in clear contravention of their legal requirements, under national and international law, to carry out a proper investigation into her death. The inquest into her death returned an open verdict, the strongest available at the time, and that was the end of any investigation into the death of a mother of six young children.

In June 1980, Mrs Thompson's family were given £84.07 in compensation. Her husband, Patrick, tore up the cheque.

---

160 *Derry Journal*, 29 October 1971.
161 *Derry Journal*, 5 November 1971.

But Kathleen Thompson's children refused to accept this as the end of the matter and have campaigned since to have a proper investigation into the death of their mother. In 2001, the RUC confirmed that they could not find any investigation file into the death of Mrs Thompson, although under media pressure they eventually produced an 'investigation file' which contained nothing more than the inquest documents.

At the time of writing, the death of Kathleen Thompson is subject to a further investigation by the HET.[162]

Local reaction to the death of Kathleen Thompson was one of great anger. The Creggan and Foyle Hill Tenants Association claimed that the harassment of the people of Creggan by the British Army had been replaced by a policy of 'intimidation and murder' and claimed that the shooting of Mrs Thompson was just the soldiers' way of venting their anger at not being able to arrest their intended target. They compared the soldiers to the Black and Tans, the notorious British Army regiment from the War of Independence of 1919–1921.

In the days following the death of Mrs Thompson, violence across the city increased even more. There were numerous IRA gun attacks on the British Army, including one on a helicopter flying over the Brandywell, and the British claimed to have wounded four republicans involved in the gun attacks, though they offered no evidence to back up this claim. On 9 November, another British soldier was killed in Free Derry.

Lance Corporal Ian Curtis

The 23-year-old single man, serving with the Royal Anglian Regiment, was shot dead by the IRA while on his last patrol before going home on leave.

Curtis, from Fareham near Portsmouth, was part of a foot patrol on waste ground by the bank of the River Foyle when two burst of shots were fired near the junction of Foyle Road and Bishop Street. Ian Curtis was hit by the second burst.[163]

On 12 November, the Bogside Vigilante Association called for more volunteers to patrol the Bogside and Brandywell 'to protect their families and homes in the event of an influx of British troops into the area'.[164]

On 17 November, a 14-year-old schoolboy was seriously wounded during rioting that followed an attempt to demolish a barricade. The boy was shot just after a warning that the soldiers would open fire on anyone with a petrol bomb. The British Army claimed that the only shots fired were by the IRA and that one of them must have hit the boy. Civilian witnesses claimed that the soldiers had opened fire. The boy was reported to be 'improving' in hospital.[165]

---

162 Pat Finucane Centre fact file on the death of Kathleen Thompson.
163 *Lost Lives* 178.
164 *Derry Journal*, 12 November 1971.
165 *Derry Journal*, 19 November 1971.

In the last four days of November alone, nine IRA bombs exploded in Derry's city centre as the bombing campaign against business and economic targets gathered momentum. The Provisional IRA claimed responsibility for all the attacks, in which six people were injured.[166] Locals joked of the need to 'buy now while shops last'. There were seven more bomb attacks in the following three days, with a further eight people injured.[167] It could be regarded as amazing that in a bombing campaign of this intensity that no-one was killed, but it has always been claimed that PIRA units in the city were under strict instructions at the time to avoid civilian casualties.[168] Martin McGuinness, currently Deputy First Minister in the Stormont Assembly, has admitted being second-in-command of the PIRA in Derry during this time.

In early December, the British Army decided to move away from its containment policy for Free Derry and adopt a more combative approach. It was agreed that they would continue arrest operations 'at the highest possible intensity . . . to harass the IRA to such an extent that they do not know where to turn to next for a safe bed for the night' and that battalion-strength patrols of the Bogside and Creggan would begin 'as soon as the Brigade force levels allow'.[169] The increase in the number and intensity of British Army raids began immediately.

On 6 December, 500 troops carried out a raid into Creggan. Both wings of the IRA, who said they had operated together to attack the raiding party, claimed that four soldiers were shot during the raid, with one killed. The British Army claimed that they had shot four gunmen. There was no actual evidence of injuries on either side.[170] The raid had been met with gunfire, bombs, bottles, bricks and stones for the two and a half hours it lasted. It resulted in the discovery of a small amount of arms and ammunition.[171]

On 9 December, around 400 troops raided the Bogside. On 10 December, there was another 500-strong raid into Creggan. Local MP John Hume warned that the raids were only turning local people more and more against the British, and that their indiscriminate use of CS gas would eventually lead to 'open rebellion on the streets'. During the raid into Creggan, a three-year-old girl and a 52-year-old man were shot and wounded.[172]

Attacks and counterattacks, raids and riots, claims and counterclaims, continued throughout the month of December, but on 27 December, the Official IRA gave the people of Free Derry a belated Christmas present when they raided the offices of the Housing Executive and destroyed hundreds of files. They then made off with another few hundred files which they symbolically burned in front of an assembled press corps at the roundabout at the top of the Eastway entrance to Creggan. The files were

---

166 *Derry Journal*, 30 November 1971.
167 *Derry Journal*, 3 December 1971.
168 Patrick Bishop & Eamonn Mallie *The Provisional IRA* (Heinemann, 1987) p154.
169 OP Directive 4/71 from Brigadier McLellan, senior British Army officer in Derry, quoted in BSI 8.119.
170 *Derry Journal*, 10 December 1971.
171 *Derry Journal*, 7 December 1971.
172 *Derry Journal*, 10 December 1971 & 14 December 1971.

said to contain details of people who owed the Housing Executive money because of the ongoing rent and rates strike.[173]

Gunner Richard Ham

On 29 December, Richard Ham became the last fatality of 1971 in Derry. The 20-year-old single man from Glamorgan, who was serving with the Royal Artillery, was shot by an IRA sniper while on foot patrol on the Foyle Road.

Gunner Ham's mother said she had offered to buy him out of the army several times, and that he did not want to be sent to the North of Ireland but that he loved the army and refused to leave.[174]

So as 1971 drew to a close (with two bombs exploding and widespread rioting on New Year's Eve), the situation was almost unrecognisable from the year before. Derry was truly now a city at war. Nineteen people had been killed during the year: eight civilians killed by the British Army (including two children who do not appear officially as victims of the conflict); one Provisional IRA volunteer had been killed in action and another in an accidental shooting and nine British soldiers had been shot dead by republicans. The barricades were back up and strengthened around Free Derry and large parts of the city centre had been reduced to rubble by the escalating IRA bombing campaign.

It would get much worse. In terms of violent death, 1972 would be the worst year of the entire war, not only in Derry but across the North of Ireland. If 1970 had been a prelude to war, and 1971 the descent into war, then 1972 was going to be all-out war.

---

173 *Derry Journal*, 28 December 1971.
174 *Lost Lives* 228.

The Darkest Year Dawns

By the end of 1971, 229 people had lost their lives in the burgeoning conflict in the North of Ireland. In 1972, 496 people would lose their lives, by far the highest total in any year of the entire conflict.

The year would include Bloody Friday, Claudy and the Springhill Massacre among the 10,631 shooting incidents and 1,853 bombs planted that year.[175] It would also include the darkest and most pivotal day in the modern history of the city of Derry: Bloody Sunday.

The year began as the previous one had ended. On 4 January, two PIRA bombs exploded in the city centre and on 6 January a British soldier was shot and wounded on the Lone Moor Road. NICRA announced that they would defy the Stormont ban on marches as People's Democracy and Sinn Féin had already done on Christmas Day of the previous year. The OIRA called on local people involved in the rent and rates strike to destroy their rent and gas books, and helped them along by continuing their policy from the previous December and raiding the offices of the Derry Gaslight Company, destroying thousands of customer files.[176]

Another British soldier was shot and wounded on 9 January during rioting in the Bogside, when the British Army claimed to have hit two republican snipers.[177]

As Unionist politicians fumed about the continuing existence of Free Derry and the other No Go areas – two Unionist MPs had already resigned from the Stormont Government in protest at what they regarded as the 'softly-softly' approach being taken against them – the British Army decided they had to come up with a harder strategy. This was framed in a document written by Major General Robert Ford, the Commander of Land Forces for Northern Ireland, the most senior British soldier in the North of Ireland:

> I visited Londonderry on Friday 7th January with ACC (Ops) and held discussions with Commander 8 Brigade, Commanding Officer the City Battalion (22 Lt AD Regt), and the Police Divisional Commander . . . I was disturbed by the attitude of both the Brigade Commander and the Battalion Commander, and also, of course, by Chief Superintendent Lagan. All admitted that 'The Front' was gradually moving northwards and, in their view, not only would Great James Street go up in time but also Clarendon Street unless there was a change of policy . . .
>
> The IS situation in Londonderry is one of armed gunmen dominating the Creggan and Bogside backed and protected by the vast majority of the population in these two areas, and of bombers and gunmen making occasional sorties out of these hardcore areas to cause incidents . . .

---

175   Paul Bew & Gordon Gillespie *Northern Ireland: A Chronology of the Troubles 1968–1999* (Gill & MacMillan, 1999) p57.
176   *Derry Journal*, 4 January 1972.
177   *Derry Journal*, 11 January 1972.

However, the Londonderry situation is further complicated by one additional ingredient. This is the Derry Young Hooligans (DYH). Gangs of tough, teenaged youths, permanently unemployed, have developed sophisticated tactics of brick and stone throwing, destruction and arson. Under cover of snipers in nearby buildings, they operate just beyond the hardcore areas and extend the radius of anarchy by degrees into additional streets and areas. Against the DYH – described by the People's Democracy as 'brave fighters in the republican cause' – the army in Londonderry is for the moment virtually incapable . . .

The weapons at our disposal – CS gas and baton rounds – are ineffective . . .

As I understand it, the commander of a body of troops called out to restore law and order has a duty to use minimum force but he also has a duty to restore law and order. We have fulfilled the first duty but are failing in the second. I am coming to the conclusion that the minimum force necessary to achieve a restoration of law and order is to shoot selected ringleaders among the DYH, after clear warnings have been issued. I believe we would be justified in using 7.62mm but in view of the devastating effects of this weapon and the danger of rounds killing more than the person aimed at, I believe we must consider issuing rifles adapted to fire HV .22 inch ammunition to sufficient members of the unit dealing with this problem . . .

If this course is implemented, as I believe it may have to be, we would have to accept the possibility that .22 rounds may be lethal . . . I am convinced that our duty to restore law and order requires us to consider this step . . .[178]

In this document, Ford basically admits that the British Army were losing the battle to contain Free Derry, and that its sphere of influence was actually expanding. He also claims that the only way to stop this was to shoot members of the DYH, ie rioters, not gunmen or bombers, and that they may have to be shot dead. The discovery of this document and of Ford's suggestion for shooting unarmed rioters, written just twenty days before Bloody Sunday, is very telling, showing, as it does, willingness on behalf of the command of the British Army to shoot dead unarmed people. They also showed no regard for what Ford called the 'devastating effects' of 7.62mm ammunition when they used it on Bloody Sunday against a crowd of innocent civilians.

On Saturday 22 January, the North Derry Civil Rights Association organised an anti-internment march along Magilligan Strand, about eight miles from the city, to the internment camp that was housed in the army base there. Up to 1,500 people took part in the march, which was not technically illegal under the ban because it did not take place on a public road.

The perimeter fence of the internment camp was being patrolled by members of the 1st Battalion of the Parachute Regiment, who had a reputation for brutality and who had been involved in the killing of eleven civilians the previous August during

178 Major General Robert Ford, *The Situation in Londonderry as at 7th January 1972*, quoted at BSI 9.104. It is believed to have been written on 10 January 1972.

the Ballymurphy Massacre in Belfast. The people of Derry were about to have their first encounter with them.

As the marchers approached the camp, the 'Paras' opened fire with rubber bullets, then baton charged the crowd. According to Derry doctor Raymond McClean, who was on the march:

> . . . the soldiers charged forward with batons waving, smashing into everyone in sight. The crowd broke in panic, and we started running back across the sand, through water, sand, seaweed and whatever came in the way. The army onslaught was brief but violent and we had several severe skull lacerations to deal with when we got organised again some way along the sand. The army charged again – more lacerations and more running in panic.[179]

Other witnesses gave similar accounts of the violence of the Paras. A *Daily Telegraph* reporter described how he saw soldiers firing rubber bullets into the chests of marchers at very close range, which was against all the rules for the use of such weapons. He also reported how he saw some officers having to physically restrain their men from attacking the marchers even more.[180] Even a military witness, a captain from the Royal Green Jackets, described what he regarded as 'an awful lot of unnecessary violence by the Paras . . .'[181] and a Para stated that he had seen an officer from the Royal Green Jackets hit a Para with a baton and call him an animal.[182]

The marchers retreated back to the safety of their buses. Their first encounter with the 1st Battalion of the Parachute Regiment had not been a good one.

The following Tuesday, the Derry branch of the Civil Rights Association announced that the violence used against the marchers the previous Saturday would not put them off and that they would hold another anti-internment march in the city the following Sunday, 30 January.

On Thursday 27 January, the IRA killed the first two RUC officers to die in Derry.

Sergeant Peter Gilgunn and Constable David Montgomery

The two RUC officers were travelling with three others up Creggan Hill towards Rosemount RUC Barracks at just before 8.30AM when three gunmen opened fire on their car from two different side streets. The car was hit seventeen times. The driver was able to keep going and reach the barracks, but the two officers were already dead and a third injured. A British soldier opened fire on the IRA men from his position in Rosemount Barracks but did not claim to have hit any of them.

Peter Gilgunn (26) was a married man from County Fermanagh with an eight-month-old son; David Montgomery (20) was a single man from Belfast.[183]

---

179 *The Road to Bloody Sunday*, p116.
180 BSI 9.207.
181 BSI 9.211.
182 BSI 9.212.
183 *Derry Journal*, 28 January 1972; *Lost Lives* 240, 241.

On 28 January, a British cabinet committee approved security plans for the march planned for Sunday 30 January. The march organisers advertised the march in the local press and called for people to travel from across the North to join the march:

> A call for a massive turnout at the Civil Rights Demonstration planned for Derry tomorrow has been made by the Executive of the Civil Rights Association. Making the call, the Executive pointed out that the British Government are now full-tilt on repression and coercion and that a massive peaceful demonstration was vital if world opinion was to be impressed by the justice of the democratic cause in Northern Ireland.
>
> The twin major aims for Derry is a demonstration that is both huge in numbers and perfectly peaceful and incident free. It is pointed out that any violence can only set back the civil rights cause and play straight into the hands of the Tory-Unionists by providing a justification not only for any violence they may contemplate against the demonstration itself but also for the daily violence of the security forces.[184]

On 29 January, a joint British Army/RUC statement warned that any violence at the march the next day should be blamed on the march organisers. By this time, the RUC had been informed by local sources that both wings of the IRA intended to stay away from the march, and the senior RUC officer in the city, Chief Superintendent Frank Lagan, had already passed this information on to the British Army.

But that Saturday afternoon provided a well-timed example of how the British Army felt towards shooting unarmed men, and how Ford's memo from earlier in the month was being put into practice. During rioting in William Street, in which two teenagers were shot and wounded by British soldiers, a number of nail bombs were thrown at British armoured vehicles. Local radio enthusiast Jimmy Porter, who owned a shop on William Street and regularly recorded non-secure British Army radio transmissions, picked up the following communication between an officer and a soldier, 1.9 being the officer in command:

1.9: 6.1, this is 1.9. Did you see that last nail bomb, where it came from?

6.1: No, but we presume it was thrown from my right, from the alleyway along the Grandstand Bar, over.

1.9: Say again, over.

6.1: The nail bomb came from my right, in the alleyway to my right.

1.9: Roger. Is there anything you can do to improve your fire position?

6.1: No, it is a very good one actually.

---

184 NICRA press statement, quoted at BSI 9.732.

1.9: 6.1 this is 1.9. I want you to move, move back so that you can see down the alleyway by the maroon lorry, over.

6.1: I can see the whole of the alleyway, over.

1.9: I understand you to say you are already covering this alleyway, is that correct?

6.1: This is correct. The last nail bomb that was just thrown came from the alleyway alongside the Grandstand Bar. Thrown by a youth in dark clothing, over.

1.9: Roger. Why didn't you shoot him? Over.

6.1: My sights were not on him, and he was only in view for a second, over.

1.9: Roger, have the place covered, out.

6.1: I can see the nail bomber. Do you want me to shoot him? He has nothing in his hands at the moment, over.

1.9: Say again, over.

6.1: This is . . . I can see the nail bomber but he doesn't appear to have anything in his hands, over.

1.9: Roger, out.

1.9: 6.1, this is 1.9. Are you absolutely certain that the person you can see is the nail bomber? Over.

6.1: Positive. Over.

1.9: Shoot him dead. Over

6.1: 1.9, this is 6.1. Missed him by about two inches, over.

1.9: Bad shooting, out.[185]

The transcript clearly shows a British officer ordering a soldier under his command to shoot dead a youth who has just been clearly identified as unarmed. This was the British Army attitude in Derry on 29 January 1972, the day before Bloody Sunday.

---

185 British Army radio transmission, recorded 29 January 1972, William Street. Transcript from statement of Jimmy Porter to BSI.

Bloody Sunday

Sunday 30 January 1972, Bloody Sunday, was to be a day that would shape the course of modern Irish history, the day that all semblance of hope for peaceful change was replaced by the certainty of a long and bloody struggle ahead.

The Northern Ireland Civil Rights Association had called on people from across the North of Ireland to come to Derry to protest against internment without trial, and on that bright, crisp afternoon, 15,000 people gathered in Creggan to march against internment. Reports circulated through the crowd of barbed wire across all exits from the Bogside, and of paratroopers (Paras) behind the barriers, but the good mood of the marchers was enhanced by satisfaction at the turnout.

The intended route was from Bishop's Field and through Creggan, down Southway, then through the Brandywell and Bogside and out from Free Derry into Guildhall Square in the city centre. Shortly after 3.00PM, the march set off.

But the men, women and children who made their way from Creggan that Sunday afternoon to take part in the banned anti-internment rally had no idea of the events that were to unfold that fateful afternoon or of the carnage they were about to endure.

As the marchers were leaving the Creggan estate, General Ford, the officer commanding the British Army in the North, was finalising preparations to prevent the march from reaching Guildhall Square. Twenty-six barricades had been erected around the Bogside to stop the march, and the 1st Battalion of the Parachute Regiment, the 'elite' regiment of the British Army who had attacked peaceful Derry marchers the week before at Magilligan, had for some reason been drafted in to the city to bolster the already substantial British Army presence.

These preparations went largely unnoticed by the marchers, who knew that both wings of the IRA had given assurances to the organisers that they would stay away from the march. Feeling safe in this knowledge, the marchers expected a peaceful day, by Derry standards, as evidenced by the large numbers of women and children who took part.

As the march approached the army barricades at the bottom of William Street, the lorry leading the parade and the bulk of the marchers swung to their right, into the Bogside and towards Free Derry Corner, to hear speakers including Bernadette Devlin and Lord Fenner Brockway. A group of several hundred, mostly young people, continued along William Street and came to Barrier 14, which was blocking the road into the city centre.

There followed the standard Derry riot: stones and bottles against rubber bullets, CS gas and water cannon. This was an almost daily occurrence in Derry at the time, and as 4.00PM approached, the riot was 'petering' out. Nothing seemed out of the ordinary, and even well-known local press photographer Willie Carson, who had got soaked by a water cannon, went on home, feeling that he had photographed hundreds of such riots, so there was no point in hanging around in soaking wet clothes just to photograph another one. Just another ordinary day, with an ordinary march and an ordinary riot. Just another day in Free Derry.

Then the day became anything but ordinary.

At 3.55PM, away from the riot in William Street, two Paras opened fire with five live rounds at a teenager who had run from the crowd to try to grab a rubber bullet as a souvenir. Damian Donaghy (15) was hit in the leg. **John Johnston** (59) was hit in the arms, legs and hand.

John Johnston, a married man with no children and who had worked as a draper all his life, was a keen supporter of the civil rights movement and attended as many marches as he could. His other passion was golf, and he was a member of Lisfannon Golf Club, where he once won the captain's prize. He died from his injuries on 16 June 1972.

The OIRA fired one shot in response to this burst of army fire, *after* the soldiers had already opened fire.

At approximately 4.07PM, the order was given for the Paras to begin an 'arrest' operation. Their commander, Colonel Derek Wilford, deployed one company of Paras through Barrier 14 in William Street. A second company, Support Company, was ordered through Barrier 12 in Little James Street in armoured personnel carriers (APCs). Support Company were responsible for all of the deaths that day.

The crowd ran as the armoured vehicles roared into Rossville Street. The first APC turned left, into the waste ground in front of Rossville Flats. Alana Burke (18) was crushed against a wall by an APC, receiving serious internal injuries. She was the first of only two women to be injured on Bloody Sunday. Thomas Harkin (32) was hit by the same APC. The Paras dismounted from the APCs and opened fire with live rounds.

Jackie Duddy (17) was one of a family of fifteen from Creggan. He worked at French's factory, though his real passion was boxing and he was a member of Long Tower Boxing Club and had fought throughout Ireland and represented the club in Liverpool. He had no interest in politics and attended the march against his father's advice. He was running through the courtyard of Rossville Flats, alongside Fr Edward Daly, when he was shot in the back. The photos of his body being carried by a group led by Fr Daly waving his white handkerchief are among the most iconic photographs of that day.

The second woman to be injured was Margaret Deery (33), a mother of fourteen whose husband had died just four months earlier. She was shot in the leg as she sought safety at the end of Chamberlain Street. Patrick McDaid (25) was shot and wounded after he helped carry the wounded Mrs Deery to safety.

Michael Bradley (22), and Mickey Bridge (25), were shot and wounded as they confronted the Paras after they heard of the shooting of Jackie Duddy. Pius McCarron (30) was injured by flying debris caused by British Army rifle fire, and Patrick Brolly (40) was injured by gunfire in one of the Rossville Flats.

A second wave of Paras dismounted and advanced along Rossville Street on foot as some marchers tried to take cover at the rubble barricade. The Paras took cover behind a pram ramp at Kells Walk and opened fire towards the barricade.

Hugh Gilmour (17) was the youngest of a family of eight and the son of a former Derry City player. He worked as a trainee tyre fitter in Northern Ireland Tyres in William Street. Living in Rossville Flats, Hugh had found himself at the forefront of the civil unrest that swept across the North in 1969, and he was active in the defence of the Bogside in August 1969. He was an avid Liverpool supporter, who had just bought a car and was learning to drive. He was shot dead as he ran towards the safety of the Rossville Flats, dying just below the windows of his own home. The banner of the Derry Civil Rights Association was laid over his body.

Michael Kelly (17) was the seventh child in a family of thirteen. He was training to be a sewing-machine mechanic and spent his weeks in Belfast, returning to Derry at the weekends. At the age of three, he had been in a coma for weeks and his family was told not to expect him to recover. He had no interest in politics and the Bloody Sunday march was the first he had ever attended. He was shot dead at the rubble barricade in Rossville Street.

Michael McDaid (20), from Tyrconnell Street in the Bogside, was the second youngest of a family of twelve. He worked as a barman in the Celtic Bar. He was described by his family as an affectionate young man who was very close to his parents and especially close to his young nephews. He was shot dead at the rubble barricade in Rossville Street.

John Young (17) was the youngest of a family of six. He worked in John Temple's menswear shop and had a passion for showbands. In September 1971, he had witnessed the death of Annette McGavigan, who was shot dead by the British Army just a few hundred yards from where he himself died. He was shot dead at the rubble barricade in Rossville Street.

William Nash (19) was the seventh child in a family of thirteen. He worked with his father at Derry docks, and loved country-and-western music. He had just celebrated his brother Charlie's success at the National Boxing Championships in Dublin and the marriage of his brother James the day before. He was shot dead at the rubble barricade in Rossville Street. His father Alex (51) was shot and wounded as he tried to reach his dying son.

Kevin McElhinney (17) was the middle child in a family of five. He had a keen interest in athletics and soccer and worked at Lipton's supermarket from the time he left school. He regularly attended dances but didn't smoke or drink, and his real passion was music, especially T-Rex. He was shot in the back and killed as he crawled from the rubble barricade towards the doorway of the Rossville Flats.

Other marchers had tried to find shelter in Glenfada Park, opposite the Rossville Flats, unaware that a group of Paras were heading that direction. Residents of the Rossville Flats shouted warnings that the Paras were coming. When those in Glenfada Park tried to run, the Paras opened fire on them.

A group of four Paras had advanced into Glenfada Park, firing as they moved. These four soldiers were, between them, responsible for between fourteen and seventeen deaths and injuries that day, and for all of the shots fired in and from Glenfada Park.

Joseph Friel (22) was shot and wounded in the chest as he tried to get out of Glenfada Park. Daniel Gillespie (32) was hit by a bullet in the head and fell unconscious. Michael Quinn (17) was wounded by a bullet in the shoulder that exited through his face. Joseph Mahon (16) was wounded in the leg and feigned death as the Para who had just executed Jim Wray passed him by.

Patrick O'Donnell (41) was wounded as he threw himself across a woman to protect her from the gunfire.

William McKinney (27) was the oldest in a family of ten. He worked as a compositor with the *Derry Journal* and was interested in music, particularly Irish music, and played the accordion. His true passion was photography and he used his film camera to record many of the major events of the civil rights era in Derry, including the earlier stages of the march on Bloody Sunday. At the time of his death, William was 'going steady' and had just passed his driving test. He was shot in the back and killed as he tried to help those already wounded.

Jim Wray (22) was the second oldest in a family of nine. He had worked in England for some time and had become engaged to an English girl. He attended the civil rights marches in Derry and the entire family went on the march on 30 January after attending Mass together. He was lying on the ground, wounded and paralysed by the first burst of fire when a Para shot him again in the back from point-blank range just in front of his grandparents' home.

Gerard McKinney (35) was the father of eight children, the youngest of which, also called Gerard, was born eight days after his father's death. Other than his family, Gerard's main interests were soccer and roller skating. He managed a junior soccer team and ran the Ritz roller-skating rink on the Strand Road. He worked in John McLaughlin's on the Strand Road and had no particular interest in politics.

Gerald Donaghey (17) was the youngest of three children and had been orphaned at the age of ten when his mother and father died within the space of four weeks. Gerald witnessed at first hand the creation of the civil rights movement in Derry and was involved in the civil unrest that was so common at the time. Sentenced to six months for rioting in the Bogside, he had been released from prison on Christmas Eve 1971. After his death he was acknowledged as a member of Fianna na hÉireann.

The two were killed by the same bullet, fired through the alleyway that led from Glenfada Park to Abbey Park. The bullet passed through Gerard McKinney, who had both hands in the air when he was shot, and hit Gerald Donaghey, who was just behind him. Thinking the shooting had ended, the two were trying to reach the dead and wounded who lay in Glenfada Park. A number of nail bombs were allegedly found on Gerald's body after his death. For more on this, see below.

As the Paras left Glenfada Park, they opened fire again towards Rossville Flats.

Patrick Doherty (31) was the father of six children between seven months and eleven years. He worked in Du Pont and was a strong supporter of the civil rights movement who had attended all of the protests in the late 1960s and early 1970s. He had been at Magilligan the week before Bloody Sunday and witnessed the brutality of the Parachute Regiment. He was shot from behind as he tried to crawl to safety in the forecourt of the Rossville Flats at Joseph Place. As he lay dying, Paddy Walsh tried to crawl out to help him, even though he was fired at himself. The sequence of photographs of Mr Walsh's brave attempt to rescue the dying man highlight the bravery displayed by many that day as they tried to help the injured and the dying.

Barney McGuigan (41) was the father of six children. He had worked in the BSR and as a general handyman at Cedric's factory on Carlisle Road. He had no real interest in politics but had attended many of the early civil rights marches in the city. He had been sheltering at the corner of Rossville Flats, and became the oldest fatality on Bloody Sunday when, ignoring warnings for his own safety, he stepped out waving a white handkerchief and tried to get to the dying Patrick Doherty. He was shot in the head as soon as he stepped from cover.

Patrick Campbell (51) was shot and wounded as he ran for the safety at the Rossville Flats. Daniel McGowan (38) was wounded as he tried to help Patrick Campbell to safety.

The shooting eventually stopped.

In less than half an hour, in an area not much larger than a football field, British soldiers had killed thirteen unarmed men and wounded another two women and sixteen men, one of whom would later die of his injuries.[186] All but the first two casualties – Damian Donaghy and John Johnston – had been hit in the space of less than

---

186 Three of the wounded – Pius McCarron, Patrick Brolly and Thomas Harkin – did not appear on the list of wounded from Bloody Sunday until after the second Bloody Sunday Inquiry began sitting, hence all references over the years were to thirteen dead and fifteen injured on the day.

ten minutes. During this time, the OIRA had fired three ineffectual shots in response, none of which have been claimed to have led to any of the Paras shooting unarmed civilians that day.

The people of Derry were left in a state of shock as they slowly learned of the rising death toll, while the British propaganda machine immediately swung into operation.

As the bodies were still being picked off the streets, General Ford appeared on television claiming that his soldiers had only fired four shots, and stated that if there were any more than four bodies then they must have been shot dead by the IRA.

That evening, Captain Michael Jackson (then adjutant of 1 Para, later to become General Sir Michael Jackson, the most senior officer in the British Army) prepared a list of shots fired by the Paras, in which he claimed each shot was aimed at a clearly identified gunman or nail bomber. The British Army and Government claimed that hundreds of shots had been fired at the soldiers. They claimed that four of the dead were on the British Army's 'wanted list'. This was the version that went to the media around the world, courtesy of the British Information Service.

The quieter voices from Derry that were trying to get the truth out were drowned out by the propaganda. Seven Derry priests who had been in the Bogside accused the British Army of wilful murder. They were unequivocal:

We accuse the Colonel of the Parachute Regiment of wilful murder. We accuse the Commander of Land Forces of being an accessory before the fact. We accuse the soldiers of shooting indiscriminately into a fleeing crowd, of gloating over casualties, of preventing medical and spiritual aid reaching some of the dying.

It is untrue that shots were fired at the troops in Rossville Street before they attacked. It is untrue that any of the dead or wounded that we attended were armed.

We make this statement in view of the distorted and indeed conflicting reports put out by army officers. We deplore the action of the army and government in employing a unit such as the paratroopers who were in Derry yesterday. These men are trained criminals. They differ from terrorists only in the veneer of respectability that a uniform gives them.[187]

It would be decades before the world would fully accept their words.

People wanted to fight back, and there were queues to join the IRA. Factories, schools, shops and offices across the city shut down in protest and anger and a fund was set up to help the families of the victims.

NICRA and the National Council for Civil Liberties (NCCL) took hundreds of statements from civilian eyewitnesses to the massacre on Bloody Sunday. The British Army took statements from their own soldiers, then, over the following weeks, coached the soldiers through a process of changing their statements until they all matched the 'official' version of events.

On 1 February, British Prime Minister Edward Heath announced that a public inquiry into the events of the day would he held, to be chaired by the Lord Chief

187 *Derry Journal*, 1 February 1972.

Justice, Lord Widgery. In a memo discovered by accident by researchers for the Bloody Sunday families in the late 1990s, Heath told Widgery to remember that they were 'fighting not just a military war but a propaganda war', a clear direction to Widgery to come to the right conclusions. Another secret memo said that Widgery would 'pile up the case against the deceased', further evidence that the result of his inquiry was a foregone conclusion.

The Bloody Sunday funerals on 2 February were mass events, attended by political, civic and religious representatives from around the world. Family members had to be given tickets to ensure that they were able to get into St Mary's Church in Creggan, where the funerals were held. Twelve of the thirteen dead were laid to rest in the nearby city cemetery. Gerard McKinney was buried in a family plot in Donegal.

Under the headline 'The skies wept too as Derry laid its dead to rest', the *Derry Journal* described the funerals:

> Ireland was united in grief on Wednesday. St Mary's Church in the Creggan estate was the centre of world attention for a poignant hour as Derry buried its murdered dead.
>
> Church and state, priests and people, joined in a unique ceremony which expressed the emotion of a sorrowing nation.
>
> From north and south, from east and west they came, the mourning thousands, to honour the dead, to comfort the bereaved, to pledge by their living presence a Christian response to horrific tragedy.
>
> There were few dry eyes among the distinguished congregation. Outside, the thronging thousands ignored the bitter cold, and even the driving rain seemed heaven's tears.
>
> There were 200 priests from every corner of the land . . .
>
> There were hundreds of stricken relatives, sustained, however, by the overwhelming manifestation of a national sharing in their individual grief.
>
> There were thousands of people from all parts of the land, many of whom had made long and arduous journeys to be present.
>
> There were the deeply affected thousands of local people from every area, every street in the city, present in mourning accord to share in yet another tragic yet historic occasion in the serried story of their city, on ground hallowed centuries ago by the blood of martyrs . . .
>
> Seven of those [twelve priests conducting the Mass] had, seventy-two hours earlier, shared with their people in the Bogside the terror unleashed on the streets and risked injury and death to bring succour and the last rites of the Church to dead and dying.
>
> And before the high altar, thirteen coffins reposed, the stark reminders of the purpose of the sombre gathering, containing the remains of thirteen young men, struck down ere they could experience a normal life span . . .[188]

---

188 *Derry Journal*, 4 February 1972.

On the day of the burials, protestors in Dublin burned the British embassy to the ground. Throughout the South and in nationalist areas of the North, schools and workplaces closed in support of the families. The Southern Government designated the ad hoc general stoppage 'a national day of mourning'.

The Widgery Tribunal decided not to sit in Derry, where the killings had taken place, but instead set up shop in the County Hall in Coleraine, a staunchly unionist town about thirty miles away. It was not a comfortable place for family members and civilian witnesses to visit, and there were loyalist protests outside the Hall some days when they arrived. It opened on 21 February, with the very narrow remit of only looking at the moments when the shooting took place, and not at any of the background to the day. Widgery heard evidence from only 114 witnesses, of whom only thirty were Derry civilians, despite the fact that hundreds had witnessed the events and had given statements to NICRA and NCCL. Widgery rejected these statements but leaned heavily on the doctored statements and evidence provided by the Paras.

The Tribunal finished on 20 March, after just seventeen days of hearings. The Widgery Report, all of thirty-nine pages long, was published on 18 April, eleven weeks after the events of Bloody Sunday. Its contents were greeted with dismay, if not surprise, in Derry, where 'Widgery washes whiter' was used to describe his whitewash of the truth. Widgery had followed the direction of his political masters and produced a report that matched their version of events. While he could not definitively find any of the victims guilty, no matter how hard he tried, he clearly implied that they were and laid all of the blame for the deaths anywhere but on the British Army and Government. In his Summary of Conclusions, he stated that:

1. There would have been no deaths in Londonderry on 30 January if those who organised the illegal march had not thereby created a highly dangerous situation in which a clash between demonstrators and the security forces was almost inevitable.

2. The decision to contain the march within the Bogside and Creggan had been opposed by the Chief Superintendent of Police in Londonderry but was fully justified by events and was successfully carried out.

3. If the Army had persisted in its 'low-key' attitude and had not launched a large-scale operation to arrest hooligans, the day might have passed off without serious incident.

4. The intention of the senior Army officers to use 1 Para as an arrest force and not for other offensive purposes was sincere.

5. An arrest operation carried out in Battalion strength in circumstances in which the troops were likely to come under fire involved hazard to civilians in the area which Commander 8 Brigade may have underestimated.

6. The order to launch the arrest operation was given by Commander 8 Brigade. The tactical details were properly left to CO 1 Para who did not exceed his

orders. In view of the experience of the unit in operations of this kind, it was not necessary for CO 1 Para to give orders in greater detail than he did.

7. When the vehicles and soldiers of Support Company appeared in Rossville Street, they came under fire. Arrests were made; but in a very short time the arrest operation took second place and the soldiers turned to engage their assailants. There is no reason to suppose that the soldiers would have opened fire if they had not been fired upon first.

8. Soldiers who identified armed gunmen fired upon them in accordance with the standing orders in the Yellow Card. Each soldier was his own judge of whether he had identified a gunman. Their training made them aggressive and quick in decision and some showed more restraint in opening fire than others. At one end of the scale some soldiers showed a high degree of responsibility; at the other, notably in Glenfada Park, firing bordered on the reckless. These distinctions reflect differences in the character and temperament of the soldiers concerned.

9. The standing orders contained in the Yellow Card are satisfactory. Any further restrictions on opening fire would inhibit the soldier from taking proper steps for his own safety and that of his comrades and unduly hamper the engagement of gunmen.

10. None of the deceased or wounded is proved to have been shot while handling a firearm or bomb. Some are wholly acquitted of complicity in such action; but there is a strong suspicion that some others had been firing weapons or handling bombs in the course of the afternoon and that yet others had been closely supporting them.

11. There was no general breakdown in discipline. For the most part the soldiers acted as they did because they thought their orders required it. No order and no training can ensure that a soldier will always act wisely, as well as bravely and with initiative. The individual soldier ought not to have to bear the burden of deciding whether to open fire in confusion such as prevailed on 30 January. In the conditions prevailing in Northern Ireland, however, this is often inescapable.[189]

Widgery had just confirmed what Free Derry already knew; that the entire British Establishment stood behind the Bloody Sunday killers. Their commander, Colonel Wilford, was awarded the Order of the British Empire just nine months after the massacre, decorated by his queen for services to the crown.

The Derry coroner, Hubert O'Neill, took a different view than Widgery. Addressing the inquests held that August he was unequivocal:

It strikes me that the army ran amok that day without thinking what they were doing. They were shooting innocent people. The people may have been taking

---

189 The Rt. Hon. Lord Widgery OBE, TD. *Report of the Tribunal appointed to inquire into the events on Sunday, 30ᵗʰ January, 1972, which led to loss of life in connection with the procession in Londonderry on that day* (HMSO, 1972).

part in a march that was banned, but that does not justify the troops coming in and firing live rounds indiscriminately. I would say without hesitation that it was sheer, unadulterated murder. It was murder.[190]

NICRA organised the first two Bloody Sunday commemorations, and the Bloody Sunday memorial in Rossville Street was unveiled at the second in 1974. From 1975 to 1989, the annual commemoration march was organised by Sinn Féin. The issue was forced largely underground by the ongoing conflict, but the march continued year after year as the people of Derry refused to forget what had happened on Bloody Sunday.

In 1987, a small group of relatives and campaigners came together to form the Bloody Sunday Initiative in an attempt to reopen the subject of Bloody Sunday in the wider public consciousness, outside of its traditional republican support base, and to place it in the context of wider human rights issues. The Bloody Sunday Weekend Committee was then set up to take on responsibility for the annual commemoration.

As part of a major series of events to mark the twentieth anniversary of Bloody Sunday – under the theme of One World, One Struggle – a meeting was organised in Pilots Row, to which members of the Bloody Sunday families and others were invited to discuss the way forward. Out of that meeting the Bloody Sunday Justice Campaign (BSJC) was born. (The Bloody Sunday Initiative soon became the Pat Finucane Centre (PFC), named after the human rights lawyer shot dead by UDA members working for the British security services in 1989. The PFC continues to work on wider human rights issues in Ireland and with many of the families of those killed in the conflict in the North of Ireland.)

The BSJC was set up with three main aims:

1. That the British Government should publicly and unambiguously acknowledge that all those killed or injured were totally innocent.
2. That the British Government publicly repudiate the Widgery Report in its entirety.
3. That those responsible for the murders and attempted murders on the streets of Derry on 30 January 1972 be prosecuted.

For the next six years, the BSJC campaigned relentlessly for the truth to be told about the events of Bloody Sunday. A seemingly hopeless campaign at times, it had its high points as hitherto secret documents came to light exposing the British Government and army's intentions on Bloody Sunday and afterwards and the wider media began to take an interest in the story. Slowly, support for the campaign began to grow well beyond its Derry base.[191]

By the latter part of the 1990s, the campaign was beginning to gather an unstoppable

---

190 Quoted in Eamonn McCann, *The Bloody Sunday Inquiry: The Families Speak Out* (Pluto, 2006) pp3-4.
191 For a full account of the BSJC, see Julieann Campbell *Setting the Truth Free: The Inside Story of the Bloody Sunday Justice Campaign* (Liberties Press, 2012).

momentum. On the twenty-fifth anniversary, 40,000 people marched in support of the BSJC. In the same year, the publication of *Eyewitness Bloody Sunday* by Don Mullan placed the original witness statements taken by NICRA and NCCL back in the public domain. The Bloody Sunday Trust (BST) was set up to aid the families' campaign, and it commissioned Professor Dermot Walsh to write *The Bloody Sunday Tribunal of Inquiry: A Resounding Defeat for Truth, Justice and the Rule of Law*, an unanswerable destruction of Widgery and the soldiers' evidence which again showed the Widgery Tribunal up for the farce that it was. The Irish Government came on board and in the summer of 1997 presented their own analysis of Widgery and the new evidence that had come to light to the newly elected Labour Government in Britain.

On 29 January 1998, British Prime Minister Tony Blair announced the setting up of a new inquiry into the events of Bloody Sunday. It was an unprecedented move – never before in British legal history had a second inquiry been set up into any event. The inquiry would eventually also become the longest in British legal history.

The inquiry, under the chairmanship of Law Lord Mark Saville, held its first hearing in the Guildhall in Derry in April 1998. It heard its last witness at the same venue in January 2005.

In the intervening years, it was dogged by legal challenges and obstructions from the British Ministry of Defence and had to move its entire operation to London for a year, ostensibly because the military witnesses had security concerns about coming to Derry, but more likely to save the embarrassment of having senior political figures summonsed to come and explain their actions in the city where Bloody Sunday had happened.

During the 435 days that it was sitting, the Bloody Sunday Inquiry (BSI) heard evidence from 505 civilians, 245 military witnesses, forty-nine journalists, thirty-nine politicians and civil servants, thirty-five IRA members (OIRA and PIRA), thirty-three police officers, nine 'expert witnesses' (forensic scientists etc) and seven priests. Evidence was also taken into account from a further 1,563 witnesses who were not called to give oral evidence. The Inquiry generated around 160 volumes of statements, documents and photographs, comprising 20-30 million words. In terms of scale, it completely dwarfed the Widgery Tribunal.

The years between the end of the Inquiry in 2005, and the eventual publication of its report in 2010, were frustrating ones for the families, who just wanted to see what the report was going to say. As the publication date eventually grew nearer, many of them were involved in the long, drawn-out negotiations over how the publication of the report would be handled, who would have prior access to it and early access on the day etc. A new campaign was set up, 'Set The Truth Free', to try to put pressure on the British Government to release the report without interference or censorship.

On 15 June 2010, the report was finally released. Two members from each family were allowed into the Guildhall from 10.00AM that morning to see the report that their legal representatives had seen just a few hours earlier. Once they entered the Guildhall, they were under a complete 'lockdown', unable to let anyone else, even their own families, know what was in the report. The first announcement of the content of the report was scheduled to be made by the British Prime Minister at 3.30PM, and no-one would be allowed to steal his thunder.

But as the clock ticked towards that time, the families managed to sidestep all the security precautions, twice. About fifteen minutes before Cameron was due to speak, word reached the small coterie of Bloody Sunday Trust support workers gathered on the city's Walls. Family members on lockdown had been in the apparently not so secure smoking area set aside for them, and had managed to get a whispered message to a colleague just outside. The message reached the small group on the Walls, who were surrounded by the world's media: 'Don't show any reaction, but it's a good report.' Then, a few minutes later as thousands waited outside in the sunshine to hear the news, raucous cheers greeted the sight of upraised thumbs in the windows of the Guildhall. The families had beaten all the British security precautions and got the first word out themselves.

The 'thumbs up' from the families lifted the mood of the crowd, and made them all the more receptive to Cameron's words when they came at 3.30PM:

> There is no doubt. There is nothing equivocal. There are no ambiguities. What happened on Bloody Sunday was both unjustified and unjustifiable. It was wrong.
>
> Lord Saville concludes that the soldiers of Support Company who went into the Bogside '. . . did so as a result of an order . . . which should not have been given' by their Commander . . . on balance the first shot in the vicinity of the march was fired by the British Army . . . that 'none of the casualties shot by soldiers of Support Company was armed with a firearm' . . . 'that there was some firing by republican paramilitaries . . . but . . . none of this firing provided any justification for the shooting of civilian casualties' . . .
>
> What's more, Lord Saville says that some of those killed or injured were clearly fleeing or going to the assistance of others who were dying . . .
>
> The families of those who died that day should not have had to live with the pain and hurt of that day – and a lifetime of loss.
>
> Some members of our Armed Forces acted wrongly. The Government is ultimately responsible for the conduct of the Armed Forces. And for that, on behalf of the Government – and indeed our country – I am deeply sorry . . .[192]

When Cameron finished speaking, the families emerged from the Guildhall into the bright sunshine to give their initial response:

> Unjustified and unjustifiable. Those are the words we have been waiting to hear since 30 January 1972 and I think, Derry, you have been absolutely brilliant in this.
>
> The victims of Bloody Sunday have been vindicated and the Parachute Regiment has been disgraced. Their medals of honour have to be removed. Widgery's great lie has been laid bare. The truth has been brought home at last.

---

192   David Cameron to House of Commons, 15 June 2010. (Original in MoFD collection.)

It can now be proclaimed to the world that the dead and the wounded of Bloody Sunday, civil rights marchers, were innocent one and all, gunned down in their own streets by soldiers who had been given to believe they could kill with perfect impunity. The Parachute Regiment are the front-line assassins for Britain's political and military elite. The report of the Saville Tribunal confirms this. It was the Paras' mission in Derry to massacre people they thought of as enemies of the state. They will have known that murder is what was expected of them when they erupted onto our streets.

Bloody Sunday wounded Derry very, very badly. We may hope that from today we can begin to bind up those wounds. But we recognise, too, that the issues arising from the Report go wider and deeper than Derry's concerns. When the state kills its citizens, it is in the interest of all that those responsible be held to account. It is not just Derry, or one section of the people of Derry, it is democracy itself which needs to know what happened here on 30 January 1972. The British people need to know. The Irish people need to know. The world now knows.

Our campaign in the first instance was for justice for our loved ones. But we didn't fight only for ourselves. We have tried to stand in the place of others who have suffered the same grief and the same grievous wrong at the hands of unaccountable power and who may never win any official inquiry, who may never have their truth told. We are mindful of the victims of the Ballymurphy Massacre by men of the Parachute Regiment in August 1971, of the families of the two men murdered by the Paras on the Shankill Road in September 1972. And of all families bereaved by the paratroopers and other state forces over the course of this bloody conflict. And of all who have died here, from whatever background, at whomever's hand.

Bloody Sunday was the price the Bogside paid for Free Derry. So it is, always and everywhere. Just as the civil rights movement of forty years ago was part of something huge happening all over the world, so the repression that came upon us was the same as is suffered by ordinary people everywhere who dare stand up against injustice. Sharpeville. Grozny. Tiananmen Square. Darfur. Fallujah. Gaza. Let our truth stand as their truth, too.

Bloody Sunday was a great injustice. But the fight for truth and justice has also been an inspiration to us and to the people of Derry. It has deepened our sense of who we are and made us more aware that we are also citizens of the world. Nobody who struggles for justice will be a stranger here. Nobody who dies in the struggle for justice will be forgotten here. Thank you, Derry.[193]

After this statement was read out, representatives of each family lined up, one by one, to declare their loved ones innocent, each announcement greeted with cheers from the thousands gathered in Guildhall Square. The wounded were also all declared innocent.

The family members and their supporters, their years of campaigning finally vindicated, left the Guildhall knowing that they had achieved most of what they

---

193 Collective family response, 15 June 2010. (Original in MoFD collection.)

had set out to do: the Widgery Report was in the bin, their loved ones innocent in the eyes of the world.

The report of the Bloody Sunday Inquiry had indeed repudiated Widgery in many important ways. Where Widgery had implied guilt, the BSI was unambiguous about innocence. Where Widgery had laid the blame for the first (and many more shots) at the feet of the IRA, the BSI was clear that the first shots had come from a British rifle and that there was no republican shooting that impacted on the events of the day.

In terms of the individual deaths, the BSI found that:

John Johnston had been shot by either Corporal A or Private B, who had opened fire on Damian Donaghy in the mistaken belief that he was about to throw a nail bomb.

Jackie Duddy had probably been shot by Private R of Mortar Platoon. Private R claimed he had opened fire at a man who was about to throw a bomb, but the BSI concluded that he could not have been sufficiently confident about this to justify his opening fire.

Hugh Gilmour was shot by Private U, who claimed to have fired at a man armed with a handgun. The BSI rejected his account as 'knowingly untrue'.

Michael Kelly was killed by Lance Corporal F, who claimed that he had fired at a nail bomber. The BSI found that F had opened fire either in the clear belief that no-one at the rubble barricade was posing any sort of a threat, or not caring whether or not anyone at the barricade was posing a threat.

Michael McDaid, John Young and William Nash were shot by one or other of Corporals P or E or Lance Corporal J, who all claimed to have fired at armed men. Again the BSI rejected each of these claims as knowingly untrue.

Kevin McElhinney was killed by either Private L or M, who claimed that they had seen someone with a rifle crawling away from the barricade. The BSI found that neither soldier could have been properly satisfied that they had identified an armed man before they opened fire.

William McKinney was shot dead by one of the four soldiers – Corporal E, Lance Corporal F and Privates G and H – who had entered Glenfada Park. All four claimed they had identified and shot at men who were about to use guns or nail bombs, but the BSI found that none of these soldiers could plausibly have had that belief when they opened fire, and that they had opened fire either knowing they were firing on unarmed men, or not caring if they were or not.

Jim Wray was shot by one of the same group of soldiers who killed William Mc-Kinney. All four denied firing at anyone lying on the ground, but the BSI found that the soldier who did must have known there was no possible justification for shooting him as he lay wounded on the ground.

Gerard McKinney and Gerald Donaghey were killed by Private G who, according to the BSI, opened fire knowing that Gerard McKinney was not posing any threat. Gerald Donaghey was also not posing any sort of a threat when he as shot.

Patrick Doherty was shot dead by Lance Corporal F, who claimed to have fired at an armed man. The BSI found that his claim was knowingly untrue and that, as in the other cases, he had fired neither knowing nor caring whether or not his target was armed.

Barney McGuigan was shot in the head by Lance Corporal F who, as in the case of Patrick Doherty and others, had opened fire neither knowing nor caring if the person he was shooting at was armed.[194]

But the report was not also without major problems. In terms of the guilt of those responsible, it was very weak. The BSI restricted all blame to one small group of soldiers and their commanding officer, exonerating those who were involved in the political and military decision-making processes in the run-up to the day. It also made clear that the Widgery Report was wrong, but did not investigate why it was so wrong. This was not a surprise, since this was left out of the Inquiry's remit at its announcement in 1998, but it did allow all of those involved in the cover-up that followed Bloody Sunday, from those who prepared the initial information and statements on 30 January 1972 to those who directed Widgery in his findings, to escape any blame for their actions.

Perhaps the flaw that hurt the most in Derry was the BSI's findings in relation to Gerald Donaghey. In 1972, the British Army had claimed that he had four nail bombs in his pockets when his body was searched in their base below the Craigavon Bridge. His family and others claimed that the bombs had been planted in his pockets in the army base. Widgery found that 'on a balance of probabilities, the bombs were in Donaghey's pockets throughout.' Despite all the available evidence – the civilian and military eyewitnesses who had close contact but didn't see any nail bombs in the tight clothing he was wearing, the fact that the bullet that killed Gerald Donaghey passed though a pocket in which there was allegedly a nail bomb but did not hit it, the fact that the British Army were only ever able to produce one photograph of one nail bomb in one pocket without ever explaining why they never thought to photo-graph all of the supposed nail bombs in place on his body – the BSI made the same

---

194 *Principal Conclusions and Overall Assessment of the Bloody Sunday Inquiry* (TSO 2010) 3.94 – 3.113.

finding, that he was 'probably armed with nail bombs' when he was shot, although 'he was not a threat at the time'. This finding qualified the innocence of Gerald Donaghey and left his family with a great deal of hurt to deal with. They have vowed to continue to fight until his name is completely cleared.[195]

But nothing could diminish the overall achievement of the Bloody Sunday families and their supporters. They had fought for over thirty-eight years to clear their loved ones' names and they had just done that. They had forced the British Government to go against all precedent and set up a second inquiry. They had forced their successors in government, the same Conservative Party who were in power at the time of Bloody Sunday, to apologise. The world now knew most of the truth about what had happened that day. Their long campaign had been vindicated.

At the time of writing, the BSJC's last demand – that those responsible for Bloody Sunday be prosecuted – has not been met, although it has been announced that the Police Service of Northern Ireland are to launch the first-ever criminal investigation into the events of the day, so prosecutions are still a possibility.

At the end of the executive summary of their report, the BSI outlined the impact of Bloody Sunday on the North of Ireland. It echoed what many people had been saying all along, that Bloody Sunday was a day that changed the course of history and that the actions of the British Army that day had sentenced the North of Ireland to decades of conflict:

> The firing by soldiers of 1 PARA on Bloody Sunday caused the deaths of 13 people and injury to a similar number, none of whom was posing a threat of causing death or serious injury. What happened on Bloody Sunday strengthened the Provisional IRA, increased nationalist resentment and hostility towards the Army and exacerbated the violent conflict of the years that followed. Bloody Sunday was a tragedy for the bereaved and the wounded, and a catastrophe for the people of Northern Ireland.[196]

---

195 For further information see *Gerald Donaghey: the truth about the planting of nail bombs on Bloody Sunday* (Bloody Sunday Trust/Pat Finucane Centre/Creggan Enterprises, 2012).
196 *Principal Conclusions and Overall Assessment of the Bloody Sunday Inquiry* (TSO 2010) 5.5.

DERRY CIVIL RIGHTS ASSOCIATION

MASSIVE ANTI-INTERNMENT MARCH AND RALLY

Assemble at 2 p.m. in The Bishop's Field,
Creggan, and march to the Guildhall Square
for Public Meeting.

★ **LORD FENNER BROCKWAY**

★ **THE REV. TERENCE McGAUGHEY**
  PRESBYTERIAN MINISTER

★ **EDWINA STEWART**
  HON. SECRETARY, N.I.C.R.A.

★ **MARGO COLLINS**
  EXECUTIVE COMMITTEE, N.I.C.R.A.

★ **MISS BERNADETTE DEVLIN, M.P.**

★ **MR. FRANK McMANUS, M.P.**

★ **RORY McSHANE**
  (CHAIRMAN) NICRA EXECUTIVE COMMITTEE.

Derry Journal advertisement for the anti-internment march on 30 January 1972.

Thousands gather in the Bishop's Field in Creggan for the march against internment on 30 January 1972, Bloody Sunday. (Robert White)

The march passes the gasworks in the Brandywell. (Robert White)

Marchers at the top of Westland Street in the Bogside. (Robert White)

British Army water cannon repel the marchers in William Street. (Robert White)

The Parachute Regiment moves into the Bogside in armoured vehicles on Bloody Sunday. Within minute thirteen men and boys would be shot dead. (Robert White)

Michael Kelly lies mortally wounded at the rubble barricade on Rossville Street. Entering the picture from left is Michael McDaid, who was shot dead just seconds later. The boy looking down on those trying to help Michael Kelly is Daniel Hegarty, shot dead by British soldiers six months later during Operation Motorman. (Robert White)

British paratroops attacking unarmed marchers in the Bogside. (Fulvio Grimaldi)

Hugh Gilmour, third from left, runs for the safety of Rossville Flats just after he was shot. He made it to the corner before he died, just below the window of his own home. (Robert White)

Thirteen coffins line the altar in St Mary's Church, Creggan. (*Derry Journal*)

Thousands march in Derry in support of the Bloody Sunday families in the late 1990s. (Hugh Gallagher)

A thumbs-up from the families on 15 June 2010 reveals the outcome of the Bloody Sunday Inquiry, mome: before British Prime Minister David Cameron announced it in Westminster. (Lorcan Doherty)

The Bloody Sunday families emerge triumphant from the Guildhall after the publication of the report. (Lorcan Doherty)

Motorman and the End of Free Derry

Bloody Sunday failed in its objective. If the intention was to draw the IRA out into a gun battle they couldn't win, it failed: the IRA stayed away; if the intention was to cow the people of Free Derry so that they would return quietly to their homes and accept a return to the old ways, it failed, for the people were not deterred, they were defiant. Hundreds queued to join the two IRAs, desperate to fight back against the army that had tried to shoot them off the streets. NICRA, and its ideal of peaceful protest, was dead. Constitutional nationalism was in a state of catatonic shock, for a while at least.

Republicans held off until after the Bloody Sunday funerals, then returned to war. On 5 February, five British soldiers were injured when a land mine exploded under their vehicle on the Lone Moor Road. The IRA opened fire on the soldiers as their vehicle crashed into the wall at West End Park. [197]

On 8 February, the British Army claimed to have wounded four republicans during a gun battle at Eastway in Creggan. The claims were rubbished by local sources. On 10 February, the IRA attacked the army post in the Brandywell, while gelignite and nail bombs were thrown at soldiers in the city centre. The OIRA claimed responsibility for wounding a British soldier.[198]

On 12 February, the PIRA bombed the Woodleigh Hotel on Asylum Road while a wedding reception was taking place. No-one was injured by the bomb, but the best man tried to intervene and was injured when one of the bombers opened fire. The PIRA said in a statement that the hotel had become a haunt for British intelligence agents and RUC Special Branch. The attack led to a war of words with the OIRA, who accused the PIRA of 'crass stupidity' for bombing the hotel, while the PIRA accused the OIRA of 'callous cowardice' for their failure to protect the people of Free Derry. By this stage, the PIRA were refusing to refer to the OIRA by name and called them instead the 'National Liberation Front'.[199]

In a statement issued on 14 February, the PIRA claimed responsibility for aiding the return of bus services to the Free Derry area, saying they had pledged their protection so that buses could operate freely.[200] But two days later, a bus driver and off-duty UDR soldier became the first fatality in the city since Bloody Sunday, showing just how much the mood in the city had changed and how anyone connected to the British Army was now considered a 'legitimate target'. This was just six months after RUC Constable Daniel Barr had been escorted from Free Derry by the IRA.

Private Thomas Callaghan

Thomas Callaghan (47), a married man from Limavady, was a part-time member of the Ulster Defence Regiment and a full-time bus driver. On 16 February, he was

---

197 *Derry Journal*, 8 February 1972.
198 *Derry Journal*, 11 February 1972.
199 *Derry Journal*, 15 February 1972.
200 *Derry Journal*, 15 February 1972.

driving his bus through Creggan when he was dragged from his vehicle by the IRA and bundled into a waiting car.

His body was found a few hours later at the junction of Foyle Road and Brooke Street. He had been hooded, gagged and shot in the head.

In a statement, a number of local priests condemned the killing of Thomas Callaghan:

> We have condemned publicly and privately the indiscipline and excesses of the army, but we also are greatly saddened by the senseless acts of violence of some of our own people . . . the people responsible sometimes claim to be our protectors, but what irresponsible protectors they are showing themselves to be.

Bus services in the area were suspended for some time after his shooting. The local Ulsterbus manager said that services had been returned to Creggan the previous October after a long break but that they could not go back now no matter what assurances were given by the PIRA.[201]

On 17 February, the IRA destroyed four shops and a services club in bomb attacks in the city centre. On 19 February, the OIRA shot and wounded a British soldier who was stationed on top of the Embassy building in the city centre. The shot was fired from Rossville Flats. In a statement claiming responsibility, the OIRA said that this was 'the beginning of the retaliatory action after the massacre of 30 January'. On 20 February, the British Army fired around thirty shots at the spire of St Eugene's Cathedral, claiming that IRA snipers were firing from there. The administrator of St Eugene's denied the claim, calling it a 'slur and a slander'.[202]

Óglach Gerard Doherty and Captain Marcus McCausland

Gerard Doherty (16), a member of the OIRA, died after a gun went off in his hand on 25 February. He was found lying in Central Drive in Creggan and taken to hospital by a priest.

He was given a republican funeral, at which a statement was read out that no other person was involved in Gerard Doherty's accidental death. When the remnants of the OIRA staged a commemoration march on the third anniversary of the boy's death in 1975, his parents condemned the event, saying that the circumstances of his death 'were never cleared up'.[203]

On 4 March, the body of Marcus McCausland (38), a captain in the UDR, was found on the Braehead Road, between Free Derry and the Donegal border. The Limavady man had been shot three times in the head. The OIRA claimed responsibility for his death and claimed he had been working for British military

---

201 *Lost Lives* 270; *Derry Journal*, 22 February 1972.
202 *Derry Journal*, 22 February 1972.
203 *Lost Lives* 285.

intelligence and had been involved in trying to set up an intelligence network in the Free Derry area.

Friends of Marcus McCausland, who was Eton-educated and had been appointed high sheriff for County Derry in 1967, dismissed the claims and said that he was actually in the process of leaving the UDR because he disagreed with recent British Army actions.[204]

The PIRA called a short truce over the weekend of 11 and 12 March and stated that 'in accordance with the directive from our headquarters in Dublin, military operations will be suspended during the truce period. In the event of a British Army incursion into the Free Derry area, we will have no choice but to defend the people of the area.' There were a number of shooting incidents between republicans and the British Army over that weekend, but the PIRA denied any involvement in them.[205]

On 14 March, the British Army attempted a major raid into the Bogside and ended up in a major gun battle with the PIRA, during which more than 200 shots were fired. After the gun battle was over, the bodies of two PIRA members were found in nearby Dove Gardens. The PIRA denied that either man had been involved in the gun battle.

Óglaigh Colm Keenan and Eugene McGillan

Colm Keenan (19) and Eugene McGillan (18), both single men and volunteers in the PIRA, were found dead in Dove Gardens shortly after a long gun battle between the PIRA and the British Army on 14 March. The PIRA denied that either man was involved in the gun battle.

At the inquest, a forensics expert testified that both men had lead traces on their hands, which was consistent with having fired a weapon, but also agreed that this could have been transferred from someone else. Similar forensic tests used in the case of some of those killed on Bloody Sunday were later discredited.

The inquest heard from a British representative, who said that the British Army were planning a search of a house in Stanley's Walk when the IRA opened fire on them. It is believed that the soldiers were actually escorting staff of the Widgery Tribunal through the area when the gun attack began. As the soldiers retreated, they fired back and claimed to have hit two armed men, who were dragged away after they fell. A civilian witness said he had seen the two men earlier and they were not armed.

An ambulance was called to Dove Gardens, where it picked up Colm Keenan and Eugene McGillan. Both men were dead on arrival in hospital. In death notices, Colm Keenan was described as a lieutenant in the IRA.

Colm Keenan – the son of veteran Derry republican Seán Keenan, who was interned in Long Kesh at the time – was given a full military funeral, and despite what was described as 'one of the strictest security operations mounted in Derry

---

204 *Lost Lives* 292.
205 *Derry Journal*, 14 March 1972.

since the Troubles began', two leading members of the Provisional movement, Seán Mac Stiofáin and Martin Meehan, managed to get through to attend, with Mac Stiofáin delivering the oration at the graveside. Eugene McGillan had a private funeral.[206]

On 16 March, children in St Cecilia's Secondary School in Bligh's Lane had to be sent home after shots were fired into the school from the British Army post opposite the school. The shots were fired as the funeral of Colm Keenan was taking place just a few hundred yards away. The British Army gave assurances that there would be no repeat of the incident.

It was also reported that one of the Derry internees, Seán McShane from the Waterside, had to be moved to the camp hospital in Long Kesh. He had been on hunger strike since 2 March, protesting against internment.

Four British soldiers were injured, one seriously, in shooting incidents in the Bogside and Brandywell on 18 March. The PIRA claimed responsibility for the attacks.

Rifleman John Taylor

John Taylor (19), a single man serving in the Royal Green Jackets, was shot by an IRA sniper at Lower Road, near the City Baths in William Street, on 20 March. He was hit in the stomach and was dead on admission to hospital.

There was rioting in the area at the time and a number of shots had been fired at the British Army. The PIRA said in a statement that Taylor, from Wanstead in London, had been shot by a member of its Bogside Company, firing from the Little Diamond, and that the shooting was in retaliation for Bloody Sunday.[207]

On 21 March, up to twenty members of the OIRA were involved in a two-hour-long gun battle with British soldiers who had been flown in by helicopter to examine a barricade on Southway. The OIRA claimed that they had killed two soldiers and wounded six more, but the British Army stated that they had not suffered any casualties. The principal of nearby St Peter's Secondary School said that he had to keep all 600 pupils inside the school because of the intensity of the gun battle.[208]

On 24 March, British Prime Minister Edward Heath announced that the Unionist Government at Stormont would be suspended for a period of one year, after it refused to relinquish power over law and order to the London government. There had been tension between the two governments for some time over law and order in the North, and especially over who had control of the British soldiers based here. Heath said that the move would help in finding a political solution to the problems in the North and appealed directly to nationalists to support the new arrangements. Unionists organised protest rallies across the North. Stormont Prime Minister Brian Faulkner resigned, saying that the removal of control of law and order completely undermined

---

206 *Lost Lives* 304, 305; *Derry Journal*, 17 March 1972.
207 *Lost Lives* 317; *Derry Journal*, 21 March 1972.
208 *Derry Journal*, 24 March 1972.

his government. William Whitelaw became the first Secretary of State for Northern Ireland under the new arrangement.

One of the main demands of the civil rights movement had just been achieved, but in the changed situation in the North, their demand was now completely irrelevant. So was the initial suspension period of one year, and Westminster retained direct rule over the North for the next thirty-five years, with intermittent breaks for attempts at setting up some form of government in the North.

Attacks on the British Army continued throughout the rest of March and into April. British soldiers wounded a Derry pensioner in her own home when they opened fire on a car they said gunmen were using. An 11-year-old boy and a 65-year-old woman were injured when the IRA opened fire on British soldiers on Northland Road. A British soldier was injured by a nail bomb when rioters from the Bogside moved into Waterloo Place. Another was injured by IRA gunfire at the junction of Barrack Street and Bishop Street, and another while he was travelling along the old railway line at Foyle Road. A young Derry woman was injured during a gun battle between the IRA and British soldiers in the Brandywell.

On 10 April, two more British soldiers were killed just outside Free Derry when the OIRA planted a bomb in the doorway of the pavilion of the City of Derry Bowling Club, which the army were using as a base. Lance Bombardier Eric Blackburn (24), from Maidstone in Kent, and Bombardier Brian Thomasson (21), from Bolton, were killed instantly in the blast. Both were serving with the Royal Artillery.[209]

Private Martin Robinson and Corporal Gerard Bristow

In the violence that spread across the North of Ireland following the Parachute Regiment shooting dead OIRA leader Joe McCann on 16 April in Belfast, two soldiers were shot dead by the OIRA in Derry.

Royal Welsh Fusilier Gerard Bristow (26), a married man with one child, was on patrol near the junction of Ferguson Street and Bishop Street when he was shot by an OIRA sniper firing from the grounds of St Columb's College. Gerard Bristow was from Newport in Monmouthshire.

Martin Robinson (21), from Sutton-On-Sea, Lincolnshire, was serving with the Worcestershire and Sherwood Foresters. He was in an observation post in the Brandywell when it came under attack by an OIRA sniper firing from the city cemetery.

Twenty minutes later, two more soldiers were injured in a gun attack in Little James Street.

In 1979, three Derry men were jailed for the shooting of Corporal Bristow.[210]

Meanwhile, life in Free Derry went on. The area already had its own taxi service, but the Foyle Hill and Creggan Tenants Association announced that they would need to change their departure point in the city centre from Guildhall Square to Great

---

209 *Derry Journal*, 11 April 1972 & 14 April 1972.
210 *Lost Lives* 336, 337.

James Street to avoid the long delays being caused by having to negotiate too many British Army checkpoints. The OIRA refuted claims made by a *Financial Times* reporter that the area behind the barricades was beginning to deteriorate without essential services:

> Ambulance services are regular . . . Dustbin and refuge collections are regular as far as we are able to ascertain . . . These allegations are evidence of a despicable Tory attack by the British Tory press and its paid agents on an area which has enjoyed the fruits of liberation since the barricades were erected on 9 August. We hardly expect agencies like the *Financial Times*, which is the organ of the rich business class, to be sympathetic to the cause of national liberation for which the people of the Free Derry area are fighting.[211]

The PIRA decided to issue their own press cards to visiting journalists. They said that they had been giving journalists free access for some time but now had to place 'strict sanctions' because of what they described as the 'twisted and warped' stories appearing in some of the right-wing British press. 'The Command has no intention of inhibiting the freedom of the press,' they said, 'and would have no objection to reports that were objective, even if not necessarily favourable to the Provisional viewpoint.' According to the report, Martin McGuinness, described as 'OC Derry Battalion of the Provisional IRA', had taken particular exception to a *Daily Express* story that supposedly quoted him because he had not given an interview to the paper.[212]

As if to prove the point about how well Free Derry was working, Provisional Sinn Féin decided to hold elections for a 'community government for Free Derry'. The election was announced at a public meeting held on 16 April. Activist Barney McFadden called for all political parties to take part in the election and said that of the nominations already received, the SDLP were so far the only ones refusing to do so.[213]

A committee was set up to oversee the elections, in which it was reported that up to 15,000 people would be eligible to vote. The area was divided into wards, and there were originally to be eighteen candidates contesting the thirteen seats available in the election. Thirteen of the candidates were from Provisional Sinn Féin, the others independent of any organised political party. The wards were No1, which included most of the Bogside and part of Creggan, No2, Lower Creggan and Rosemount, No3, Upper Creggan and No4, Brandywell, Bishop Street and Foyle Road.[214]

At the end of nominations on 17 July, it was announced that since only thirteen candidates had finally been nominated for thirteen seats there was no need for an election, and the thirteen candidates were duly elected. The new 'Free Derry Community Council' would comprise of seven members of Sinn Féin, five Independents

---

211 *Derry Journal*, 14 April 1972.
212 *Derry Journal*, 14 April 1972.
213 *Derry Journal*, 18 April 1972.
214 *Derry Journal*, 9 May 1972 & 2 June 1972.

and one Nationalist. (Two of the five 'Independents' then identified themselves as members of the Nationalist Party.[215]) Since Free Derry ended less than two weeks later, the 'Community Council' never had an opportunity to function.

Bus services to Creggan were resumed on 17 April, two months after the shooting dead of bus driver and part-time UDR member Thomas Callaghan. The resumption followed negotiations between Ulsterbus and several organisations from Creggan.

* * *

The ongoing violence in the city was having a marked affect on its Protestant population. While the violence had been aimed directly at the British Army and RUC, and there had been many calls from nationalists and republicans for there to be no attacks on Protestant residents, some were now living in fear and many more had left their homes on the Cityside. A deputation of Protestants from Abercorn Road went to the RUC to demand greater protection. One resident later recalled the feeling of the time:

> The Cityside was made up of small enclaves of Protestants surrounded by a large Catholic population. When civil unrest came onto the streets, Protestants felt threatened and they were nervous going through some of the barricades. It was only natural that they would think about moving to a safer environment. The barricades around the periphery of the Bogside meant Protestants in the Northlands, in the Glen, and even Ballymagroarty would have had to go through them. If they were collecting children from school and taking them through the barricades, they would have feared for the children's safety. With the tension on the streets, sides were being taken and Protestant children felt threatened on the streets, even by their former playmates . . .[216]

In the last local-government elections in Derry, Unionists had, as usual, secured a majority in the North Ward and taken all the seats, though in the South Ward, which roughly corresponded to Free Derry, they had so few votes they had not even bothered to stand a candidate. This still shows a significant unionist electorate in the Cityside in the late 1960s, which by the 1990s, however, had reached such low numbers that there wasn't a single unionist representative on Derry City Council from the Cityside.

While the movement of the majority of the pre-Troubles Protestant population is without doubt, it is not down to the large-scale 'ethnic cleansing' that some unionist politicians like to claim. There was undoubtedly some direct threat to individual Protestants and Protestant families, and many more would have perceived a threat to themselves, which would be just as compelling, and moved because of it. Also, the general atmosphere in the Cityside was undoubtedly becoming very uncomfortable

---

215 *Derry Journal*, 18 July 1972.
216 William Temple, quoted in Adrian Kerr, Paul Hippsley & Declan Carlin (Eds) *Perceptions: Cultures in Conflict* (Guildhall Press, 1996) p158.

for them. Many Protestants regarded Derry city centre as 'theirs', containing, as it did, so many symbols that they held dear – the city's Walls, the war memorial, St Columb's Cathedral, the Apprentice Boys' Memorial Hall – and they now watched it coming under constant attack from rioters and the IRA. It was also a fact that many of the businesses being bombed belonged to Protestants, even though that was not the reason they were bombed. So Protestants felt that they were under attack, even though the attacks were not directly aimed at them.

Once the population movement started, it soon reached a point where it became unstoppable. As people left small Protestant communities, they then became smaller again, and those left behind felt even less secure and so followed their erstwhile neighbours across the river. As the population on the Cityside dropped, Protestant churches and halls, with less people to use them, began to close and follow their former users. A vicious circle was created that continued throughout the conflict until, whatever the cause, the Protestant population of the Cityside dropped from around 18,000 in the late 1960s to around 500 now. While the term 'ethnic cleansing' is over-emotive and completely inaccurate, there is no doubt that the onset of the conflict in the city had a major impact on its minority Protestant population and caused the mass movement of that population from the Cityside to what was regarded as the safety of the Waterside. Now the Cityside has only one Protestant enclave left, the Fountain estate, home to less than 300 families.

* * *

The new Northern Ireland Secretary, William Whitelaw, visited Derry near the end of April and said that there were no plans for a military invasion of Creggan and the Bogside because he was 'not prepared to put innocent women and children at risk'. His visit followed calls from unionist politicians for a military invasion. John Hume said that the unionists wanted Whitelaw to fail and that it was their military tactics that had caused the situation in the first place.[217]

On the last day of April, the PIRA shot a man who they claimed had been involved in a robbery, and at the beginning of May released a statement warning that they would not tolerate any sort of crime in Free Derry:

We have information to the effect that prowlers are operating in some areas of the barricaded districts . . . We take this opportunity to issue a warning to people involved in these activities that we will not tolerate anyone who perpetrates crimes against the people of the Free Derry area. We will deal with anyone found guilty of such actions in a very severe manner . . . We hope that the shooting of the two men in the leg by us recently for crimes against residents of the barricaded areas will serve as a deterrent . . .[218]

217 *Derry Journal*, 25 April 1972.
218 *Derry Journal*, 5 May 1972.

On 5 May, a 10-year-old boy was shot in the face by a rubber bullet fired by a British soldier. Richard Moore was left permanently blinded by the bullet, which hit him as he made his way home from school.

Richard decided not to give in to his blindness and was eventually able to return to the school he had attended before he was shot. He became determined to help others in similar situations and in 1992 founded the highly regarded Children in Crossfire charity, set up to help children in conflict zones in Africa.

Free Derry suffered its next fatality on 13 May, when a young PIRA volunteer was shot dead by the British Army.

Óglach John Starrs

John Starrs (19) was a former Irish soldier from Hamilton Street in the Brandywell who had returned to Derry and joined the PIRA after Bloody Sunday. He was shot dead by the British Army at the junction of Chamberlain Street and William Street on 13 May. The British Army claimed that they had fired two shots at two identified gunmen and hit them both. They initially claimed to have fired from positions on the ground but then changed their statement to say that the fatal shots were fired from an observation post. The IRA said that their men were ambushed from behind while 'engaging British forces'.

Rioting broke out just after John Starrs was shot, and the four-storey building from where the soldiers had fired was burned to the ground.

John Starrs died two hours later in hospital and was given a full IRA funeral. The IRA said that another man, who was wounded going to the aid of John Starrs, had received treatment in the Bogside and recovered.[219]

Within the next week, there were two more deaths in Free Derry which showed how the local community would react when local people were killed, regardless of whether their killers were in the British Army or the IRA.

Manus Deery and Ranger William Best

Manus Deery (15) lived with his parents and family in Limewood Street in the Bogside. He had just started working, and on the night of his death had just got his first pay packet.

On Friday 19 May, Manus left his home at about 9.15PM to go to the local chip shop. He met up with some friends near the Bogside Inn and was standing talking to them when, at around 10.00PM, they heard the crack of a shot from the city's Walls. The bullet ricocheted off a wall and hit Manus on the side of the head. He was taken to hospital, where he was pronounced dead soon after admission.

A few hours after Manus was shot, around 150 women marched from the Bogside to Victoria RUC Barracks to demand that action be taken against the soldier who had fired the shot. A deputation that met the RUC described the shooting as

---

219 *Lost Lives* 357; *Derry Journal*, 16 May 1972.

'a cruel, calculated and brutal murder', carried out as a reprisal by the army for a bombing earlier that day in which two soldiers were injured. Over 2,000 people attended his funeral.

Two soldiers, A and B, who were positioned in 'Sniper's Corner' (a section of the northwest side of the Walls well known for British Army sniper fire at the time), claimed to have seen a gunman near where Manus was standing and that they had fired at him. Their statements, given to military investigators, were unchallenged at the time, and there was no actual police investigation into the death of Manus Deery. The Director of Public Prosecutions (DPP) marked the file 'no prosecution'.

The HET released their report into the death of Manus Deery in February 2012, which concurred with the soldiers' versions of events. Manus's family flatly rejected the report. In June 2012, the Attorney General ordered a new inquest into the boy's death, a move which was welcomed by his family.[220] At the time of writing the new inquest, along with a number of others into controversial state killings, has been postponed.

William Best (19) was serving with the Royal Irish Rangers in Germany and had returned to his Creggan home on leave in May 1972 at a time in the aftermath of Bloody Sunday when anyone connected to the British Army was considered a legitimate target by republicans.

It was later revealed that William Best had received a telegram telling him to come home because his mother was ill but that his family had never sent any such telegram.[221]

He left his home to make a telephone call and is believed to have been picked up, beaten and killed by the OIRA. His body was found on the morning of 21 May on waste ground in William Street.

An OIRA statement said that he had been 'tried by an IRA court and sentenced to death'. Unofficially, they said that 'once we had him, there was nothing we could do but execute him. Our military orders after Bloody Sunday were to kill every British soldier we could. They didn't say anything about local soldiers. He was a British soldier and that is all there was to it.' The PIRA called on the OIRA to leave the Bogside and Creggan. The OIRA said that they would cease 'offensive shooting' in the city. This announcement was a prelude to a permanent ceasefire by the organisation.[222]

Around 5,000 people attended William Best's funeral in Creggan.

The death of William Best caused a major outcry in Derry. Around 200 women from Free Derry marched to the OIRA headquarters to protest against the killing

---

220   Pat Finucane Centre fact file on the death of Manus Deery; *Lost Lives* 364; *Derry Journal*, 23 May 1972.

221   *Londonderry Sentinel*, 30 May 2012.

222   Members of the OIRA opposed to the ceasefire went on to form the Irish National Liberation Army (INLA), a smaller paramilitary organisation than the PIRA but one which was responsible for a number of major incidents during the conflict. The two hunger strikers from the city of Derry who died in 1981 – Patsy O'Hara and Michael Devine – were members of the INLA.

of the local man, including Kathleen Doherty, the mother of Gerard Doherty, a young OIRA volunteer killed earlier in the year (see above). The protest generated a lot of media attention, and for a short while the women who led it found themselves the centre of political attention, even being invited to meet the British Secretary of State for Northern Ireland, William Whitelaw. The outcry and the pressure it put on the OIRA was a major factor in their decision to declare a ceasefire.[223]

One man was charged in connection with the death of William Best in 1973, but the case was dropped due to lack of evidence.

On 23 May, around 2,000 people attended a public meeting in Creggan, where the recent acts of violence in the city, from all sides, were condemned. At the meeting, organised by a number of priests and former members of the Nationalist Party, two resolutions were passed. The first condemned the shootings of Manus Deery and William Best and the ongoing upsurge in violence, and the second condemned all use of violence. The meeting ended early when there were angry exchanges between some of those attending and members of the OIRA.[224]

A few days later, around 5,000 people took part in a march to endorse peace terms outlined by the PIRA. Their terms included the release of all internees and other political prisoners 'whether republican or Protestant', an amnesty for all on the wanted list, withdrawal of the British Army to barracks and a declaration of intent that they would be withdrawn completely in a very short time.[225]

At the beginning of June, the local leader of Ian Paisley's Democratic Unionist Party (DUP) in the city, the Reverend James McClelland, called for a blockade of the Bogside and the cutting off of essential services to force people to leave the area. A secret discussion document on Free Derry, put together by a British civil servant at the time and forwarded to the Northern Ireland Office, shows that their thinking was remarkably similar to that of the DUP. It also gives an amazing insight into how the British Government viewed Free Derry at the time:

> The most intractable problem facing HMG in Northern Ireland is that posed by Londonderry. This city, though of only relatively minor importance in the economic and social life of Northern Ireland, has a special significance in the minds of Roman Catholics and Protestants alike, which makes the question of who controls it important politically. The failure of earlier attempts in 1970/71 to maintain government control of the main Roman Catholic areas on the west side of the River Foyle by peaceful persuasion has allowed the IRA to achieve the initiative in the area to a degree unparalleled elsewhere in Northern Ireland. The IRA has caused some £6m of damage in the city since August 1971 and within the 'No Go' areas of the Bogside and the Creggan, the IRA are building up their defences and consolidating their political position . . .

---

223 *Lost Lives* 367; *Perceptions: Cultures in Conflict*, pp40-43; *Derry Journal*, 23 May 1972.
224 *Derry Journal*, 26 May 1972.
225 *Derry Journal*, 30 May 1972.

The aim of this paper is to consider the options open to HMG with regard to Londonderry . . .

The maintenance of law and order in Londonderry, 67% of its population Roman Catholic and only four miles from the Republic, has always been difficult. Today the Bogside and Creggan are controlled by the IRA and with the exception of the posts at Bligh's Lane and Brandywell, both of which are frequently under attack, these areas are 'No Go' to the Security Forces . . .

It is estimated that there are 250–300 IRA gunmen in these areas who include in their armoury a number of AP [armour piercing] weapons which are capable of penetrating lightly armoured vehicles . . . this had necessitated the deployment of Saracen APCs in Londonderry . . . the gunmen operate in packs and are supported by the 'Derry Young Hooligans' who are used to lure the Security Forces into exposed positions . . .

The gunmen are better trained and have developed defences which include dug-in positions and an efficient warning system . . .

After this summary of the position of Free Derry as it stood in June 1972, the paper then goes on to outline a number of options open to the British Government to try to solve the problem.

The first was to continue with the present policy of containment and sporadic raids. The advantages listed for this option were that it would not increase bloodshed and would give an opportunity for a political solution to be developed. The disadvantages were that it would allow the IRA to consolidate its hold on the area and prevent the British Army from regaining control.

The second was the same as the first but to include a withdrawal from military posts in Free Derry. This had the advantage of removing British soldiers from the line of fire but would hand a massive morale boost and propaganda victory to the IRA.

The third option was to tighten the ring around Free Derry to make it more difficult for the IRA to operate outside the area. This might reduce the level of violence, but could also induce a 'siege reaction' in Free Derry and increase support for the IRA.

The fourth option was to impose sanctions on the Free Derry area. This was in line with the DUP's earlier call for a blockade of Free Derry, and was discussed in more detail later in the document.

The fifth option was to offer the west bank of the River Foyle to the Republic of Ireland, accompanied by a financial grant to the Republic. This was rejected because of the impact it would have on other border areas of the North, most of which had a nationalist majority, and also because 'it is extremely unlikely that the Government of the Republic would be prepared to accept the Londonderry Enclave which in its way would be as great a problem to the Republic, both politically and economically.'

The sixth and final option was the military occupation of Free Derry. This would have the advantage of restoring British authority and pleasing unionists, who had called for an end to the No Go areas, but had the disadvantage of requiring a great increase in troop levels; would take some time to organise and therefore would be difficult to carry out by surprise; would have major political ramifications and would hand the IRA a propaganda victory when they could present Free Derry as being invaded by a massive military force. This, they said, would have to be balanced by advance propaganda to give the British Army a head-start on the reporting of the event.

Despite the disadvantages listed, what the document describes as the sixth option is basically a blueprint for what happened at the end of July, even down to the British Army making it clear in advance what was intended so that they could generate a propaganda campaign of their own ahead of the operation.

Returning to the issue of sanctions against Free Derry, the briefing document summarises a range of options first raised in May 1972, and includes the original document outlining the May proposals (which was described as being of 'especial secrecy'):

> At some stage a policy of 'containment' while moderating influences work may have to be supplemented, or in the event of failure, replaced by other measures short of a massive use of force . . .
>
> In our view, the first possible steps in an ascending order of difficulty and unpopularity would be to withdraw or curtail a number of public facilities at present available within the enclaves, at a cost of inconvenience rather than real hardship to the residents, whether law-abiding or not. Such steps could include the following:
>
> (i) Total suspension of letter- and parcel-post deliveries within the areas. Letters or parcels to be either held for collection outside the area or returned to sender.
>
> Such a suspension could be justified on the grounds that the Post Office no longer have the obligation, or even the right, to expect their employees to traverse daily an admittedly lawless area. There is a parallel here with the withdrawal of bus services, which has taken place on a number of occasions on similar grounds. There would, of course, be a risk, if letters etc could be collected outside the enclaves that the IRA themselves would set up an unofficial postal service as part of their plan to establish an alternative 'government'.

Other sanctions discussed at this level included the closure of post offices in Free Derry, suspension of the telephone service and the jamming of radio and television signals, and possible present and future penalties against residents' social security and other benefits. But then the document moves on to much more serious matters:

> We now turn to measures of such severity and divisiveness that they are only to be contemplated in a situation where hope for a gradual 'withering away' of IRA influence had been abandoned, extreme military measures were still ruled out but other means sought to reduce the enclaves by creating a virtual 'state of siege'. Even in such a situation, it is not to be assumed that a combination of such measures would necessarily achieve the desired results, since the application of

draconian measures short of the use of force could lead quite rapidly to a physical confrontation making its use inevitable.

It might, in a number of cases, be impracticable for technical or other reasons wholly to sever services in the enclaves, or alternatively to do so without affecting consumers in other areas of the city. Moreover, the suspension of certain services and benefits would involve the abandonment of statutory responsibilities, which would require legislative sanction.

In general, a wide range of public services continue to operate in the enclaves. Attempts at rent collection have had to be wholly abandoned; the repair and reinstatement of footpaths, which are constantly torn up, has been given up as a hopeless task; there are some difficulties in street cleaning and in repairs to street lighting; and house repairs were abandoned for a time, though they have now resumed. Otherwise, valiant efforts have been made to maintain services at as near a normal level as possible. In terms of possible sanctions, the services might be considered under the following broad headings:

(i) Supplies essential for the maintenance of normal life. This would encompass gas, electricity and water. Their total cut-off is virtually unthinkable, except *in extremis*, and even their curtailment to limited hours of the day would be a most drastic step.

(ii) Services whose abandonment or curtailment could involve public health risks. These would include water supply (again), sewerage, street cleansing and the services of the health clinic, the old people's home, district nurses, health and welfare visitors, midwives and public health inspectors. Any action in this field would be extremely emotive in terms of national and international opinion.

(iii) Services whose abandonment would not involve public health risks. These would include:

(a) The library service.

(b) The payment of grants for provision of bathrooms etc under the House Improvement Scheme.

(c) Advances of money for house purchases under the Small Dwellings Acquisition Act (made more significant by the unwillingness of Building Societies to advance money in the areas concerned).

(d) House repairs.

(e) Repairs to street lighting.

(iv) Payment of welfare and social security benefits. To abandon this would be another drastic step, involving legislation. A less drastic step would be to imply a threat of action by introducing special vetting or interviewing of claimants, who would have to come out of the enclaves to draw benefits . . .[226]

While these sanctions are rejected in the document, it is obvious that most were rejected not because of the impact they would have on the people of Free Derry but because of the impact that they would have outside Free Derry – 'action in this field would be extremely emotive in terms of national and international opinion . . .' – or because of the difficulty in introducing them, 'would require legislative sanction' or 'impracticable for technical or other reasons . . .' This document was considered serious enough to be forwarded to the Northern Ireland Office for discussion on 7 June 1972. One senior British civil servant went even further when he wrote around the same time: 'I have always been in favour of encouraging the No Go areas to rot from within. There is no reason why we should not encourage the breakdown of essential services and the spread of disease . . .' So it is clear that at this stage, the British Government were giving at least some consideration to the use of basically a siege to bring Free Derry to its knees – seventeenth-century tactics in the late twentieth century.

As would soon become clear, they opted instead for one of the other options rejected in this, and previous documents: military invasion.

On 9 June, the IRA shot a 45-year-old UDR private in a gun attack on the Buncrana Road. Edward Megahey, from Drumquin, outside Omagh, was hit by a single shot to the head and died two days later in hospital.[227]

On 12 June, they struck at the symbolic heart of Unionist misrule in the city when they shattered the entire interior of the Guildhall with a 200lb bomb. The bomb was planted by seven men: six of them entered the Guildhall, carrying two large plastic rubbish bins stuffed with explosives while the seventh held the staff at gunpoint. The bomb went off twenty-five minutes later, causing extensive damage. Just to complete the job, they bombed it again four days later. The PIRA claimed responsibility for both attacks.[228]

Speaking in Westminster, William Whitelaw said that the position in the Bogside and Creggan was 'intolerable' and that he had no intention of allowing it to spread 'like a cancer'. Announcing that more British soldiers were to be sent to the North, he said that 'the sternest measures' would be taken against Free Derry.[229]

On 18 June, the PIRA fired over 200 shots at British Army posts in Free Derry in a three-hour period. The British Army returned fire but neither side claimed any hits.[230]

On 21 June, the PIRA shot and killed a soldier on guard duty at Strand Road RUC station. Kerry McCarthy (19), a private in the Royal Welsh Fusiliers, was hit by a single shot to the chest.

226 *Northern Ireland – The Problem of Londonderry*, dated June 1972 and forwarded to Northern Ireland Office 7 June 1972 by AW Stephens. Also *Policy Options for Londonderry*, dated May 1972. Both documents are marked as secret and only came to light during the proceedings of the Bloody Sunday Inquiry.
227 *Lost Lives* 396.
228 *Derry Journal*, 13 June 1972 & 20 June 1972.
229 *Derry Journal*, 13 June 1972.
230 *Derry Journal*, 20 June 1972.

British Army fortifications in and around Free Derry in 1972, at Creggan Hill (above) and Butcher Gate.
(Peter Moloney, Eamon Melaugh)

British Army post on Bligh's Lane, Creggan, 1972. (Peter Moloney)

Barricade at Howard Street in the Long Tower area. (Peter Moloney)

Civilian barricades around Free Derry in 1972, at (top) Anne Street in the Brandywell, Beechwood Crescer Creggan and (bottom) Fahan Street in the Bogside. (Peter Moloney, George Sweeney)

IRA leaders hold a press conference in Free Derry in June 1972 to announce a temporary ceasefire. From left: Martin McGuinness, Dáithí Ó Conaill, Seán Mac Stíofáin and Seamus Twomey. (Willie Carson)

IRA volunteers operate a vehicle checkpoint in Creggan, 1972. (Eamon Melaugh)

British Army armoured vehicles pour into Creggan during Operation Motorman in the early hours of 31 July 1972. (Eamon Melaugh)

British Army Centurion tank adapted with dozer blade for demolishing barricades enters Creggan during Operation Motorman. (Eamon Melaugh)

On 22 June, the PIRA announced a ceasefire to allow for talks between republicans and the British Government. During the ceasefire, which would last for two weeks, a PIRA delegation, which included Martin McGuinness and Gerry Adams, travelled to London for talks with the Northern Ireland Office. The Provisional delegation demanded a British withdrawal from Ireland, which Whitelaw described as impossible. The meeting ended without any sort of agreement.

Rifleman James Meredith

James Meredith (19), a soldier in the Royal Green Jackets, was shot by the PIRA as he stood at a checkpoint on Abercorn Road on 26 June. He died a short time later. According to the British Army, he was the hundredth soldier to be killed since 1969, giving Derry the unenviable title of having had the hundredth person, hundredth civilian, and now the hundredth soldier to die. He was shot dead by the PIRA just hours before their ceasefire was due to come into effect.

James Meredith was from Kirby-in-Ashfield in Nottinghamshire. Seven years later, two men were jailed for manslaughter after admitting driving the man who fired the fatal shots.[231]

On 29 June, the PIRA announced that some of the barricades in Free Derry would be taken down but emphasised that the general framework of barricades would remain. The announcement followed a meeting in the Bogside between John Hume, officials from the Northern Ireland Office and local community representatives. In a statement, the PIRA said:

In order to facilitate the people of the area and to relieve inconvenience, we have decided to remove certain barricades. These barricades are ones which not only inconvenience the general public but in some cases have become health hazards. Work on clearing the barricades will begin tomorrow.

We have noted the outcome of the meeting held in the Bogside today and the request made by community leaders. As always, the interests of the people are our primary concern in the decision.

We wish to emphasise that the general framework of barricades in the Free Derry area will remain.[232]

On 7 July, two British Army officers were 'arrested' by the PIRA after they were found walking around the Bogside. They were interrogated and released after eighteen hours. The PIRA said they were released because of the ongoing ceasefire, and both officers signed statements that they had not been mistreated in any way. The British Army suspended both officers, pending an investigation.

On 10 July, the PIRA announced the end of their ceasefire in Derry, saying that it had broken down because of the British Army's actions in Lenadoon in Belfast, where

---

231 *Lost Lives* 421; *Derry Journal*, 27 June 1972.
232 *Derry Journal*, 30 June 1972.

they were accused of using force to help the Ulster Defence Association (UDA)[233] prevent nationalists from moving into vacant houses near a loyalist area. The following day, the PIRA shot dead Terence Jones (23), a member of the Royal Artillery, in Great James Street.[234]

The OIRA carried out a survey in Free Derry which, they claimed, showed a majority of people in the area were in favour of keeping the barricades up. Ten thousand copies of the survey were distributed and the results showed that residents felt the barricades should only come down once the British Army and RUC were completely removed from the area and a locally recruited police force, with no connection to the RUC, put in place.[235]

On 12 July, five separate explosions rocked Derry's city centre with one, a 200lb car bomb, detonated in Waterloo Place, causing what was described as 'the biggest explosion in the city since the Troubles began'. At least fifty buildings were damaged in the explosions.[236] The British Army began to strengthen their barricades around Free Derry, with brick walls being proposed to seal off William Street and Waterloo Street.

On 20 July, the PIRA blew up a British Army scout car in the Brandywell, claiming to have killed or seriously injured the occupants. The British Army claimed that they had suffered no casualties but had hit five PIRA members in the gun battle that followed. The PIRA said that they had not suffered any casualties.[237] Later statements, including one from a local priest, claimed that one of the 'gunmen' hit was an unarmed civilian wounded in Great James Street.[238]

James Casey

James Casey (57), a married man with a family and a former British soldier and prisoner of war in World War II, was a passenger in a car returning to Derry from Donegal on the night of 24 July 1972. His son-in-law, who was driving the car, said that while they were entering Creggan along Westway in the early hours of the morning they heard a shot from behind.

James Casey urged him to drive on, and it was only when they reached their home in Melmore Gardens that anyone realised he had been shot. He died two hours later in Altnagelvin Hospital.

The British Army initially claimed Mr Casey was hit by IRA gunfire. Three other civilians were injured by gunfire that night in Creggan, which the British Army also blamed on the IRA.

In 1978, Mr Casey's widow was awarded compensation from the Ministry of Defence for his death, but in the same year, the DPP ruled that there should be no prosecutions.

---

233 Formed in 1971, the UDA was the largest loyalist paramilitary organisation throughout the conflict which, despite being linked to hundreds of deaths, remained a legal organisation until 1992.
234 *Lost Lives* 449.
235 *Derry Journal*, 11 July 1972.
236 *Derry Journal*, 14 July 1972.
237 *Derry Journal*, 21 July 1972.
238 *Derry Journal*, 21 July 1972.

As gun and bomb attacks continued in Derry, and as Free Derry continued to thrive despite any attempts by the British Army and Government to bring it to an end, a change of policy was decided upon.

Whereas before, a full-scale military invasion of Free Derry had been rejected as being too costly in terms of troop numbers and public opinion, it now came to be seen as their only option.

A briefing document – signed off by Brigadier McLellan, the British commander in Derry – stated that the British Government had decided on 'resolute action' against the PIRA and its strongholds and that moves would be taken to 'root out the terrorists once and for all'.[239]

That 'resolute action' was to be Operation Motorman, the codename for the invasion of all of the republican No Go areas in the North of Ireland. The specific operation against Free Derry was codenamed Operation Carcan.

In the early hours of 31 July, the British Army sent 21,000 troops, supported by tanks and bulldozers, into nationalist working-class areas across the North. The soldiers had been warned to expect a pitched battle:

> There may be fierce fire-fights lasting perhaps 2/3 hours. Thousands of rounds may be fired and there may be some civilian casualties. IRA positions will be quickly pinpointed and effective action will be taken against them, including hot pursuit. Thereafter, sporadic sniping and the occasional ambush or bomb attack is likely to be the extent of IRA operations . . .[240]

But the operation was not a secret, deliberately so in light of the statement about advance warning and propaganda in the June document quoted above and the fact that William Whitelaw announced it on the television news twenty-four hours in advance, and the IRA, well aware that they weren't ready for a pitched battle with such a formidable force, had left the No Go areas, so no real resistance was offered.

More than 1,300 soldiers, backed up by 300 armoured vehicles, advanced into the Bogside and Creggan. A warship waited on the Foyle. Converted tanks simply drove over the top of the barricades, flattening them. The *Derry Journal* described it as a 'Prague-like invasion of Bogside and Creggan':

> Not since Russian troops entered Budapest and Prague in the 1950s and 1960s to suppress risings of the Czechoslovakian and Hungarian people, have sights been seen in any European city like those in Derry yesterday morning as 1,500 British soldiers followed 300 army vehicles in a massive invasion of the Bogside and Creggan estate . . .
> 50-ton Centurion tanks, adapted as bulldozers, rumbled up battle-scarred

---

239 Document quoted in *Derry Journal*, 3 February 2012.
240 Document quoted in *Derry Journal*, 3 February 2012.

William Street . . . other battalions streamed into the Creggan estate as warning sirens sounded the invasion alarm . . .

But the IRA had opted not to fight a pitched battle with the massive British force . . .[241]

Despite the absence of armed resistance, British soldiers shot two teenagers dead in Derry during Operation Motorman.

Daniel Hegarty and Óglach Seamus Bradley

Daniel Hegarty (15) had gone out with his two cousins in the early hours of 31 July to see the tanks that were invading his estate. As a teenage boy, he was naturally excited at the thought and wouldn't have seen any great danger in his actions.

The three boys were walking along Creggan Heights when they were warned by a neighbour not to go any further because there were soldiers coming into the area, so they turned for home. As they walked back along Creggan Heights, they crossed the road and stepped onto the footpath outside 114 Creggan Heights. As they did so, they heard a burst of four shots ring out. Daniel was hit twice in the head at point-blank range by two bullets from a heavy-calibre general-purpose machine gun and died instantly. His cousin Christopher was grazed in the head and fell to the ground.

Two soldiers, known at the inquest as A and B, claimed that they had shouted a warning and then fired at three armed figures running towards them, at a distance of about twenty-five metres. Civilian witnesses were adamant there was no warning given, and all the evidence showed that Daniel was shot at a distance of less than three metres. The soldiers then pulled out without checking the dead or wounded boy, or trying to arrest the third boy, whom they claimed they thought was armed.

The RUC investigation supported the soldiers' versions of events, including the fact that the shots were fired at a distance of about twenty-five metres, and the DPP decided on no prosecutions.

Not long before Daniel's death, his father, Alex, had saved the life of an RUC officer who had become surrounded by a hostile crowd in Creggan.

Daniel's family never gave up on trying to get to the truth about his death and, following a report from the HET, eventually managed to force a second inquest, which was held in December 2011. During the second inquest, the jury completely rejected the soldiers' accounts, and the coroner asked the Public Prosecution Service to review the case to see if the soldiers involved should now be charged with his death. At the time of writing, the Police Service of Northern Ireland have announced that they will be reviewing the case.[242]

Seamus Bradley (19), a volunteer in the PIRA, was at Central Drive in Creggan in the early hours of 31 July as British soldiers were pouring into the estate.

At close to 5.00PM, a British soldier, identified only as Soldier A (not the same

---

241 *Derry Journal*, 1 August 1972.
242 Pat Finucane Centre fact file on the death of Daniel Hegarty; *Lost Lives* 516.

one as above), claimed that he saw a figure leave a group of about ten people and run towards the trees in Bishop's Field, carrying what he claimed to be a Thompson sub-machine gun. The figure then climbed into one of the trees. Soldier A said he then fired four shots at the figure from his position in Linsfort Drive, about 175 metres away, and saw the figure fall from the tree.

About an hour later, soldiers were sent in to search the area and found Seamus Bradley lying wounded at the base of the tree. Controversy still surrounds what happened next. The soldiers claimed they took Seamus Bradley straight to St Peter's Secondary School and that he was dead on arrival. Members of Seamus's family still believe that he was alive for a lot longer and that medical attention was deliberately denied and that a considerable time had elapsed between his being taken away in an armoured vehicle and his arrival at St Peter's school. Forensic tests proved that Seamus Bradley was unarmed when he was shot dead.

In 2012, his family received a HET report into his death, which stated that if the soldiers' accounts were true, then they had acted lawfully, but that it was also clear that the soldiers' accounts had not been properly investigated at the time of his death and there was no way now of testing their veracity. The report speculated that Seamus may have survived if he had been given prompt medical attention.[243]

By daylight, Free Derry was under complete armed occupation. The British Army set up more camps, like Piggery Ridge in Creggan, and expanded and consolidated others. For the next twenty years, Free Derry was one of the most militarised areas in Western Europe, encircled by camps and watchtowers and crisscrossed by constant military patrols.

Thus ended Free Derry, the final phase, 9 August 1971 to 31 July 1972.

---

243 Pat Finucane Centre fact file on the death of Seamus Bradley; *Lost Lives* 515.

Epilogue

Operation Motorman was designed to break Free Derry and the other republican No Go areas in the North, and to defeat the PIRA by removing its main bases of support and operation. But like Bloody Sunday before it, it failed, and the PIRA were able to carry on the war for more than two more decades until the first ceasefire was announced in 1994.

Free Derry suffered inordinately during that time. By the time of the 1994 ceasefire, 122 people had lost their lives in and around the Free Derry area, including seventy-three civilians and republican volunteers and forty-nine members of the security forces or civilians working for the security forces. This works out at over three per cent of the total deaths in the conflict occurring in an area with less than one per cent of the population of the North of Ireland. The area also experienced a very high rate of security-forces killings, with forty-six of this total being killed by the British Army or RUC, and thirty-three of these being noncombatant civilians. To date, no British soldier or RUC officer has ever been charged in connection with killing anyone in the Free Derry area, while in contrast, there have been charges brought in twenty-five per cent of the cases where the victims were members of the security forces. At the time of writing, this may be about to change, as a number of the cases covered in this book, eg Bloody Sunday and Daniel Hegarty, are about to be reviewed by the PSNI with criminal charges to be considered.

Free Derry may have ended as a physical entity on 31 July 1972, but just as the slogan remained on the gable wall of 33 Lecky Road, so too did the spirit of Free Derry remain in the stubborn independence of its people. The lessons of self-reliance learned during the years of Stormont repression, which were first evidenced in the emergence of the early civil rights organisations like the DUAC and the DHAC, are now apparent in the strength of the community sector in the area and in how the people of this area continue to look to themselves to look after their own interests. This is especially important, since it is still one of the most economically and socially deprived areas in the North of Ireland.

And just as the Free Derry area was central to the emergence of the conflict in the North, so too was it central to the political process which ended it, with prominent Derry figures like John Hume and Martin McGuinness playing a major part, and the early talks about peace – the Hume-Adams talks – taking place in Hume's home in West End Park – in the centre of Free Derry – in the late 1980s and early 1990s.

The majority of visitors to the area these days come in holiday clothes rather than camouflaged uniforms, and the Bogside, especially around Rossville Street and Free Derry Corner, has become one of the main tourist attractions in the city as people come to learn about what happened here directly from the people who were involved, knowing themselves that the media has given them a partisan version of events for decades. Where armoured vehicles were once a common sight, it is now tourist buses, and SLRs[244] with barrels and bullets have been replaced by SLR cameras (single lens reflex) with lenses and filters. Free Derry Corner is now a place to come and have your picture taken, one for the holiday album.

But Free Derry Corner also remains the political and emotional epicentre of the area, symbolising the long years of struggle for civil rights and the years of armed conflict that followed, and it remains today as a symbol of the same, and as a marker for civil and human rights struggles around the world. It is still the focal point for marches and protest, for highlighting injustices. It is still the symbol of Free Derry, and the spirit of Free Derry.

---

244 Self-Loading Rifle, standard British Army-issue weapon during most of the conflict in the North of Ireland.

Northern Ireland Civil Rights
ASSOCIATION

A CIVIL RIGHTS
MARCH

WILL BE HELD IN DERRY
ON SATURDAY, 5TH OCT.

COMMENCING AT 3-30 p.m.

ASSEMBLY POINT: WATERSIDE RAILWAY STATION

MARCH TO THE DIAMOND

Where a PUBLIC METTING will take place

...ter for the 5 October 1968 march in Derry, the first civil rights march in the city. The violent police attack
...n the march that day was a major factor in the descent into conflict in the North. (Charlie McMenamin)

Poster highlighting the dire situation in Derry in the 1960s. (MoFD collection)

original hand-drawn design for the Derry civil rights logo, created by Sheila McClean. (MoFD collection)

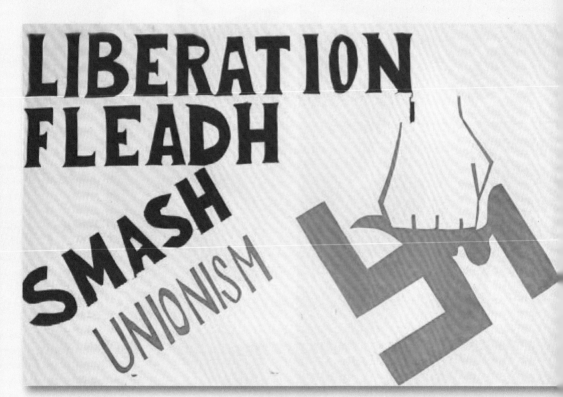

Poster for the 1969 Liberation Fleadh after the Battle of the Bogside, comparing Unionism to Nazism. (Peter Moloney)

Screen-print poster opposing the removal of the barricades around Free Derry in September 1969.
(MoFD collection)

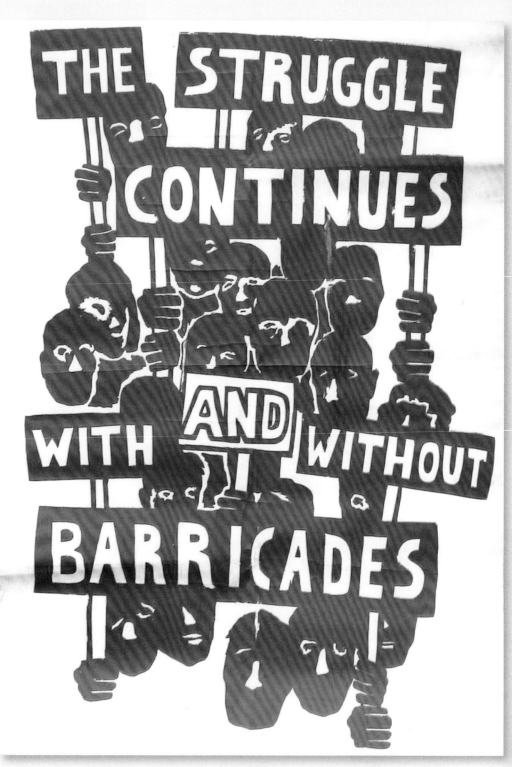

Screen-print poster announcing that resistance would continue, October 1969.
(MoFD collection)

Poster attacking the Unionist Government's political control of the B Specials and law and order.
(MoFD collection)

A 1969 poster satirising Stormont Prime Minister James Chichester Clark's futile attempts to placate nationalists without annoying unionists. (MoFD collection)

Screen-print poster calling for an end to the Stormont Government. (Peter Moloney)

FERRYQUAY GATE

FERRYQUAY GATE WILL BE CLOSED TO VEHICLE TRAFFIC FROM 1 A.M. TO 7 A.M. DAILY

VEHICLES SHOULD USE SHIPQUAY GATE.

A TURNSTILE IS AVAILABLE AT FERRYQUAY FOR PEDESTRIANS.

Issued by

British Army poster advising of traffic restrictions in the city centre. (Charlie McMenamin)

Anti-internment poster comparing Stormont Prime Minister Brian Faulkner to Adolf Hitler. (Peter Moloney)

Urging a rent and rates strike to protest against the introduction of internment. (MoFD collection)

A 1971 Christmas card highlighting internment. (Peter Moloney)

MASS RALLY

NEW YEAR REDEDICATION
FOR
THE PEOPLE OF DERRY
SATURDAY 2nd JANUARY, 1972

Bishops Field   :=:   Creggan

AT 3 p.m.

Speakers:

B. DEVLIN Mid-Ulster M.P.
TOMAS MAC GIOLLA President, Sinn Fein, Dublin
J. WHITE Republican Movement, Derry
M. MC GURRAN Republican Movement, Lurgan
T. ROBINSON Republican Movement, Derry
SEAMUS O' TUTHALL Ex-Internee, Dublin

Unite to Fight!   Unite to Win!

JAMES CONNOLLY REPUBLICAN CLUB

Poster advertising a 1972 protest in Derry, on the same day that the civil rights march was attacked on Magilligan beach. Bloody Sunday would be just eight days later. (MoFD collection)

People's Democracy poster produced soon after Bloody Sunday, the thirteen skulls representing the thirteen civil rights marchers killed that day. (MoFD collection)

REMEMBER BLOODY SUNDAY!

DON'T FRATERNISE

Poster warning against fraternisation with British soldiers after Bloody Sunday. The thirteen printed crosses represented the thirteen killed; the fourteenth was added by hand after the death of John Johnston from the wounds he received that day. (MoFD collection)

Poster advertising an anti-internment meeting at Free Derry Corner on 30 July 1972, the last day of Free Derry. (MoFD collection)

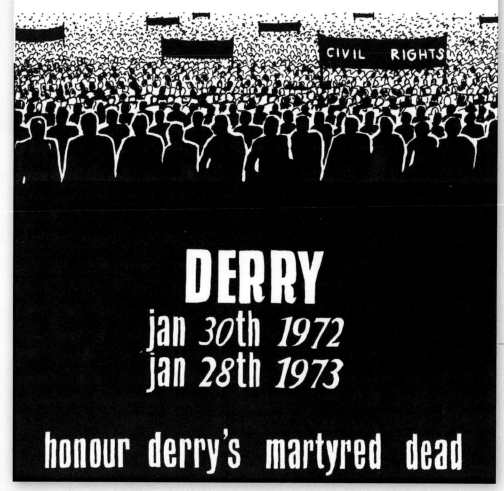

northern ireland civil rights association

CIVIL RIGHTS

DERRY
jan 30th 1972
jan 28th 1973

honour derry's martyred dead

From 1973 on, posters were produced to promote the annual Bloody Sunday remembrance march and th[ey] soon became an integral part of the commemoration. While earlier posters were more militaristic and focus[ed] mainly on the situation in the North, they began to show a wider outlook in the early 1990s with the emerge[nce] of the Bloody Sunday Weekend Committee. In some years two posters were produced, one in Irish and [the] other in English. The following pages illustrate their development over time. (MoFD collection)

BLOODY SUNDAY

memorial   unveiling   ceremony

A MARCH
bishop's field to free derry corner
assemble 2-30p.m jan. 26th.

northern ireland civil rights association

BLOODY SUNDAY MARCH

BRITS OUT!

8th Annual Commemoration
BLOODY SUNDAY
DERRY
SUNDAY 27th JANUARY

Assemble: 2.30p.m. Creggan Shops
MARCH AND RALLY
Prominent Republican Speakers

9th ANNIVERSARY

BLOODY SUNDAY
COMMEMORATION MARCH

All Bands Welcome — Organised by Sinn Fein

DERRY
FEBRUARY 1st.

Assemble Creggan Shops - 2.30pm.

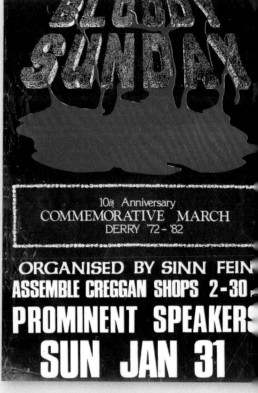

1983

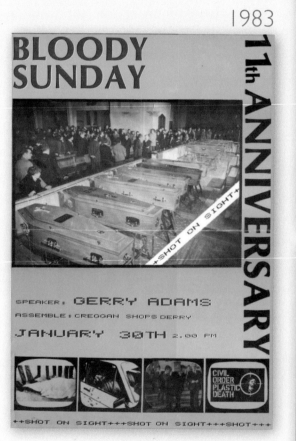

1984

1986

BLOODY SUNDAY

14th Anniversary
COMMEMORATIVE
MARCH
1972—1986
ORGANISED BY SINN FÉIN
MAIN SPEAKER
JIM McALLISTER
ASSEMBLE CREGGAN SHOPS 2-30 PM
SUN JAN 26

198

TOWARDS JUSTICE

REMEMBE
BLOOD
SUNDA

CREGGAN SHOPS 2
SUN 27 JA

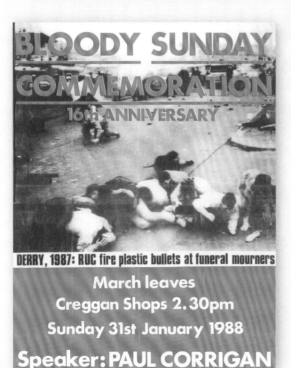

BLOODY SUNDAY
COMMEMORATION
16th ANNIVERSARY

DERRY, 1987: RUC fire plastic bullets at funeral mourners

March leaves
Creggan Shops 2.30pm
Sunday 31st January 1988
Speaker: PAUL CORRIGAN

1988

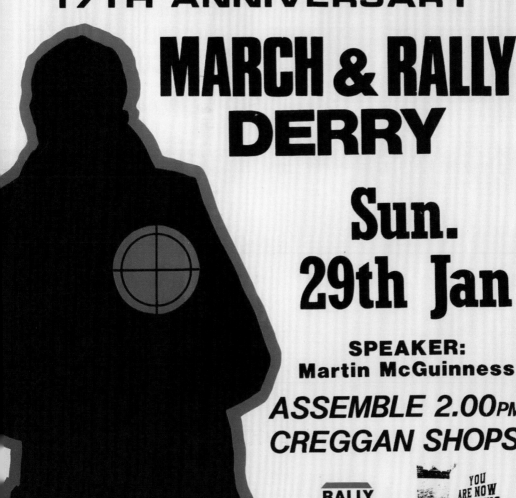

Bloody Sunday commemoration
17TH ANNIVERSARY

MARCH & RALLY DERRY

Sun. 29th Jan

SPEAKER:
Martin McGuinness

ASSEMBLE 2.00PM
CREGGAN SHOPS

RALLY AT FREE DERRY CORNER

YOU ARE NOW ENTERING FREE DERRY

1992

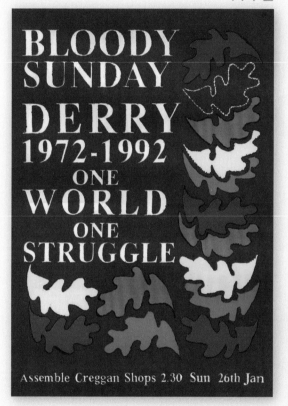

BLOODY
SUNDAY
DERRY
1972-1992
ONE
WORLD
ONE
STRUGGLE

Assemble Creggan Shops 2.30 Sun 26th Jan

BLOODY
SUNDAY

18th COMMEMORATION
MARCH & RALLY

Speakers:
PAUL HILL
GERRY CONLON

FREE THE
BIRMINGHAM 6

Creggan Shops 2.30pm
Sun 28th Jan

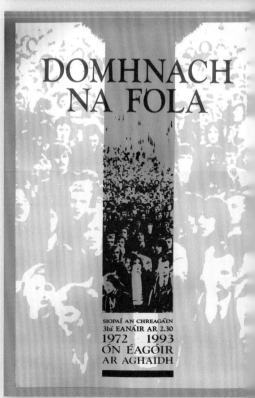

DOMHNACH
NA FOLA

SIOPAÍ AN CHREAGÁIN
31ú EANÁIR AR 2.30
1972 - 1993
ÓN ÉAGÓIR
AR AGHAIDH

1993

1994

JUST PEACE

Killers walk free
Caraher murder whitewashed

The widow, father and relatives of Fergal Caraher walked out of Belfast High Court in silent protest against presiding Judge Brian Hutton's acquittal of two British marines last week.

Lance Corporal Richard Elkington and Marine Andrew Callaghan, both from 45 Commando, were acquitted on the grounds of "reasonable doubt" of the murder of 21-year-old South Armagh Sinn Féin member Fergal Caraher and the attempted murder of his brother Micháil in December 1990.

Margaret Caraher, widow of Fergal, described herself as being "disappointed" by the judge's decision. She continued: "We have come to expect nothing more from the legal system."

BLOODY SUNDAY
SUN. 30 JAN 1994
ASSEMBLE CREGGAN SHOPS 2.30

BLOODY SUNDAY

YOU ARE NOW ENTERING FREE DERRY

DECOMMISSION INJUSTICE
SUN: 28th : JAN : CREGGAN : 2.30

1995

TIME FOR JUSTICE

BLOODY SUNDAY
SUN 29 JAN
CREGGAN SHOPS 2·30

1996

Domhnach
na fola

Máirseáil ar son na Córa

Uair na Fírinne **25**ú *Cuimhneacháin*

Siopaí an Chreagáin 2.30 Dé Domhnaigh 2ú Feabhra 1997

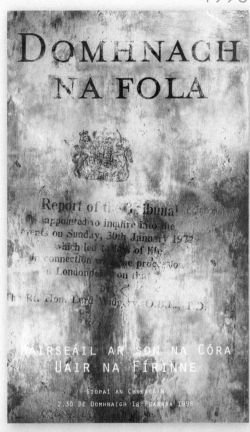

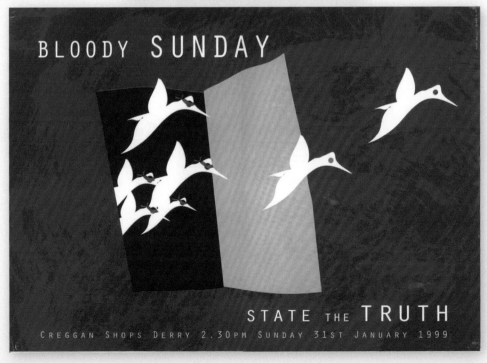

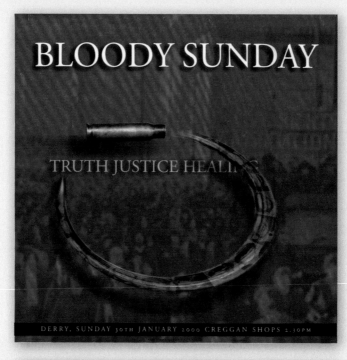

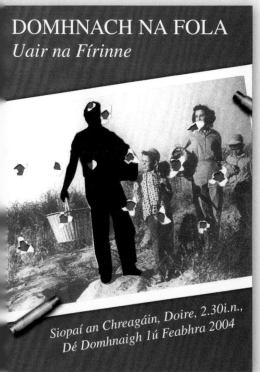

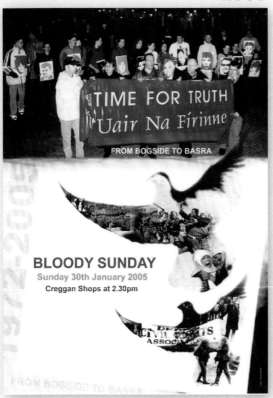

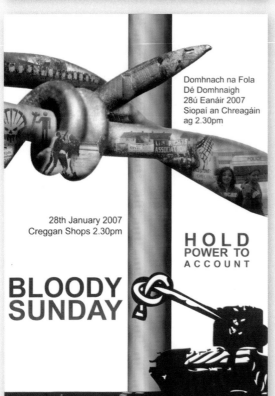